A SHARED JOURNEY

'An air-balloon regularly passes over my house and I under-stand it often travels long distances. It is very multi-coloured. It is like Ann Daniels' life, full of colour in producing great things for God's glory.

'Ann was a most extraordinary woman. In the world's way of assessing things she didn't have all the ingredients necessary to produce a most remarkable life. However, her achievements for God were outstanding. Her life was a challenge to everyone who met her.

'Her wonderful story is here lovingly told by her devoted husband, Norman. It is a story that will challenge anyone who reads it. If you are someone who is settling in for a tranquil life, beware. This story might just blast you out of your safe boltholes.'

– Peter Fenwick

Dedication
To
Ella Ann
(All God's Favour)
Introducing the Granny you
never knew

A Shared Journey

Changing worlds one person at a time

NORMAN DANIELS

THANKFUL BOOKS

First published 2006

Published by Thankful Books
c/o P.O. Box 2118, Seaford BN25 9AR.

ISBN-13: 978 1 905084 09 8
ISBN-10:   1 905084 09 9

The song, *For the joys and for the sorrows* by
Graham Kendrick, on page 259 is reproduced by
permission of Make Way Music.

The song, *When it's all been said and done* by James
Cowan, on page 318 is reproduced by permission of
Integrity's Hosanna! Music/Sovereign Music UK.

Book design and production for the publisher by
Bookprint Creative Services, <www.bookprint.co.uk>
Printed in Great Britain.

CONTENTS

FOREWORD

The Hebrew word *Ebenezer* (meaning thus far the Lord has helped us) refers in the Scriptures to a memorial or milestone set up on a journey as a permanent record of the distance travelled and, in that journey, of the grace of God.

In a similar way I set out to chronicle the journey of Ann's life and very soon realised that it had to be the plural "us" rather than the singular "she". A unique individual, Ann did not live her life only for herself but was always at the centre of events, whether as a teenager, a young mum or as director of various works at home or abroad. Her influence affected others' lives too and whilst this is an account of our personal journey together, I realise that the tremendous privileges we experienced were not merely the result of our enthusiasm or energy but were due also to the direct help of so many people.

These pages represent a travel brochure (or photographic album), recording incidents and events, some trivial but memorable, others perhaps memorable but trivial in reality. They are experiences along our journey; reminders of how far we have come and yet how far each one of us has yet to travel.

Travellers in Romania will often hear the farewell greeting *Drum bun*, which basically means "have a good and safe journey". I pray that as you read through these pages your journey will be an enjoyable one and that these words will assist you in your personal walk, much like Christian in *Pilgrim's Progress*, in arriving at your own God-ordained destiny. "Do two walk together unless they have agreed to do so?" (Amos 3:3 NIV).

Norman Daniels
October 2002

ACKNOWLEDGEMENTS

Although my name is recorded as the author of this work it is true to say that I could not have written it purely by myself. Life is far too complex to be exclusive – and so too within society and within the Christian community we live our lives in an interdependent balance.

Many of the key players in life are often anonymous but much is owed to their input, reliability and unselfish service. In these pages the names of many individuals receive no record, but I do want to acknowledge their invaluable contribution to our lives and ministry. Naturally, over the years these numbers have been far too many to count – but too many to ignore. I therefore say thank you for your help in our personal lives.

I am grateful to the church family at Poplars for their unstinting support for Ann and myself and our family through the years. I particularly appreciated this opportunity to record the incidents of our full life. Thanks, Derek and Pete, for allowing me time to write in the midst of all the demands on our shared lives. I am especially grateful to those many friends and volunteers for their anecdotes of experiences, some of which I have included.

Were it not for the invaluable skills of the Poplars office staff these pages would have remained mere long-hand scrawl. Thank you all . . . Kate Russon, Diane Cornelius and Pat Caunt especially for your patience. Thanks too Bill Caunt for the planning and transfer to disk and to Ruth Hardy for her reading and helpful comments. Thank you Vivien Culver from Sheffield for your professional editorial obser-vations – your tremendous and diligent hard work – I never realised how much was involved.

What wonderful children and grandchildren God has given me – thank you all for your love, support and genuine interest in the project. This record is for you as a reminder of a godly saint – a woman of faith, one whom we loved and whose memory we cherish.

And finally thanks and glory to the Lord Jesus – the Author and Perfector of my faith, to the Holy Spirit for His continuing presence and enabling and to Father God for His consistent heart of love through the experiences of life.

She has done what she could . . . that which this woman
has done shall be spoken of in memory of her.
Mark 4:8–9 (NASB)

Were not our hearts burning within us
While He was speaking to us on the road . . . ?
Luke 24:32 (NASB)

EDITOR'S NOTE

To preserve the privacy of those concerned, names of some individuals have been changed in parts of this book relating to the fostering of children.

PROLOGUE

August 1999

"This hospital has a policy of openness with patients," began the nurse, "and I'm taking up your case as part of my further studies towards my degree; perhaps I could ask you a few questions?"

"That's fine," said Ann, "but maybe first you could explain to me what is wrong; what is my diagnosis?"

"You mean you don't know?"

"No . . . you see I've had a biopsy and other tests over these last two or three weeks – but no consultation – in fact I've not seen a consultant yet – you're the first person I've really sat down with and spoken to about my condition."

The young man blushed and was obviously embarrassed – somehow he'd unintentionally compromised his position, unaware that his seniors had not yet seen Ann to discuss her symptoms, treatment or prognosis. As he puzzled over what he should do next, Ann intervened to rescue him and suggested that she look at her medical file.

As a trained nurse she could understand its contents, and thus relieve him of his embarrassment. She quickly scanned the paperwork; the diagnosis was not yet definitive but could either be primary leukaemia or mantle cell lymphoma in transformation – in a nutshell she had cancer.

Trained to deal with emergency situations, Ann thanked the nurse for his help and collected herself for the trip home. Somehow, in the grace of God, this chilling diagnosis had been leaked to her in a somewhat indelicate way whilst she was making what she thought was a routine hospital visit on her own. A number of immediate concerns crossed her mind – first for the young professional and how he would explain to his superiors that he had breached the ethical patient/doctor structure; and secondly, what was this dreaded disease? What implications would this impose on her, the family and her work? Driving the fifteen miles home alone seemed one of the longest journeys of her life.

CHAPTER ONE

MOVING NORTHWARDS

In the last chapter of the Book of Proverbs, King Lemuel asks many questions, one of which is: "An excellent wife . . . who can find? For her worth is far above jewels." Over the years I have come to appreciate and value the relationship that Ann and I had enjoyed since our marriage in 1963. I had discovered a jewel of exquisite value, but like all precious stones its formation had taken place under considerable heat and pressure over many years. Ann's development was no exception.

She was born in Hendon, North London, during the middle of the Second World War where the family rigidly resisted sending their children as evacuees, as defiant Londoners carried on their lives as best they could under the threat of bombing from the German Luftwaffe. Ann's parents did whatever was necessary in those dark and trying times to rear their two children. John was five years Ann's senior, a typical older brother but always protective of his little sister. Her father, Ted, was unable to do military service on health grounds and as a result he spent hours each day crossing London to work. Her mother Nance cared for the children in the cramped quarters – resorting to the garden air-raid shelter with her charges as and when air-raid sirens demanded. In spite of several near misses from incendiary devices the family came through the ravages of war, toughened but together, like many other Brits savaged by the blitz and its consequences. Nor was all the fighting restricted to the war; it later overspilt to school when Ann was given an eye patch to her National Health spectacles in order to straighten squints in both eyes. Her brother John fought many battles defending his sister, called "four eyes" by fellow pupils.

Growing up on rationing and in restricted space somehow was normal and Ann often recalled her memories of hours spent playing with friends in and around the many nearby bombed premises. As times passed and as war-time restrictions slowly lifted, she remembered the family routine, particularly on Sundays when dad enjoyed a nap after dinner and the kids were sent up the road to the Baptist Sunday school to give the parents space and a bit of peace and quiet. These may have been human mixed motives but there was also divine overruling, for it was this regular weekly input from dedicated Christian teachers that set the example and challenge for her later commitment to Jesus.

Encouraged by her Sunday school teachers and alongside her friends, Ann attended the last day (22 May 1954) of the Greater London Billy Graham Crusade, which was held at the nearby Wembley Stadium. That cold wet evening witnessed the greatest religious congregation, 120,000, ever seen until then in the British Isles. Billy Graham ended his message with these words: "You can go back to the shop, the office, the factory, with a greater joy and peace than you have ever known. But before that can happen you must commit yourselves to Jesus Christ. You must make your personal decision for Him. And you can do that now. Choose this day whom ye will serve!" The *News of the World* described the scene that followed:

> There was no emotional hysteria, no tension . . . only a very deep reverence . . . Within minutes thousands of men, women and teenagers were moving to the track. They were of all ages, of all classes of society. Husbands and wives were hand-in-hand with their children, young men walked forward alone . . .

To the newspaper it looked like 10,000; in fact 2,000 with their counsellors stood before the platform. That evening Ann stepped forward on to the famous Wembley turf to commit herself and her life to Jesus. This commitment was the opening of an intimate relationship with her Saviour that continued throughout her life.

Her return home from Wembley was not, however, to the welcome she might have expected. Her parents resented this step of youthful exuberance and she was to be given a few weeks to outwork this passing fad. The pressure had begun – but the jewel was already under divine preparation. Ann's family was not in any way spiritually minded, merely typical Londoners enduring the hardships of life and enjoying the relief the weekends brought. Her father didn't drink alcohol, because of his stomach ulcer, whereas grandfather Bert (a typical cockney – using the term as a generalisation for Londoners rather than those born within the sound of Bow Bells) was an avid imbiber. On one occasion he sent Ann on an errand for his drink and this led to her being knocked over by a passing car whilst she was crossing a nearby road with her arms full of Granddad's bottles of beer.

Coming from a non-Christian home had its difficulties but gave Ann an understanding and love for people generally, especially those who were not yet sure of the need for salvation. Bible reading in this hostile environment was never easy, so Ann devised a plan (typical of many experiences later); press on rather than be put off. She would read under the bedclothes each evening with the aid of a torch. Not ideal, certainly not confrontational within the family, but a method which enabled her to feed her spirit with Scripture, an appetite she never lost as the years passed by. She, however, always received the encouragement of her church leaders and owed a lot to the input provided by the Girls' Life Brigade (GLB), as it was then called. One of Ann's mentors of that time, Pat Price, described her as

> a most enthusiastic little girl always wanting to serve her Saviour and learn more about Him, an eagerness quite remarkable at her age. In the GLB she was always to be relied upon and serving with excellence all the time and there was always plenty of laughter when she was around.

The country had embarked upon a national rebuilding programme and this meant change for Ann as she approached secondary school age. Change was often a challenge for Ann and at the newly built Whitefield's School in Cricklewood she soon made friends and, thankfully, one of these proved to be a Christian too. Ruth Tate (then Ruth Blow) remembers with gratitude their first encounters:

> It was the first day and the first time that she spoke to me as we were going out to break. God was so good to bring her into my life then. I had been feeling very insecure, as the school seemed so big and there were only three of us from my junior school in

that class and the other two were boys – all my other friends were in other classes. From that day on we spent a lot of time together. Ann was always an encourager, a gift she never lost. Ann was the first person that I had known who hadn't been brought up in a Christian home, who had a living and vibrant faith in God and for me who went to church every Sunday, I was challenged by that and it provoked me to want and seek what she had.

Spiritual encouragement developed naturally and her long friendship with Ruth continued beyond school, through nurse training, marriage, rearing of children and church life even though distance separated them surprisingly quickly. Letter writing, telephoning and, much later, attending conferences together strengthened those childhood bonds.

Adolescence seemed idyllic but once again further change was imminent. It was however with little notice that Ann was told in the spring of 1957 that the family was leaving Hendon to move to Yorkshire. Dad had decided to leave his maintenance work at a local hotel to assist his brother in his electrical business up north in Maltby. Her personal world somehow seemed to be falling apart. Now she would have to leave her established friends, church and school, for what? . . . a totally unknown environment. Her sad farewells were soon made to friends and neighbours, to school and church and it was off at the age of fourteen from the suburbs of North London to the coal mining villages of the West Riding of Yorkshire – to a culture a million miles apart in an impressionable period in her adolescence, a factor which in those days was not even considered.

The family, except for brother John (who had at this time taken up an apprenticeship with North London aeroplane makers De Havilands), squeezed into a small flat above uncle's wallpaper and paint shop, from which he also ran his electrical maintenance business. He too had moved north a few years before, a decision which proved financially advantageous since the electrical work and decoration demands expanded as new homes were now being constructed and all this of course prior to the DIY boom of years to come. Within months of their arrival, unfortunately, Uncle Alf died and Ann's father was given the responsibility and ownership of the electrical sector, piling on further pressure as the family adjusted to a new location, new contacts and a new way of life.

An end-terraced house in the colliery "model" village was soon purchased and modernised in their spare time and it was change yet again. The house had three bedrooms, a central staircase out of the living room, a very small, virtually non-existent, "garden" to the front and a rear yard finished in tarmac; no palace, but home. Ann had her own bedroom for the first time, a haven where she could be herself. She had managed to bring with her from London two prized possessions: a small upright piano, which had to remain in the downstairs front room, and her newly acquired Singer electric sewing machine, both of which received almost constant use as years progressed.

The village of Maltby lies six miles east of Rotherham in what was then the southern part of the West Riding of Yorkshire, whilst its district stretched eastward up to the Nottinghamshire border.

Until the twentieth century [wrote former vicar of Maltby Clifford Auckland] it was a small, poor but beautiful agricultural village located in an area of rolling hills. It boasted a derelict Cistercian monastery and several large estate and manorial dwellings of which Sandbeck House (the home of the Lumley family and seat of the 11th Earl of Scarbrough, the Lord Chamberlain to the Queen until his death in 1969) was the sole survivor. The village's future was however sealed and its tranquillity transformed when half a mile or so beneath the surface rich deposits of coal were discovered by turn of the century geologists. Once the technology had been developed Maltby saw an influx of thousands of miners and their families. From 1911, when coal production began, the village grew rapidly into a flourishing township. The community was fiercely socialist with a rich mixed mining community life, combining the input of mining families from Staffordshire, Scotland, Durham and Derbyshire, amongst others. It was a community that worked hard, played hard, and drank hard, a community of twelve thousand who knew one another. There were still the stalwart colliers who attended the chapel, plus those who would not cross the threshold of any church building. It was also a place of contrasts, on the one hand regularly hosting members of the Royal Family at Sandbeck House and on the other hand glorying in its famous son, fiery Freddie Trueman, the Yorkshire and England Cricketer.

Maltby had no Baptist church so Ann sought out the nearest similar group, which happened to be the Methodists. She set off for a Sunday evening service unaware that there was one problem she had not countenanced; the meeting did not start at 6.30 pm as she expected but earlier at 6.00 pm. Nervously she opened the doors to find the meeting in full flow. Not put off she sidled into a space at the back, slightly embarrassed and obviously the centre of attention. It was the annual Sunday School Anniversary, a musical collection of songs sung by the young people for the benefit of the old. I was one of those young people, and distinctly remember Ann's entry.

Thronging with teenagers, the church boasted a very active youth club on Friday evenings and it was to this that Ann was naturally attracted. She was goaded mercilessly for her London accent, especially when she collected everyone's "sabs" (subscriptions), but soon became one of the in-crowd, always full of ideas and ever keen to speak of her relationship with her Lord.

Ann had not passed the then notorious eleven-plus examination to enter grammar school, so her lot was to attend the local girls' secondary school which sadly was much inferior to Whitefield's in London. Fortunately school life was soon over, Ann leaving at the age of fifteen. She decided, with the encouragement of her father, to enter cadet nursing at Rotherham Moorgate Hospital, which included attending the local Technical College for studies prior to being let loose on patients and the wards. Her horizons were expanding, with new colleagues entering the scene, and new friendships developing. Like most young people starting in the adult world, Ann's faith and values were tested and she confided later that this was the most trying time of her Christian walk. Inevitably, amongst her colleagues, she promoted the youth club and some of them soon began coming to the Friday night or other special activities.

One memorable event in 1959 was the participation in a youth club bed-push along three miles of the main arterial road, the A630 – all dressed in pyjamas or nightgowns and collecting on behalf of Refugee Year. This had been designed so as to assist the late relocation of those dispossessed through the ravages of the Second World War. I distinctly remember the somewhat hair-raising journey since I happened to be the patient in the bed pushed by a handful of noisy nursing cadets. We didn't win the race but the time was enjoyable and the collecting tins soon filled with cash! I shudder to think what would happen today if such a venture was countenanced with all the necessary permissions, the emphasis on risk analysis and safety and the much-increased volume of traffic, but then it was not a problem, you just did it and it was all good-natured.

The youth club was the hub of our teenage activities and Ann's spiritual contribution was exceptional. Another of her visionary ideas took place in April 1958 just after her fifteenth birthday. She heard that evangelist Joe Blinco was coming to take a series of meetings entitled Tell Rotherham, to be held at the Sheffield Road swimming baths – I'm still not sure whether the water was drained out or not. Her idea was to take as many youth club members as possible to hear the good news about Jesus, since she herself was so thankful that she had been taken to hear Billy Graham years before. Needless to say the bus was quickly filled through her enthusiastic encouragement. Twelve of the young people responded publicly to the evangelist's message that night . . . of which I was one! Already, even before we were emotionally committed to one another, her ventures of faith had brought me to the point of decision. From then on we took it upon ourselves to start a Scripture Union group during the youth club time for those who had responded. Today we would call it a cell group, for nurturing young Christians. Instinctively Ann knew that study, fellowship, prayer and worship were vital for growth. Somehow Ann's own spiritual hunger and input to her peers made a noticeable difference for, sadly, within many church structures of that time the emphasis seemed to be on social rather than spiritual needs. This emphasis plainly failed to produce the environment for conversion, commitment and spiritual growth.

Encouragement did come from individuals who obviously flourished in their personal relationship with Jesus, but some of these were getting old and their influence was diminishing.

One notable exception was a bachelor, Pastor Cock, a man who related to and encouraged the young people by holding Sunday evening meetings in the manse. Unfortunately he soon moved on to serve other circuits, highlighting another repeated problem in the church system of the time. Looking back, the use of pastors training on the job, beginning like apprentices (disciples with mentors) and going through to full ministerial positions, seems to have emulated the methods promoted by Jesus, whose disciples learned by doing, whether successfully or unsuccessfully. They then returned to Jesus to learn by analysis, discussion and correction – a very different system from the current scheme of full theological and academic training and then learning by doing.

The popularity of the youth club and its obvious success was amazing – well over one hundred young people from fourteen to twenty met from seven till nine each Friday evening, to let off steam, play table tennis, listen to music, hang around. Quite tame in respect of today's essentials but the start of many relationships that led to marriages that have lasted forty years later.

Before the introduction and popularity of package holidays the youth club offered new horizons that attracted young people. One such jaunt was held in the summer of 1959 when the venue chosen was North Devon, taking in the beauty of Wells, Cheddar Gorge, Morthoe Bay, and Woolacombe. A week's holiday under canvas with outings to local beauty spots, beaches, and places of interest,

all with the youth leaders and out of the gaze of protective parents. Norman and Sybil Holmes and Ron and
Shirley Woodhouse, themselves only a few years our
seniors, managed us well and except for minor hiccups we
not only arrived safely but also returned without a scratch.
Into an old privately hired coach we crammed marquees,
tents, poles, food and all the paraphernalia of camping,
whilst thirty young people sang themselves hoarse all the
way there and back. For me the significance of the event was
not the beauty of the Gothic cathedral at Wells, or the splen-
dour of the limestone gorge at Cheddar or even the beautiful expanse of beach at Woolacombe – but the beginning of
our relationship which started with a dare and a kiss in the
village of Mortehoe, innocence which would change both
our lives.

As young people, with no outlets for earning, and no
parents' cars, even the cost of public transport to the Tell
Rotherham Crusade follow-up meetings proved difficult
and beyond our means. The literature sent to us in the
mail after the event did prove helpful but the welcome given
to the news of the twelve responses was somewhat muted at
the local church. A pat on the back and a public acknowledgement were given, but personal nurture sadly was
nil. The Scripture Union group, therefore, became even
more vital. Sometime later it was a shock of monumental
proportions to us as young people when I received a letter
from a visiting preacher, Mr Vaughan, asking that I find two
young people who would step forward and publicly share
their story of faith when he hoped to come to Maltby in two
weeks time. He requested confirmation that this was in
order. What a bombshell this was. We were not used to
attending the evening services but we could not remember

the last time someone shared a testimony. I'm sure it must have happened, but for us this was a first! Although everything within us wanted to pass it on to someone else, as leaders of the Friday evening group (and especially since I had been a responder at the crusade) we knew it ought to be us. This produced a spiritual struggle for us, but one we could not evade. We had to be the ones who stood up to testify. I realise now this was all part of the formation process of our lives, precious stones in the making.

The struggle we experienced and our determination to respond had of course virtually resolved the problem. Our time to participate came and with some fear and trepidation we gave our stories. The sharing went with little trouble, and what a sense of relief after we had discharged our responsibility. We had publicly testified of our relationship with Jesus before our own church members. Unknown to us, however, that particular evening a visitor, recently moved from Sheffield into the village, attended the service for the first time. He introduced himself as Keith Foster, married to a Maltby girl, Gwen, and father of two young boys. He thanked us for sharing and encouraged us by inviting us both for a meal at their home the following weekend.

This proved to be the first visit to their home but by no means the last, for Keith and Gwen took us under their wings and became our mentors for several years in things spiritual. Under their friendship and help we flourished, attending many interdenominational groups and widening our horizons even further. Keith had been involved in the Youth for Christ movement and was up-to-date on what was then the contemporary communication of the gospel. Gwen had come from a Pentecostal church background and this input, plus that of Gwen's parents, Mr and Mrs Mann, showed us there was much more to experience in the Christian life than we had appreciated. We were introduced to the lives of other Christian pioneers, which further unlocked so much more of God and practical spiritual experience.

The natural outworking of our enthusiasm was to serve in the church and this meant at that time to become Sunday school teachers both at the morning and Sunday afternoon sessions. Later, Ann's work shifts often made it difficult to keep to this pattern, but it was this regular studying and sharing in a public role that gave us confidence before others, helped us grow in our faith and taught us what Christian preparation and service involved.

Keith and Gwen encouraged us, and many others, to visit the Filey Convention held annually under the auspices of MWE (Movement for World Evangelisation) and the leadership of Lindsay Clegg, the Reverend George Duncan and the Reverend Ben Peake. Quite radical in those days, the movement sought "to foster and carry out evangelism within the Christian church, both at home and overseas" and "to bring the claims of Christ to the unconverted, to challenge the individual Christian to a life of devotion and to lay before the church as a whole the needs of the world in which we live." The convention itself was held out of season at the Butlin's Holiday Camp at Filey and included all the amusements and facilities of the camp except the bars and nightclubs. It proved to be a pioneer of what later became a Bible Week. The programme included enthusiastic and lively meetings each afternoon; Fact and Faith or similar Christian films were shown, whilst missionary exhibitions were open throughout the week. Seminars and sessions on various topics attracted hundreds. The exhibitions gave us lots of information, and we soon became aware of a strict mission regime that demanded Bible School training additional to our own professional studies. These were facts, which didn't settle lightly with two enthusiastic young Christians.

Mission had always seemed exciting and challenging, and we investigated as much as we could. Was it possibly a sense of heroism, or an appetite for more, or could it just be a divine curiosity put within? For us and for many others of our generation, interest was awakened by the account of the mission of five Americans who were killed at the hands of the Auca Indians of Ecuador in 1956 whilst attempting to share the gospel with them. The report of their death in *The Observer* read:

> There can be no doubt about the dedicated heroism of the five young Americans who lost their lives in 1956 in the jungles of Ecuador. They chose to go into the Auca country knowing it to be dangerous . . . They stood simply and unarmed on a sand bank in the Curaray River waiting for the Auca Indians to come, and when they did come the young men were not afraid to die. It is a poignant witness to the poise and purpose of a group of men who believed it to be their heavenly assignment, and having agreed on a plan went through with it to death.

One of the group, Jim Elliot, had as his motto "he's no fool who gives what he can't keep to gain what he can't lose," and this had sunk deep into our hearts.

Something far more personal had already fired Ann for mission. In the early 1950s, Gladys Aylward – the Cockney Sparrow, as she became known – had returned from China to visit her beloved London. Gladys had a call to China, but being of humble origin and theologically unqualified she had been rejected by established mission boards. Under her own steam and at her own expense she was later to travel alone on the Trans-Siberian railway to China and become God's instrument of compassion to many needy children. Ann had eagerly attended one of the mission meetings and was challenged by Gladys's question as she shook her hand before leaving: "Will you go to China?" These words never left Ann; China was never out of her thoughts or prayers. She looked forward to visiting this vast yet desperately needy country to share Jesus. It was sadly one of Ann's unrealised ambitions, a work left for others to pursue.

It was at one Filey Convention, George Duncan preached a powerful commitment message on the incident in the life of King David, recorded in the First Book of Chronicles chapter 21, where David aims to set up an altar to worship and asks Ornan, the owner of the chosen site, to let him know the cost. Ornan replied, "Take it yourself, do what you like, see here are also oxen and wood and wheat for the offering, I give it all." David however replied, "I will surely buy it for the full price, for I will not take what is yours for the Lord, or offer a burnt offering which costs me nothing." And David called to the Lord, and He answered him with fire from heaven on the altar of burnt offering. In response to the appeal at the end of the meeting Ann and I went forward to publicly offer our lives to God, as fully as we knew, to the mission of full-time sharing the good news of our Saviour wherever this might lead. But before this commitment could unfold with any clarity there were pressing things to outwork in our studies and in our relationship.

CHAPTER TWO

UP AND COMING

The duties of a nursing cadet were often menial. It's fair to say they landed all the jobs that most professionals hated, jobs that in those days nurses took as part of their duties. These were caring for patients' whole welfare, toileting, even cleaning, seeing to food distribution, individual patient's needs and the running and fetching duties that each busy ward required. Thankfully today a whole range of support workers and health care assistants supplement the nurses' role. Not always were the cadets successful and Ann often recounted the instance of the time when a colleague was asked to collect all the dentures from the bedside lockers of the elderly for cleaning. To speed up the task she took a bowl, put the teeth in, cleaned them but forgot whom they belonged to! No one complained, so presumably they were satisfied patients.

At the age of eighteen, State Registered Nurse training commenced – blue uniforms, black lace-up shoes, fob watch, starched hat and apron and, for external use, a navy blue, red-lined cape. Attractive, efficient and more than a touch of discipline! Training was to be for three years and included practical work placements, as well as in-house teaching schools and, ultimately, external examinations. Shift working, night work and bank holidays were included. The regime was strict and the rewards were minimal, from which all expenses including travel had to be squeezed. By now brother John was back on the scene and living at home after an interlude in California. He had a novel way of subsidising his recently acquired motorcar – getting as many people as possible to pay to travel with him. This also included Ann and her nursing friends paying for the privilege of not travelling on public transport. There were of course the inevitable times when the vehicle had difficulty in starting and needed a push, and who better than his passengers? On those early damp mornings, it was not unusual to see Ann and her friends running with the car whilst John let out the clutch.

This period was a very happy time, though the stresses and strains of learning and studying were obvious, and looming exams or attending at surgical operations presented their own pressures, as did the laying out of bodies or coping with the arrogance of seniors in the hospital structure. However, the system proved to be highly successful as all the student nurses qualified and later two of Ann's close friends and erstwhile bed pushers rose to be head of midwifery and matron at the later replacement district general hospital.

Finishing her duties at eight in the evening offered an opportunity for us to meet in Rotherham, not a place noted in those days for a high life, even if we wanted it. Our romantic outings were occasionally to the local Odeon or Essoldo cinemas, or for a coffee and sandwich at the very reputable local-authority-owned Whitehall café (this was before the era of fast-food outlets, although a local Wimpy bar did materialise soon after). Saturday evenings could also be occupied by a visit to the local League of Prayer, originally founded by Reader Harris QC and locally led by Albert Harper, a spiritually minded Methodist local preacher and businessman. Albert later developed the Town Mission where he and his family concentrated upon the needs of Rotherham town centre.

Soon after Ann's commencement of nurse training I sat my A-level exams – qualifying with average grades but walking straight into a place at Sheffield University to study for an honours degree in architecture. Studying nearby meant we could see each other more frequently. During this time I was also working holiday periods with Ann's father on local housing sites, which was not only developing the work ethic and bringing in much needed funding, but was also giving me real practical site experience which later became a necessary part of the Royal Institute of British Architects requirements for architectural training.

The course was for five years, plus two years' practice after-wards prior to registration, so in our minds as we contem-plated the possibility of marriage we anticipated this would not be for years to come, since the very thought was frowned upon, especially in nurse training. For my first year I lived in digs in the Woodseats district of Sheffield along with an old lady whom I had previously met when my grandparents lived close by years before. It became only a place to eat and sleep, for most of the drafting work was done in the architec-tural studio at Sherwood Road on large, practically immobile, drawing boards. Ann's shift pattern (usually three months at a time) meant split rotas with afternoons free or working nights, such that in two weeks it was possible to work twelve-hour shifts for nine successive days, as well as being responsible for one or two wards on each landing. Patient numbers could be as high as fifty, sixty or even more, quite a responsibility for a young student nurse.

Within weeks of attending the University at Sheffield I became involved in the work of the Christian Literature Crusade (CLC), which had recently opened a small bookshop on Devonshire Street. Interested in the books, I spent time browsing and enquiring about the literature ministry. Soon I was using what spare time I had to help decorate the first-floor living quarters, over the shop, occupied by two older single ladies. With enthusiasm they told me of the vision for the work by a local couple who had left for ministry in India. The names of Geoff and Pauline Williams meant nothing to me then. Years later we were to meet this couple I had heard so much about, after their return from India.

In spite of all our plans we decided to ask our parents' permission to get engaged at eighteen (the age of majority being twenty-one at that time). A little shocked, they agreed, and we set out to pray about our future. We decided, again with our parents' consent, to marry on Easter Saturday, 13 April 1963 and invited Ruth to be our bridesmaid, along with my older sister Lyn and our niece Jayne, whilst Keith performed the duties of best man. The Reverend John Bromley, who married us, was asked to make the service a time of rejoicing and outreach in view of the many unsaved people likely to be present. All went successfully and after a mid-afternoon wedding we managed to catch an early evening train from Doncaster to honeymoon in London. Young, innocent and dressed to the nines we stood out like chapel hat pegs in the carriage, since the train was packed with football supporters returning from the north to London. All the banter was good natured. Our time in London was excellent and this became just one of our frequent visits to the capital as time passed. Surprisingly, like lots of other Londoners Ann knew very little of the city of her birth.

As students we had decided to prioritise on our studies and owing to our lack of finances planned to live with Ann's parents, in two rooms, in their new sixties-built semi until we qualified. We owed a lot to their generosity and tolerance that enabled us to pursue our courses and ultimately buy the property as the in-laws moved to a new purpose-designed bungalow a little way away (yes, you guessed – one of my first designs).

Not everything was work (although it could easily have become so). We also gave ourselves the dubious pleasure of learning to drive and the acquisition of our first vehicle. Ann learned her skills through a local driving school whilst to save money I allowed myself to be taught by newly qualified Ann, economical but a definite error of judgement. We had acquired an Austin Devon (known as "the ugly duckling") for a bargain price of thirty pounds. It was well before MOT vehicle testing; otherwise I'm sure it would not have passed as being roadworthy. It had a small rear window, side arm indicators (that needed hitting to come out) and a front wing held on by string. To start, it was necessary to swing a starting handle (I never did get the hang of it!). For my first lesson Ann took me to a local hill, about one in four gradient, and then proceeded to teach me a hill start! Juddering without knowledge of clutch control, this proved to be a frightening big non-event. I was however more confident on level ground, but a visit to Matlock, Derbyshire, was far from level and running out of motion in the town centre was utterly embarrassing. After six months we came to the demise of the Devon – but so blessed were we that a neighbour came and towed it away and gave us twenty-five pounds for it in spite of a broken cylinder-head gasket. Six months' motoring for a depreciation of five pounds – if only all my vehicles were so economical.

Ann's nursing career seemed to flourish, but the local hierarchy did not appreciate the fact of her marriage during her course. They were not openly hostile, but neither did they seem to be sympathetic. Ann persisted with her course and ultimately qualified in the summer of 1964. My architectural training seemed to be unaffected by my status and that same year two other students also married – so ten percent of the year now had marital responsibilities.

Many people have expressed surprise, if not concern, at the early age at which we married but it was one of those decisions of which we were sure. Expressions of regret on our young age were passed by some to our parents, but as students together it became a mutually supporting relationship and with the aid of Ann's parents it made good economic sense. We believed, however, it was God who had brought us together; we were learning the scriptural principle that two had become one.

After qualification as a staff nurse Ann had now to decide what direction her career was to take – would it be midwifery training, medical or surgical speciality, or one of many other career opportunities? She selected none of these hospital options but was successful in obtaining a post in the education field under the county's medical officer, Dr Watts, in a local adult training centre. This was a pioneer venture bringing employment training to special needs adults, those who had suffered medical problems at birth, or in childhood, or those with special physical or educational needs such as Down's syndrome. She worked here alongside an older colleague, Hilda Brydone, who shared the same birthday but was twenty years her senior. It didn't take long for the subject of Christianity to arise between them, and it was the start of a very warm and lasting friendship, leading subsequently to the beginning of a new lifestyle for Hilda and her husband Vic. Hilda later recalled:

> When Ann and Norman first visited us, it was with an invitation: "We're off to a Christian meeting and thought you might like to come." I remember our mild protestation of "well, we're not ready, and wouldn't want to delay you" – to which excuses they cheerfully replied, "That's all right, we'll wait!" So began the first of a number of similar invitations (and acceptances) by this so sincere and enthusiastic young couple, which in due course, led to our going with them to a Billy Graham relay rally at the City Hall, in Sheffield.

The unusual career move, out of the hospital umbrella, was to set a foundation for Ann for opportunities in later days, all experiences that God used when offered to him for service. It also highlighted that Ann was a people's person and her love for individuals, irrespective of their needs or condition, was already expanding. The period at the training centre was a very enjoyable part of her career, since it provided a definite daytime work pattern, excellent conditions, new work colleagues and was merely a mile from home. "Ann's stay at the Centre," recalled Hilda, "was a tremendous time for both myself, other staff and the children, who were very happy and content. According to their parents, everyone looked forward each day to coming."

The year 1965 saw the return of evangelist Billy Graham to Britain, to hold a series of crusades at Manchester. Our enthusiasm was immense and we organised transport for all who wished to go from Maltby. Our youth club friends Ted and Joyce Stocks responded to the appeal. Once again God had used his servant to affect our lives. Within two years, my sister Margaret and her future husband, John, also gave their lives to Jesus.

The situation at the local church however was becoming less encouraging. Little spiritual input continued. Our mentoring of young Christians was discouraged, especially by one minister who said it was his job to follow up those in the church (although he didn't do it). So with misgivings we gave in our resignation as members and left to attend the Brethren Assembly in Rotherham, continuing to use our home as a base for local hospitality and fellowship.

The Rotherham assembly was different from anything we had previously experienced. Although an open meeting, there were definite rules for male and female participation, a different Sunday morning ministry (centred around the breaking of bread from the Last Supper), an evening gospel service plus a series of mid-week meetings, including those for children. We eagerly participated in the new pattern. After years of personal struggle we were publicly baptised as believing adults. Embracing this biblical command for Ann had not been the problem that it had been for me. Attending a Baptist church, she was utterly convinced of believers' baptism in Scripture, but had not proceeded because of respect for her parents' lack of enthusiasm. Believers' baptism was not, however, the theology espoused at Maltby, but as we had much discussion and prayer it became our convinced response to Scripture.

Like many places of worship at that time, the assembly had a very strong youth emphasis but since we were married and generally older than most of these we were not directly involved in their activities. We did, however, get to know the young people, many of whom later grew and took the responsibility of church leadership across the area.

It was also at this time that we became more aware of Christian activities in Sheffield. We had both passed our driving tests and had now purchased a small green Austin A30 van, to which I had added rear seating (but no rear windows) and we were far more mobile. Sheffield boasted the Youth Squash, a gathering of young people in the city centre, under the leadership of Pete and Rita Fenwick. It was the place to go, excellent speakers, vibrant worship, keen committed Christians. However 1965 saw Ann pregnant with our first child so gallivanting off to Sheffield was not always easy.

At the end of September Ann finished work at the training centre and on 22 December 1965 our first child, Martin, was born at Rotherham. Our firstborn, a son, born in Yorkshire – definitely eligible to play cricket for THE county! Only tykes know what a privilege that could be. We were further blessed when Ann was allowed home on Christmas Eve and we could spend our first Christmas time together as a family (and of course with all the extended family as well, who had turned up to see the latest addition).

Pregnancy and motherhood presented few problems to Ann; she seemed to thrive at these times, even glowed on such occasions. She was a natural at child rearing, excelling in spite of the pressures and overcoming, often in exhaustion but always with a smile. Neither did the advent of a child keep us from sharing fellowship with other Christians.

Our little green van was ideal for the carrycot with Martin tucked inside, and off we would go, speaking around the Rotherham/Sheffield area or visiting, wherever possible, to find meetings that would feed our spiritual appetites.

At the same time the pressures were building for myself, for the next few months would see the end of my five-year architectural course. The final year's graft was extensive and many hours were worked completing submissions for my finals. These submissions comprised a whole set of presentation and technical drawings, perspectives and interior designs for a College of Art and Design on a site in Rotherham, designed from a brief given by the Principal of the existing Art College. Today Rotherham has an actual College of Art and Design, built on an adjacent site to that I proposed. The examiners accepted my proposals though not without some unsuccessful representations for a higher degree by my tutor. I graduated with an average honours degree, which enabled me to start earning at last. I commenced employment with the West Riding County Council Architects Department at the Doncaster Divisional Office in Adwick-le-Street and started two days after graduation in early July. Within weeks Ann's parents moved into their new bungalow and we now had a home of our own.

CHAPTER THREE

FRIENDS AND FAMILY

Before our marriage we had naturally spoken about how we would live our lives together, what expectations we would have of each other, how many children we hoped to have and when would be the best time for them and so on. In other words, from the comfort of inexperience we would formulate principles for living. We determined that our personal relationship with God would come first, then our own relationship and finally our relationship with others. We would seek to encourage one another in the things of God and we would always honour God's word, seeking practically to implement this in our daily lives. Building ourselves up in the faith we would aim to introduce others to our Saviour. Home was to be the natural centre of our witness and we would welcome anyone, demonstrating our love and faith through hospitality. However easy it was to formulate such principles it was much more difficult to apply them, but with characteristic ingenuity we managed to have floods of visitors come through all our various homes, wherever the location.

Keith and Gwen continued to mentor us, and then Ted and Joyce Stocks came more on the scene, as did other keen active members from other churches: Elsie and Ernest Careless, Geoff and Irene Foster, Ken and Elaine Happs, more mature Christians than us but also seeking deeper fellowship. Hilda and Vic plus other family members pressed in, including Norman Norris and family members from the local Pentecostal church. The numbers began to rise and we commenced a Sunday evening fellowship group that grew, with visitors coming from all around the area. For fourteen years this powerhouse of prayer and praise, fellowship and vulnerability, impacted the lives of those who hungered after more of God. This was actually church, providing heart and spirit commitment, relationships, meeting needs and giving spiritual direction. Sadly, at the time, many local denominations were not providing this encouragement. We were not competing with the local churches but complementing and stimulating the deep needs of so many. Vic shared later about the group:

This further led to the forming with others of a Bible study group in which Ann and Norman shared in a leadership role. Importantly for me, this brought me into a different style of life because, up to that time, I was rather a nominal Christian with much to learn and in being involved in this group my eyes were really opened, particularly to my very inadequate biblical understanding. To a shy and self-conscious person like me, finding myself in a group of people much more informed than I, caused me some trepidation and embarrassment, which I made great efforts to conceal . . . It was in this situation that I recognised one of the gifts which Ann possessed, because I found it so easy to speak with her. She gave me confidence, was always ready to help explain things of which I was unsure, always with

patience and a desire to help. She gave me so much encouragement, more, I am sure, than she could ever have known or
realised. Indeed, one simply had to recognise her as a special
friend.

After only two years we were now feeling it was time to
leave the Rotherham Assembly, not in dispute but in right
standing, returning to Maltby and to the chapel, which we
had previously left! We were gladly received, our previous
youthful arrogance forgiven, and we learned lessons on
humility and God's ability to exalt. We offered to serve
where needed and soon were involved again in the life of the
church. Our stay, however, was not actually going to be for
long (we didn't know it at the time), and we soon moved on.
We continued to maintain relationships with the church
members right up to the chapel's closure many years later.

For several months alongside Ted and Joyce we ran
a Good News Club, ministering to, amongst others, the
unlikely village waifs and strays, enjoying each challenge
and every demanding minute. We would spend hours
preparing the sessions, feeling visual presentation was paramount. We would do anything to share the gospel with local
children. Ted would speak or play the guitar, Ann played the
piano, Joyce had an excellent singing voice whilst I spoke
and did the arty bits. Action choruses, crafts and stories
seemed to bring in family groups, many needy, ill-clothed
and dirty children coming for love and attention as well as
the handouts and the fun. The practical needs of food, clothing and shoes in particular were regular problems we
encountered and which we provided for out of our
own resources. For years it was working on the principle of
"inasmuch as you did it to the least of these, you did it to

me . . . ", a scripture which often became a generator for later ventures. Eternity will disclose its effectiveness. Joyce was to recall later that Ann was an inspiration; she always had what Arthur Blessit called "a one-track mind" fixed on Jesus!

In our ideal family scenario we aspired to marriage at twenty-five and having six children. Reality dictated otherwise and we actually married when Ann was twenty and myself six months younger. Ultimately we had five children of our own: Martin, December 1965; Kathryn (Kate), May 1967; Elizabeth (Liz), November 1968; Joanne (Jo) September 1971; and Peter (adopted 1991). Ann had said that she wanted lots of children as she found it so easy giving birth (a comment that raised eyebrows to say the least amongst other young mums). She also found many more besides to love, but more of that later. Each child brought such a lot into the family, as well as individual demands, which Ann took in her stride. Marriage in the sixties at such a young age plus a desire for a large family was not considered acceptable; social norms and pressures to conform to the then current practices were enormous. It was obvious that we were somehow non-conformists in many of our attitudes and actions, working out our own salvation with fear and trembling. Psalm 127 verse 3 states that "Children are a blessing from the Lord," and we were pleased that we were suitably blessed with beautiful, healthy children. My post as an architect allowed financial provision for their upkeep but like many young families we had to add faith to balance income and expenditure, especially as we had embraced the scriptural principle we had recently learned, the giving of a minimum of a tenth of our incomes.

In order to develop her own career further and to supplement our income, Ann looked for part-time employment.

She did this in three particular areas, whilst the children were small; one involved taking a post as a family planning nurse, which included further study and training. In the economy of God, this became beneficial for her later role as health educator. Clinics were held generally in late afternoon or evening each week and not only extended her knowledge of the benefits and dangers of contraception but also gave Ann contact with many anxious wives and mothers whom she could reassure. Family planning was somewhat of a taboo at this time within Christian circles; a barrier that in reality took years to break. In a small way here again Ann was breaking through in areas other Christians would not or could not openly embrace.

Ann also put her name forward to a nursing agency for the private nursing of patients in either their own homes or within private nursing home facilities. This non-National Health provision was limited but was an essential service for those able to pay for their own medical care. Generally this kind of nursing was for the elderly and from time to time Ann would build up relationships with individuals, but sadly this was usually at the end of their lives and several died whilst she was in attendance. Often her last duty was to lay out her clients prior to the relatives calling in the undertakers. In a strange way her career experiences were being expanded and her caring capacity enlarged. Once again this sphere of service would prove beneficial in her later work with the elderly.

Not all this agency work was local; often she would go to Sheffield and even to Barnsley. On one such occasion as she was driving via the motorway, off up the slip road she commenced braking, but nothing happened and the car proceeded to the roundabout and the traffic beyond. She was hit from one side and hit from the other. Somehow, she said, in those microseconds "her life passed before her" until she managed to squeeze out of our car, which by that time was a foot narrower than when she started. Apart from shaking and shock there were no injuries. In a couple of hours I was able to collect her and bring her home. No mechanical defects were discovered with the vehicle subsequently. We were overjoyed at this amazing escape.

The final area of work Ann embraced was the teaching of first aid to interested personnel, plus coal miners from Maltby colliery, in weekly evening classes based at the local comprehensive school. This suited the family situation and meant I was generally available to babysit. Initially, Ann was quite unsure about this appointment, being asked to substitute for a friend, but in fact enjoyed the sessions and never looked back. Since Maltby had a deep coal mine (and still is one of the few working coal mines in Britain) the input of miners was always a vital part of the community. Safety procedures in the work place were essential and the National Coal Board encouraged the teaching of first aid as a necessary part of individual responsibilities. The macho miners were often surprisingly squeamish at times and it was Ann's job to channel the bravado or hesitation into a positive attitude with practical skills. She learned very quickly to use the motivator or troublemaker of the group as the live model for a demonstration of bandaging. This meant she could quickly quieten and tie up potential trouble – all in a realistic demonstration for the benefit of others. She was fearless in situations like these and the lessons learned here were to be used repeatedly on occasions when she was to teach first aid later in semi-hostile classroom situations.

I'm always amazed that we humans produce and rear children generally when we are immature and inexperienced. It's like the chicken and egg syndrome; which comes first, good parenting or experience? Nature or nurture? Like all young parents we were learning on the job; what to do with crying babies and how to diagnose the needy or sick children; when to call the doctor, what injections to have and all the plethora of decisions. Our first experience of this occurred after only three weeks when we had to rush Martin by ambulance in the middle of the night to Sheffield Children's Hospital with suspected meningitis. Fortunately it proved to be a lesser viral infection instead. Inevitably many more incidents occurred, such as the problem of a piece of sponge foam up a nostril for Kate and how to get it out, or a bead lodged in an ear. In spite of this we found that two children were relatively easy to manage, one each – but then along came Liz, baby number three, a new challenge, more children than parents!

It was at this time that our neighbour found the crying of our children, especially at night, more than she could bear and whenever a child woke crying we received a banging on the separating party wall to tell us to be quiet; understandable since her husband, a milkman, rose early in the morning. The pressure became intolerable and we knew we had to move: was this to be the outworking of what we had intended years before at the Filey Convention? We had offered to go anywhere for God; was now the time and what was to be the destination?

We started to investigate mission further and the means of service abroad; neither of us was a linguist but we did have useful careers in nursing and construction to offer. Surprisingly, we were not seen as God's answer to a dying world! Careers we might have, but the path to progress in mission was through further training – Bible College, missionary orientation and linguistics – a total package that would take several more years. Admittedly we were only in our twenties, but by now we had three children and we hesitated to push further training years upon them. Since I had already trained seven years before becoming a member of the Royal Institute it all seemed too much. We declined to go down this rigid, traditional route, believing this pattern was not for our family or us. Commitment, qualifications and experience we could offer, but we did not believe God wanted us to sacrifice our family in this way. Our dilemma remained; we believed God had called us to mission, yet we did not feel it was to be via the normal route. The neighbour harassment was, however, increasing. How would we square the circle?

As change was obviously on the horizon for us again, so it was for our close friends too. Keith was successful in obtaining a place at Spurgeon's College in London to train as a Baptist minister, so he and his family moved out into small family accommodation in the Metropolis, whilst Ted took up employment with the Central Electricity Generating Board at Portishead in Bristol; so they moved on too. The way was opening up for new relationships.

CHAPTER FOUR

UP A GEAR

The sixties and seventies were important in our spiritual development but it became obvious that it was also a period when God was at work in the church both nationally and internationally. There was a sense of excitement, a looking forward to something more, beyond the often legalistic and formal religious experience prevalent in many Christian denominations.

The publication in 1963 of David Wilkerson's book *The Cross and the Switchblade* (which became a best seller very quickly) highlighted that God could use the available disciple to bring about dramatic change to people's lives; in this instance, of those affected by drugs and a gang mentality of living. Today it still has a powerful message, having been re-issued innumerable times and made into a film and a stage play. Co-author of *The Cross and the Switchblade*, John L. Sherrill, wrote *They Speak with Other Tongues* in 1964. This was "a sensitive and personal introduction to the subject . . . about a supernatural gift which is changing people today and showing that miracles still happen to ordinary people"

(Michael Harper). In a similar but perhaps more dynamic way Dennis Bennett's book *Nine O' Clock in the Morning*, again on the work of the Holy Spirit, became a blockbuster. A spin-off from the work of David Wilkerson was the ministry of one of his converts Nicky Cruz, whose own story, *Run Baby Run*, first published in 1968, also became a best seller. Nicky toured the UK several times, sharing his testimony and impacting many lives. Inevitably we attended these public meetings and took whoever would come with us.

Publications, books, meetings all gave impetus and created interest in sections of the church which were buzzing with what God was doing. Visiting ministries provided much encouragement and these meetings at various venues provided opportunity for us to take along non-Christian friends. Once again Gladys Aylward returned to Britain to share, and of course this was an essential meeting for us both to be updated on her continuing ministry in China. More and more personalities were being used publicly by God to encourage individuals to spread a message beyond the norm experienced by the local church.

Slowly the national church scene was beginning to change and a hunger for spiritual things on the part of individuals from several denominations became apparent. New local church fellowships sprang up throughout the country where body ministry, multiple leadership, plus the work of the Holy Spirit, became points of discussion, involvement and tenets of faith. Body ministry emphasised the scriptural truths that spiritual gifting in the church was not the sole prerogative of ordained leadership. Multiple and team leadership became a recognition that the "one-man band" was not the emphasis of Scripture. Was the church merely perpetuating the division between priesthood and laity, creating unreal expectations of individuals and inhibiting the priesthood of all believers? The roles and ministries of apostles, prophets, pastors, teachers and evangelists were to be explored again and again from that period onwards and Paul's letter to the Ephesian church became a much studied, preached and practised epistle. The truth of the work of the Holy Spirit, the fullness and baptism in the Spirit, enabled many to come into a new relationship with the Trinity. In the new wave of God serving the hunger of His people, the books of Chinese Christian Watchman Nee became very influential and many of these are classics.

These initial trickles and following surges for more of God were described as "streams" rather than "denominations" and ultimately the entire phenomenon became known as "the charismatic movement", which over the years was criticised for the shallowness of its doctrine or the extravagances of its adherents. This was without doubt a move of God. Our experience was one of intimacy of relationship with Father, Son and Spirit in a pragmatic way that did not suffer from the excesses and intensity of others.

The emphasis on the work of the Holy Spirit began to spread in the traditional Protestant denominations and was seen as renewal; nor was this limited to Protestants, for even sections of the Roman Catholic Church embraced the teaching and experienced the gifts of the Spirit in worship. The church in Maltby, of all places, later became a local beacon in healing gifts and ministry! Exploration into the gifts of the Spirit and whether these were still relevant resulted, and a local emphasis on healing by prayer and the laying on of hands started to filter through even to the backwaters. American Episcopalian minister Graham Pulkingham's book *Gathered for Power*, relating his experiences and those of his church in Houston, Texas, in introducing the things of the Spirit, provided guidelines for many in traditional churches. Interdenominational conferences and Christian summer camps became popular and opportunities for individual and church growth were now more readily available. In a personal way these new opportunities had to be balanced with the needs of our young family and the responsibilities of our careers.

Somehow, even in spite of early rising with wide-awake youngsters, and the demands of work, we made it a priority in our lives to explore any new exciting publications. Our daily devotions were generally taken before the children woke, and became lifelines to our further spiritual development. The norm in many churches had become the proclamation of a social gospel, but we determined to get exposure to good foundational teaching wherever and whenever possible. Alongside this we often encountered opposition but we realised, in later years, that this had merely produced a hunger for more of God and a determination at all costs to press on. We grew through this period of discipline and opposition to appreciate and value both the word of God and our relationship with Father.

A further significant event in the local spiritual scene, and possibly even within the nation at large, was the ministry of the Christian musical *Come Together* written in 1972 by Jimmy and Carol Owens. Singer Pat Boone, himself a Christian (who just happened to be one of Ann's teenage pop heroes), in his foreword to the musical score introduces John 17:20–21: "Neither pray I for these alone, but for them also which shall believe on me through their word; that they all may be one; as thou, Father, art in me, and I in thee, that they also may be one in us: that the world may believe that thou hast sent me."

Hear this plea from Jesus to His Father; intimately pouring out His deepest concerns in the very shadow of the cross, all "that the world may believe". The purpose of *Come Together* was to rediscover the fantastic thrill that swept the first-century Christians out into the streets from house to house.

Jimmy and Carol Owens introduce the work and reveal their intentions, which were fresh and sensitive and appeared to be in line with what was happening across the nation:

Come Together is an experience in Christian love. It is an opportunity for young people to lead an experiment in worship, to establish the unity of all God's people as the whole church is invited to worship and minister together. It is an opportunity for worshippers to set aside their accustomed role of observer, and to participate in active worship and ministry. It is an opportunity for people to be real in sharing their feelings and needs with the Lord and with one another. *Come Together* is a real attempt to communicate the fellowship of the saints; to demonstrate the "unfeigned love of the brethren"; to encourage every Christian to observe God's standards of purity, and challenge him to obey God's call to discipleship. It also presents the offer of eternal life through Jesus Christ to everyone who will receive Him . . .

We want people to become personally involved with Jesus and with their brothers and sisters in Christ. Since this will be a totally new kind of church experience to many people, it will be up to the performing group to present it in such a spontaneous and loving way that people will feel comfortable and free to join in. Strive for freedom, sweetness of spirit, not a show business "performance". Lead the assembly in an experience of love and fellowship. People must see the real thing, not just hear songs about it. . . Create in the audience an expectancy that God is going to do something, and when He does don't rush Him.

Somehow this encapsulated the mood of the moment and musicians and singers from across the denominations fellowshipped and learned both songs and music together prior to the public performances. Songs such as "Freely, freely, you have received", "All we like sheep have gone astray" and "Turn the hearts of the children to their parents" were so powerfully anointed that the words became a ministry both to choir members and audiences alike. The local gospel group known as Faith predominantly provided the musical input. Interest in being involved was high.

This was the time when we had heard that a local couple (a nursery nurse and scout master/mining surveyor) wanted to participate. Ann had heard of Christine through her trip to the schools and although we had not met Peter we had been praying for them both even though they were only names to us then. Meeting them at one of the singing practices proved to be our opportunity to introduce ourselves, open up about our faith and invite them for a meal. Gradually this relationship developed such that the Pilsworth family moved into Oldcotes to be part of our worshipping community. They were just a couple of years our seniors, but with children of similar ages. As our relationship progressed, we shared holidays, many adventures and much time together. Eventually our families were united as their second daughter Jenny married our eldest son Martin in 1985. Ann was able to have a special personal input into the life of Sue, Jenny's older sister, meeting with her weekly to encourage her in the faith. Sue subsequently married Junior, a Brazilian Christian, and now both are on full-time mission in France. Sue stated clearly that she owed her interest in mission to Ann's mentoring and spiritual encouragement whilst a teenager.

After the spiritual success of *Come Together* the Faith Group led the later Jimmy and Carol Owens presentation, *If My People*, which again brought the local church together from its many buildings. As before, this presentation produced a vehicle for service, fellowship and ministry, particularly to the churches in the community, and many new introductions were made and circles widened.

CHAPTER FIVE

OVER THE BORDER

Summertime was not only a period for leisure but also a time for service. How better to serve than by taking the local young people, including our own children, whenever possible on Christian camps? We were introduced by friends to the Colne Valley Children's Camps, held at various venues around the country for a number of weeks each summer. This maximised the use of camping equipment and enabled campers to have a bumper time as cheaply as possible. Ken Woodhouse and John Harris (John was married to Audrey, who just happened to be one of only two other Christians I knew at school) led the team. Various evangelists were invited annually to share the truths of the gospel with the children alongside adventure outings, camp fires, fun fixtures, sports of all kinds. Ann again was enthusiastic for these events and saw them as an ideal time of fun and fellowship, an extension of her time at Girls' Brigade camps, times which had such an impact upon her when younger. The camps continue to this day with the children of the former leaders now in charge.

As the number of our own children grew it became more and more difficult to fulfil the demands of a camp and the care of several young children. Ann eventually had to withdraw, but was wholeheartedly in favour of me continuing to serve alongside the young people we had invited. The popularity of the camps increased and the numbers locally wanting to be involved put strain on our means of transport. It was here that a local group of Christians came in to fill the gap. They were to be away on the continent and without hesitation lent us their white transit van (which they normally used for touring the country on Christian gospel group gigs). We were able to stuff all our sleeping bags, clothes, bags, food and wellies into this God-given means of transport, providing what we needed, when we needed it. It was not our first introduction to this enthusiastic and generous group of young people, and it would not be our last. The transit van belonged to the Faith Group, the ministry arm of what later became Poplars Christian Fellowship.

Although funding was limited we ensured that we always went away on a family holiday, usually under canvas and as cheaply as possible – budgeting ourselves to expenditure even as low as a pound a day for any treats. Unforgettable days loading up our vehicle with everything but the kitchen sink! It was in the mid-seventies that for our family we again hit on the idea of combining spiritual ministry and holiday together and, searching for a suitable venue, discovered the Good News Crusade Camp at Blaithwaite in Cumbria. Novices in this form of organised camping, we were allocated to a section of the camp with several other families visiting, like ourselves, for the first time. Several of these were later to become camp unit leaders themselves. One had only just made the trip, having to resort to his car being towed the last few miles, since its engine had blown up. Such was the spirit of the camp that our unit took an offering and paid for his car to be repaired for the family's return. The camp numbers were about five hundred and these were broken down for supervision reasons into sections (or units) like our own.

Speakers that year included John Hutchinson, a Scotsman from near Glasgow, a pioneer in the use of the gifts of the Spirit and a previous owner of Blaithwaite House; David Adamson, a missionary from Tanzania and an ex-artificer on the aircraft carrier *Ark Royal*; and GNC Director Don Double, a tall giant of a church leader from Cornwall, called to pioneer evangelism alongside the work of the Holy Spirit as a joint message. Meetings were also held for teenagers and these were led by Simon Matthews, later to become Don's son-in-law. Our children appreciated Simon's "no holds barred" ministry. Scriptural rights and wrongs were vehemently defended and the young people lapped up his energetic, no-compromise style of sharing. Alongside seminars and meetings for adults and teenagers, provision was also made for children, with crèches for the very young. In the evening unit supervisors enabled parents to attend the big top tent meeting once the children were settled. For us and for many more this was a liberating time, providing a formula which came to be repeated again and again as Christian family camps became more popular.

John shared his revelation on the kingdom of God and although we knew it was good teaching, and settled well as God's vision for His people, it seemed way beyond where we were at that time. As the years went by John continued to speak on this life-message and more and more we gave our assent to its implications. It is true to say that it took years before we saw the outworking of this revelation in our own experience. Don preached in a way that brought the Scriptures to life, especially in the area of the supernatural and the miraculous. The fruit and gifts of the Spirit were explained and many people responded for prayer; and miracles of healing or words of prophecy, even discernment and deliverance, occurred without excesses throughout the week.

David spoke about his work in Tanzania, and the provision of God, whilst at the Friday morning meeting based on the Christian family he spoke on the roles of husband and wife. Married for several years by now, with children of our own and committed wholeheartedly, we considered ourselves to be keen Christians. This was the first time we had heard scriptural teaching on such a subject and in such a clear practical way. Scripturally based, this teaching was revolutionary to us. We learned of both roles and responsibilities of partners and the practical way of addressing the needs of the individuals. We had somehow established our marriage on equality rather than upon two becoming one, subjugating our distinctive roles and knowing little of spiritual leadership, protection and example. Like the principles and truths of the kingdom, this teaching settled well with us but we knew there would have to be changes. We would never be the same again. Tears flowed as we responded to God's word and we held one another, committing ourselves to change yet again under the hand of God: change not meant to destroy but to create precious stones for His glory.

As the meeting finished we spoke to David and in view of his accent asked from where he originated. Imagine our surprise to find his former home was Rotherham! In view of our proximity to his hometown he asked whether we could keep an eye on his elderly father, a task which we agreed to do, and which we did for several years until his death. This practical service led to the development of a long relationship with David and his wife Jetta and family, which included visits to their home in Copenhagen once they moved from Tanzania, and later to Cornwall as they moved back to Britain.

In the desire to fulfil these new principles in our family life we read all we could on the Christian family. Noticeable at this time was Larry Christenson's book *The Normal Christian Family* which I tried religiously to implement. Ann and the children suffered my many attempts to get it right until we realised that Rome was not built in a day, and it wouldn't happen all at once. God had put a desire in our hearts to change; now we must allow Him to bring it about naturally with our co-operation. Zeal and methods would not produce lasting change; it must be our response and obedience on a daily basis. I realised my error, and repented. The changes that resulted came about in God's timing, not mine.

The ministry of our initial Good News Crusade Camp was never surpassed in our estimation. However GNC Camps became an annual outing from then onwards and we were instrumental in taking many of our friends to one or more camps as time went by. Ruth Tate remembers one such occasion:

My clear memory is of Blaithwaite 1980. During the previous years we became aware that God had done new things in your lives. Ann must have written about what was happening and told us about going to summer camp at Blaithwaite. She had also sent us a tape. This made me want to experience it for myself. We had a Bible study group in our house at that time and one of the girls had been to, or heard about, Blaithwaite camps and encouraged us to go as a group. Robert was very reluctant to go but was persuaded; so we packed our white van and trailer with five adults, two children and all the camping gear. It was a long, hot journey and we had arrived quite late. The site was very, very muddy and we were told that we could not take the van on to the site. Robert was *not* happy and he says he would have turned round and gone home. When we arrived at the site we were greeted by you with the words, "Are you still praising?"! That week was our biggest challenge. You all were such an inspiration, camping under conditions that we had never experienced before and still praising God. It was infectious! We were filled with the Spirit and I still can see Ann marching me round the field encouraging me to speak in tongues! We had old mind-sets totally shattered and experienced worship like never before. It was a week that changed our lives and we thank you both for the part you played in that.

We served under Bryan and Kath Barnes for two subsequent years until eventually we became unit leaders ourselves, always with lots of children and always with lots of helpers. To accommodate all our children our family tent seemed to annually increase in size. Camp numbers similarly increased until new venues, other than Blaithwaite, had to be found and camps doubled up to meet the demands from Christians throughout the country. It was our responsibility as unit leaders to welcome individuals and families as they arrived, offer refreshments, assist with erection of tents or positioning of caravans and to generally make campers feel at ease. This was no problem to Ann and the kettle was constantly boiling and her hospitality embraced everyone. Unit leaders were expected to be sensitive to individuals and their needs and know how best to help and release them from any spiritual hang-ups or inhibitions. Ann's boldness and anointing in sensing the needs of individuals led to many receiving healing or encouragement to press on further in God. We saw many released to move in the gifts of the Holy Spirit. On one occasion a tough army sergeant, touched by God, saw such release that tears streamed down his face. He shared that he had never cried in thirty years and definitely not in public. Amongst campers Ann's gifts earned her the nickname of "prodder"; she would not allow individuals to hide their lights under bushels.

We encouraged as many friends as possible to come to the camps, realising that they would benefit from the quality of the ministry and the exposure to dynamic teaching. Generally these were younger family groups or single persons. However we invited one pensioner friend, whose name was Leslie Thompson. We had met him on several occasions and shared meals together. Leslie was a black immigrant living in central London, on the outside an old patriarch, on the inside a vibrant, joyful personality. Years earlier Leslie had been a trumpeter with Louis Armstrong and was famous for his musical talent, playing nightclubs and venues around the world. Back in that distant past all was not well and just at the time Leslie was to launch out with his band and hit the "big-time" he encountered God in a personal way. His future plans were changed, as Leslie would say "for the better". He took up social work, ministering to offenders in prison. He never lost his talent for playing the trumpet. Here he was at Blaithwaite camp, in his late seventies, sleeping in a two-man pup tent, enjoying our hospitality and feeding on the ministry. It was Leslie who first challenged us to read right through the whole of Scripture, not portions here and there. We committed ourselves to this and it became our adopted way from then on of reading the Bible several times each year.

During the years of our camp involvement, full of many memories, two incidents other than our initial visit particularly stand out. Firstly the camp of 1980, the year of the deluge! It rained so much that the conditions under foot were, to say the least, muddy. Channels were cut in the ground for rainwater to escape downhill, whilst the surface and especially the walkways became a sea of mud. Our children eventually took off their wellington boots and just squelched around delightedly in mud up to their knees. Few, however, were discouraged and the camp continued as normally as possible. Once again the ministry was excellent; by the end of the week the rain had ceased and the fields were drying out.

Immediately after the camp we as a family and the Pilsworths (minus son Paul) continued our holiday and visited Nancy and Henry Phipps in the Orkney Islands. They had "emigrated" north to Stronsay from Carlton-in-Lindrick years earlier and before their move had been regular attenders at the Sunday evening meetings in our home. After Henry's reluctant but wholehearted conversion they too had been visitors to the summer camps (and any other meetings we could get them to). Now it was our turn to visit them. Having bought a small croft (School Brae) overlooking sea on both sides, Henry had wonderfully renovated the property. It proved large enough for two families of visitors from the south. We spent an energetic holiday – first of all keeping warm or acclimatising ourselves to the local windswept conditions, and then walking around the island collecting mushrooms or enjoying roaming on beautiful empty beaches. We visited as many highlights in and around the islands as we could, including Scara Brae, the Italian Chapel and Kirkwall on the mainland. Our return journey was via the post boat so we were able to see even more locations in this unspoilt beautiful part of Britain.Two weeks later we made our return home via Blaithwaite and were amazed to see how the camp field had survived; the ground was totally dried out, firm again with grass already emerging.

The other notable occasion for us was at a camp preparation weekend when unit leaders were invited to share and pray with the GNC team about the forthcoming camp so as to decide its theme, emphasis and ministry. Ann was particularly pleased because she felt, whilst having her devotions, that God had given her the theme from Isaiah 50:7: "Your God reigns". The meeting began by evaluating the previous camp and requesting suggestions for any changes. Likely themes for the forthcoming camp, however, seemed to falter and go nowhere. Ann shared her word (fearfully in such an august meeting), but this too was not received with any enthusiasm and the meeting broke up, to reconvene the following morning. It was then announced by Don that the camp theme was to be – "Our God reigns", just one letter different from Ann's word. This theme ultimately led to several new songs as well as re-emphasising that God was and is in control.

The camp weeks were always preceded by much preparation, such that the work became so demanding that eventually we felt God saying that we were no longer to be physically involved. We needed the time (ostensibly called leave/holiday) for rest and recuperation ourselves, especially in view of our busy lifestyles. It meant a big wrench but we knew we could not maintain this pace forever. The camp season in our lives was coming to a close; it was now time to minister within the local church scene and preserve our annual leave for family and personal relaxation. Many of those we had introduced to these camps continued to have an input over the years that followed.

Meanwhile after almost three years in post I applied for a higher position at Rotherham Borough Council. This move, I reasoned, would be of double immediate benefit: it would cut down my seventeen-mile journey each way to the WRCC Divisional office at Adwick-le-Street and give me exposure to the design and construction of local authority housing which was not available through the County. My application proved successful and I commenced employment at Rotherham in February 1969 where I stayed for almost two years. The significance of this change proved to be two-fold. Firstly, it offered a tremendous opportunity to get involved from design to completion in various sized housing projects, offering exposure to a new language of finances, grants and to local political aspirations. Secondly, at a personal level, it presented an opportunity to purchase a property from one of my new colleagues, in the village of Oldcotes just four miles from Maltby.

Oldcotes was just over the boundary of north Nottinghamshire in the district of Bassetlaw. It consisted of several farms, a hundred or so dwellings, a pub, two church buildings, a chapel, a village hall, and a pile (with resident squire) all situated on the crossroads of the A631 and the A60. Apart from the prospect of a new home, nothing initially attracted us to the place, except the plot of land and the house under construction. The property had four bedrooms, a study, ground floor cloaks area, a garage; above all it was detached, no prospect of neighbours banging on the wall! One other plus factor was that Ann's father had been successful in obtaining the electrical sub-contract on the premises, which ultimately meant we wired the house together. In October 1969 we moved into the village, with decorating, landscaping and furnishing still to complete – but another new adventure.

Since the properties were not numbered we sought for a house name and after much consultation settled on Charisma, meaning "the gift and grace of God". It was not a generally known word in our Christian or non-Christian circles at that time. It later became much in vogue, even became maligned, but for us proved to be a prophetic name for later ministry. We had offered for mission work – anywhere – expecting it to be abroad, but for this period of our lives it was merely a few miles down the road. We had yet to discover what God had in store.

CHAPTER SIX

GREAT AND SMALL

The years at Oldcotes proved to be even busier and a period in which we were to yearn for more of God and discover that He never disappoints. Almost from the start we decided that, since God had opened up our coming to the village, it was essential to get to know our neighbours. Our method of doing this was to purchase sufficient monthly copies of the *Challenge* newspaper (a Christian publication of testimony in a tabloid format) and deliver these to each house, taking the opportunity to introduce ourselves, speak of our family and our faith and if necessary ask to pray for individual needs. Emboldened by our reception and acceptance, we continued this for a number of years until we felt we had earned the trust of the residents.

Our presence at the chapel was not a total surprise but certainly increased the congregation numerically. Somehow the news of our coming had preceded us. Even my colleague from Rotherham had been confronted and asked whether he was me. The attendance at the little timber-panelled chapel was generally fewer than twenty persons, with the official membership being even smaller. The majority were over retirement age. We were welcomed wholeheartedly but there was an air of gloom since the real situation was that the society was teetering on the brink of extinction through lack of finance, vision and drive. It became apparent that this indeed would be a mission field of its own, one in which with much prayer, wisdom and sensitivity we pledged ourselves to the leading of God.

We sought to make a positive contribution by working with both the village children and adults alike. Ann's love for the people shone through and soon she had broken down several potential barriers, so often evident when newcomers enter an existing village hierarchy. Our home became a centre of activity and no one was excluded from our hospitality. Having our own children attracted others too and we threw ourselves fully into village life.

Our after-church Sunday evening fellowship continued and our friends from the Rotherham area now visited the village. Alongside this our contacts locally expanded, as we were introduced to the evangelical preachers on the circuit and soon drawn to the kindred spirit in other denominations. Within months of settling in at Oldcotes we had come to meet Arthur and Mary Simpson from Shireoaks, David and Julie Blackshaw from Whitwell, Richard and Gloria Bell plus David Ward from Worksop, as well as reacquainting ourselves with Alan and Audrey Fenton-Smith, now also in Worksop. Later David and Shirley Whitehouse moved into Worksop from Basingstoke and provided additional spiritual input, especially from their knowledge of what was happening elsewhere in the country.

As the children grew, Ann's workload inevitably seemed to increase. Admittedly her boundless energy and her love for her Lord enabled her to attempt and accomplish so much. The famous saying of William Carey comes to mind: "Expect great things from God, attempt great things for God." Her expectations were high and God continued to bless her faithfulness. Since the spiritual temperature in the area was low we were aware that for our own growth we must maintain spiritual impetus by our personal relationships, both with God and other likeminded Christians in the area.

The first way in which we did this was to meet with other Christians in the Worksop district and from our mutual desire the Worksop Evangelistic Fellowship (WEF) started meeting every Monday evening for prayer. Out of this concern for both ourselves and for others a regular weekly meeting was held. Later, a monthly series of Saturday evening meetings was started, alternating around the villages in the area, being held in village halls or chapels as suitable. Our aim was to use the day for door knocking – invite the community and blitz the area with posters and invitations. This built relationships, strengthened faith, made many contacts and increased the numbers meeting together on Mondays. In no way was this in competition with any denomination but it was an opportunity for evangelism to the area – an opportunity that at that time was rarely taken up by the established church.

Monday evenings saw David Whitehouse with his teaching ministry share on the gifts and fruits of the Spirit, whilst evangelist David Ward shared what God was doing through his work as an estate agent, contacting people, and leading them to salvation. These times fed our desire for deeper things and spurred us on in our desire to share with others. It would not be long before these desires were to be fulfilled.

Inevitably both Ann and I could not attend Monday evening meetings together so we took turns praying or babysitting as the case might be. Saturday evenings tended to be easier, when occasionally parents or friends babysat on our behalf.

Some often query whether such prayer meetings or evangelistic forays produce any lasting results. I believe eternity will reveal this but God gives us encouragements along the way. One such encouragement occurred years later. David Ward spoke on one of his recent contacts and asked us all to pray for a young journalist, Peter Hardy, who he was seeing and who was desperate. David suggested the way out of his difficulties was a new direction in Jesus Christ. Faithfully we continued to pray for this young man, unknown to most of us and, as it happens, someone we never met for years to come. His spiritual development was not ours to pursue. God had already knitted him into another group of young people, those known as the Faith Group.

Our stay in Oldcotes was a happy time but not without its challenges, for within weeks of our move, our third child Liz was born. The delivery went well and our new daughter, with a mop of dark brown hair, came into the world on bonfire night. It was a wet autumn and little could be done outside in the garden so we had time to decorate and concentrate on the expanding family needs. Within months, however, Ann's father suddenly took ill and on hearing the symptoms Ann insisted to his carefree doctor that he be taken to hospital. On visiting him at the hospital in Rotherham on my way to work the next morning I discovered he had just died of a ruptured aorta and that, as yet, the family had not been informed. Nothing could have prevented this but Ann's intervention had at least minimised the potential problems of him collapsing at home. His death was a great shock since God had given us assurance of his well-being that night in our prayers as we read John 11:4 – "This sickness is not unto death." It appeared we were wrong, but in spite of this, we still believed God's word that death was not the only outcome. The shock waves of his demise led to personal grief and loss, which threw Ann to trust even more in God for support, especially since this now meant greater responsibilities for the care of her mother on top of the demands of her family. Somehow life was so busy we had to trust to overcome our grief and deal with the loss of such a wonderful father.

We took every opportunity to get to know our neighbours and their children, several of whom became members of our young people's group. Ann made sure she got to know the mums in the village and shared their worries and aspirations. Fellowship at the chapel also became an opportunity to speak about our faith and as time passed the initial threat that we may have presented gave way to a warm embracing of our eagerness to share Jesus. Ann's prayers led to several of the mums confessing Jesus and I was thrilled to lead Ruth, then a spinster of seventy-nine and the daughter of a previous chapel stalwart, to a personal faith in the Lord. Ruth knew her hymn book thoroughly but lacked an assurance of her relationship with Jesus. Both Ruth and her spinster cousin Edith spent many hours at our home and vice versa, as they enjoyed the presence of children or gave a hand as Ann performed the hundreds of jobs a busy mother and housewife does. They even babysat on occasions, but our friendship always revolved around discussion of our faith. For them our stay in the village provided a new lease of life and we became firm friends.

Our love for them continued until physically they couldn't cope, living without support. We were able to attend both cousins whilst in hospital and later arrange the sale of their home after Edith's transfer to a nursing home prior to her death in the early nineties. Neither of them had any close family and our support met this need and widened their horizons and quality of life in its latter stages. We were of course able to introduce them to some of our friends too and for a number of years David Ward and myself were regular visitors to their home.

Not only did we have local visitors call; whenever possible we would encourage friends from farther afield to visit and if possible speak at our meetings. Each year we would invite London City Missioners, that august and dedicated group of Christians called to the Metropolis, to come to sleepy Oldcotes and tell of their work as well as the sharing of their faith. These were lovely and often hilarious times. One such event was when we all sat around the meal table enjoying our food along with the current city missioner: our eldest daughter, perhaps about five or six, asked the question "Why has he got such a big nose?" Embarrassment was overcome by laughter, innocence and curiosity being rewarded by a simple response. These visits enabled us again to use our home, busy though we were and full though it was, to welcome strangers and those in need. None of this could of course be done without Ann's remarkable energy, skills and unflappable nature. We had learned that for the sake of our family, ourselves and our witness we must always work as a team, working to our strengths and overcoming our weaknesses.

What a blessing it was to see God open up opportunities for us to become involved in the chapel at Oldcotes and to see tangible results in responses from young and old alike. We learned to love people, to break down barriers, to serve them and to use our energy and resources to encourage them to grow in their faith. In return we received the support of individuals in our ventures in the village, and at the same time our catchment area seemed to increase.

It was at this time that I was asked to survey an old farmhouse at Laxton near Newark by the Reverend Eddie Smith and his wife Marina, who along with their friends had a vision for this farm to become a Christian Centre. I remember my first visit. The farm buildings were dilapidated, the farmhouse roof was missing in parts and daylight could be seen through the ceiling in several areas. The state of the premises and the challenge to renovate them did not dampen their optimism and so, with the help of one of my colleagues at work, we produced proposals and obtained planning permission for what later became Beth Shalom, meaning the House of Peace. The family moved in and worked around themselves and it was during this time that Ann helped to teach Eddie and Marina's two sons, James and Stephen. Twice a week Ann and Ruth Hardy made the journey to Laxton whilst their own children were at school. Much hard work, generous donations, and a high degree of spiritual discipline transformed this once derelict building into a spacious home. This is now the British centre for study and expertise on the Holocaust, directed by Dr James Smith – the one time home-tutored scholar.

It was in the spring of 2003 that I revisited Beth Shalom, this time as a visitor to the centre. Dr Smith graciously gave me time out of his busy schedule and immediately recounted a personal incident in his life. He said that on one occasion when he was being taught by Ann, she asked him what his preferred career would be, to which he answered that he wanted to be a pig-farmer! Ann said she had been praying for him that day and felt he ought to become a medical doctor. James did not dismiss this comment but put it to the back of his mind and proceeded with his work, unsure whether he had the ability needed for such a calling. Two years later, he continued, his mother came to him asking the same question and on her giving a similar opinion he asked his mother whether she had been talking to Ann. "Ann who?" she responded . . . Obviously not! Realising two prayerful individuals, without collaboration, saying the same thing might have God behind it, he finally made application to medical school and was accepted. He loved every minute of the training and the work in hospital, up to the time when he felt he needed to give in his notice and continue full time with the Holocaust Centre. The volume of work demanded his whole attention. "Why I needed to train as a doctor I do not yet know – but I thank God for Ann who shared without any pressure what she believed God had revealed to her."

On one occasion we were asked to visit a home in the village since the couple were experiencing frightening occurrences. We saw this as an opportunity to serve and to proclaim the name of Jesus. Rather than go alone I asked Eddie Smith if he would accompany me, which he was happy to do. We listened to the recounting of these spooky incidents and were both sure that this had been allowed in order that we could declare the power of the name of Jesus. Desperate for change, we ministered the truths of Scripture and prayed for exorcism of malevolent spirits and for the spiritual needs of the couple. Bill and Ann Peel responded to this message and soon they became regular visitors to the chapel meetings and the fellowship in our home. Their daughters Sharon and Kerry befriended our own children and soon not only had numbers increased but resources and responses were extended.

We were unashamedly keen to speak of Jesus wherever we went in the village, whether it was Ann visiting the post office or delivering the *Challenge* newspaper or just being a family. Our activities, open home and many visitors, including speakers at various meetings, indicated that although fully integrated into village life we were by no means the average family. This did not prevent us from socialising with the range of people Oldcotes contained; we were at home both with the salt of the earth, locals or the professional commuters. Ann somehow had few inhibitions in engaging individuals in conversation at whatever level and people responded to her genuine love. I had to work to overcome my own lack of skill in this area on many occasions, but persisted, which produced results.

In the early 1970s as we devoured everything we could on the work and ministry of the Holy Spirit, Ann was herself baptised in the Spirit. One Monday evening as she babysat whilst I made my way to the Worksop Evangelistic Fellowship, she settled down in the lounge at Charisma to pray and seek God. Inevitably Ann spoke of this experience several times later. As she was praying, she actually felt something was about to happen and immediately started to fear. She was on her own and this was new. Receiving personal revelations and venturing deeper into God, there were no rules or norms. She had, however, an obvious reluctance to do anything that might grieve the Spirit. Ann sensed the presence of the Holy Spirit and repented of her fear and asked God to fill her, there and then. She later shared that this experience was emotional, intimate and overwhelming in that she definitely knew she had had a spiritual encounter.

Immediately she praised Him and the gift of speaking in tongues followed. It was an outpouring that confirmed to her she had met with God. For her the evening was real, special and awesome. Alone in the lounge sitting on the carpeted floor she and God communed. This experience was to transform her life in more ways than one.

On returning home after my meeting, I was aware that Ann was different and that something had happened. I was not in the least surprised, for I knew Ann's heart was for more of God, but I waited for her to tell me the details. How was I going to cope now? I suppose, like so many times in our lives, our individual experience and revelations became an incentive for the other to go deeper into God. We discovered later that David Ward received the infilling of the Holy Spirit at the same time as Ann and in much the same way. God was intervening supernaturally in the local church; our prayers were being answered.

I suppose I had more hang-ups to deal with than Ann, practical problems of practice and upbringing, resulting in my own filling of the Spirit following later. I was prayed for and had to move in faith, not seeking merely for tongues as the evidence. The paradox was that we often prayed for people who responded in tongues and yet I was tongue-tied! Eventually as the pressure was resisted and faith continued to kick in, I knew the liberty too of the gift of tongues, as I sought to honour and love Jesus. The camps particularly provided a platform for both of us to share our newfound experiences and our love of the Lord.

Not only did we respond to the message at the camps, but so too did our children and their friends in the village. They became ardent followers of the Scriptures, enthusiastically taught by Simon Matthews. This led to prayer meetings, fellowship times and devotions initiated and led by themselves. Doubtful music recordings with dubious lyrics were destroyed in their attempt to walk the narrow path. They sought not merely to be hearers of the word but doers also. These high standards did not, however, always lead to harmony and as only young people can they asked searching and practical questions such as "Why is it we have a tremendous time at camp, singing new songs, experiencing healings and moves of God and then come back to Oldcotes where it's predictable, and old fashioned?" They were not the only generation to raise such questions; we recognised our own feelings of years before, but they did have a point. If camp Christianity was real, why didn't we experience this each week at home? Perhaps we had compromised. Those initial times of expression in the Spirit were particularly difficult in church meetings. You sensed opposition as you suggested changes to the normal safe practice.

For a number of years however we did not feel liberty to move from Oldcotes chapel. As others of our Christian friends became thrilled with the move of the Spirit in their lives there was an understandable but tragic demarcation of opinion, and of theological and religious practices – sadly the old and the new were in conflict. The traditional felt threatened; the new charismatics (as they were to be named) became impatient and stifled. Many of the keen younger and oft times new Christians felt they could not grow. The advice of Gamaliel in Acts chapter 5 ("If it is of God, you will not be able to overthrow them; or else you may even be found fighting against God") was so relevant, but somehow forgotten.

It therefore became a time when many left the established denominations to form new churches of likeminded people. We did not feel that this was to be our response. We were to move on, rather than move out. Moving on meant fellow-ship and up-building from the local church rather than the denomination. The early days of this move of the Spirit were not always easy. For some there was a pressure either to conform to tradition or conform to the practices of the new-found liberty. Such things as hugging, hand raising, clap-ping or even movement and dancing created ripples, since they were not generally present in mainstream churches. It's true to say that the new liturgy could be off-putting for others but, for us, hugging became disarming; hand raising and clapping became an external expression of our liberty in God and movement and dance became a further worship expression.

With renewed vigour, effort and input we pressed on at Oldcotes – thrilled in our own new-found freedom and keen to share with our friends. Ann would regularly meet with the ladies of the village (plus others) and share the vitality of her faith, seeing several come into a relationship with Jesus and the fullness of the Spirit. In the busyness of my career and duties I sought to become a local preacher in order to serve and to share the good news of the gospel around the Methodist Circuits, travelling either with Ann, with some or all of our children, plus foster children, as the case might be. Realistically things were desperate in some of the churches at that time and many have since closed.

There were of course always outstanding examples of older Christians who were a great spiritual encouragement – people like George Broadbent of Dinnington, a small craggy man, a Paul-like figure. He often played his squeezebox and always testified wherever he went of the goodness of the Lord. Another such man of God was the Superintendent Minister of the Worksop and District Circuit in the late seventies, Jess Besley, a former local boy from the Rotherham area and a fellow student at grammar school with my father. He was a man of considerable compassion and was an evangelist by ministry. It was good to have a spiritual man overseeing the needs of the local circuit and to be encouraged by someone to whom you could speak of Jesus without embarrassment, one to whom relationship was far more important than religious ritual or responsibilities.

Working together as a team enabled each of us to attempt and achieve much more than would normally have occurred. For Ann the duties and demands of motherhood were her priority, but in her boundless energy she was also able to foster the needy, maintain her career interests of caring and night schools, and help at Beth Shalom. Alongside these she maintained her responsibilities as a daughter, kept an open house, spoke at various venues, offered support and encouragement to whoever chose to visit, in addition to overseeing pastoral care of the ladies of the village. She was very aware, like Susannah Wesley (mother of John and Charles Wesley) that in spite of all her activities, duties and busyness, her personal input into her children was paramount. She ensured that she prayed with them and for them, sharing her love for Jesus with each one as often as she could, giving each one personal time and personal encouragement. She faced her responsibilities as a mother with determination and zeal.

I have been reminded too by Amelia Thomlinson of Rhodesia that I also gave the children time as needed. On one occasion, she recounted, she telephoned to speak to me and was told by Ann that I was unavailable since this was the children's hour and I was busy with them. She never forgot this fatherly priority.

Charisma as our home was ideal in many ways, having a dining/lounge suitable for large meetings, if necessary, and a modern kitchen. It also had a large garden, which needed fencing, landscaping and digging when we arrived. The plot had been part of a field previously but had undergone the ravages of construction and storage of building materials. The ground was not particularly productive, having been stripped of topsoil and suffering from an impenetrable layer of limestone about a foot or so from the surface. However, over the years it did provide copious amounts of vegetables for the family needs, more than adequate space for a lawned play area for the children and sufficient room for rabbit hutches, goat pens and a goose coop. The family pets later extended to further goats, half a dozen khaki Campbell ducks, two runt pigs, several dogs (over the years) and the odd stray cat. "Odd" in that it once got to the stage where I had to say to Ann after a particularly frustrating time with the then cat (and me being anything but an animal lover), "It's either the cat that goes or me!" Ann took all this in her stride, very aware that the rearing of livestock gave our children, and particularly Martin, an avenue for development, industry and love. Needless to say neither the cat nor I did leave – but a little while later having missed it for a few days I found the animal curled up in the cupboard under the stairs. Fortunately its lifeless body did not smell and we had not come to blows.

We had become so established within the community that a local builder allowed Martin to keep his pigs, goats and ducks on a derelict plot of land in another part of the village and the building of a pig-sty became yet another father and son bonding exercise. From time to time the milking of the goats was a task dad had to do too, especially at holiday or illness times. Goats are notoriously awkward and it was frustrating to say the least when after patiently milking for thirty minutes the goat would kick over the bucket and the fruit of the labour be lost before your eyes. For the ducks the situation was ideal since at the bottom of the plot was a small beck and on opening their run in a morning they would waddle down to the water and swim off, returning faithfully each evening.

Both the ducks and the goats were productive (a picture of the good life). Duck eggs and goats' milk enabled us to supplement the family income and provided ingredients for much of Ann's baking. Goats' milk tends to taste of whatever the goats eat and the children often disliked this. Ann, therefore, used her skills to disguise its presence by using it for custard tarts (the children's favourite), which would never be refused. However, Ann, though a good cook, was not always successful in producing her custards and they often turned out as "Australian" custard tarts (as we called them), pastry and custard inverted!

During his animal phase Martin raised several goats that gave birth to kids and, on one occasion, twins. One of these was a billy; it was normal either to have this humanely put down or to pass it to other enthusiasts, since the cost of rearing would not be regained. We were able to pass this infant on via one of our local vets. The goats would eat whatever they could and often this was not beneficial. On one occasion a goat displayed symptoms of illness, a large bloated stomach and faltering breathing. We lifted it into the car and came back home; Ann suggested we place it on the floor in the kitchen next to the radiator, where she used her nursing skills to bring it back to health. Sadly it did not survive and father and son had to resort to the unpleasant task of burial.

From time to time we needed musicians to assist us in the outreach from the chapel, and who better to fulfil this than the Faith Group? We invited them to lead, and present Jesus in their own style – a mixture of gospel and country with, at times, the serious, the humorous and even the ridiculous, but always sincerely spiritual. Foot-tapping music, generally with their own lyrics and majoring on audience participation! A challenging fun-time was always guaranteed. We would invite the group and their retinue back after the event to our home for refreshments. It was after one such meeting that I was invited to meet with their leaders for fellowship on Saturday mornings. At the time we felt this would be good and so in early 1979 I began a closer liaison with the fellowship leaders.

It was not long before I was asked to assist with some architectural work on their behalf. The group members, plus many of their friends, had just moved from one local village, Woodsetts, to another one, Costhorpe. At first the group were renting but subsequently purchased a large house named Poplars. This was the former manager's house for Firbeck colliery, which had been closed in the mid-sixties, and purchased by a Muslim doctor. After several years he sought to move and rented the property to the group, who eventually were able to obtain a group mortgage to purchase. Although a large property of five bedrooms, two garages, several large reception rooms and almost an acre of land, the accommodation was beginning to be too small for the numbers that it served. It actually was home to eight adults and the meeting centre for the Faith Group and Poplars Christian Fellowship, which was regularly between forty and sixty persons. I was asked to prepare plans for extensions and provide a hall suitable for meetings and music practices, including a baptistery and all necessary facilities. This I was able to do within a few weeks, obtaining planning permission and Local Authority approval.

As they were pleased with the proposals, it seemed that what literally started as church in a home was now to become established in a more conventional building. But, in a strange way, when it came to deciding whether to proceed, each leader, along with myself, had reservations as to whether this was what God wanted – we all agreed that the proposals were too small and premature in the life of the fellowship. Acting in a professional capacity had exposed me to the workings of the leadership and laid a foundational relationship that was to continue further.

At the same time that we were feeling a need to pursue things of the Spirit at whatever cost, so too were the Faith Group. For them the direction was also not as they expected. God had spoken a prophetic word that the Faith Group was to die. Bear in mind that for almost ten years this had been virtually the entire ministry of the fellowship, within which time they had travelled thousands of miles annually and performed at countless venues. These included even the Central Hall and elsewhere around the country in church buildings large and small, plus regular performances at the Cliff College Derwent Convention. This proved to be a radical word. It was, however, gradually embraced and towards the end of 1979 several performances of "Faith's Last Stand", as they were called, were played at a number of local venues. Already the group had made three albums (long playing records) under the Kingsway label. Their obedience to the prophetic word would mean dramatic changes, so we attempted whenever possible to attend these final concerts together with our friends and invited guests from the village.

Ann and I both continued to fellowship whenever we could in either the midweek meetings or at Faith Group gigs, whilst at the same time serving the circuit and the people of Oldcotes. Keen to share our camp contacts with Poplars, we asked if Simon Matthews could be invited to speak on work with young people. This idea was enthusiastically received and Simon was able to attend. An invitation too was extended to all the churches in the area, since youth work always seems an important issue. For some reason, however, it was obviously not such a burning issue for other churches as we expected, for I was the only person in attendance, other than Poplars people! The worship time was good, participation and moving in the gifts of the Spirit was as we had come to expect and Simon knew a freedom in sharing.

Afterwards Simon, staying overnight with us at Charisma, spoke of his feelings about the meeting and how at home he felt. When we raised our children's wish to go on with God in a church situation where the work of the Holy Spirit was normal, he said he felt Poplars was for us. It was not altogether a bombshell, as we were praying about our future and where this would be, especially mindful of the pressures of loyalty to the chapel versus our desire to see our children go deeper in spiritual things. For years we had resisted coming out of an established denomination, emphasising that God's word to us was to move on rather than to move out. We were now getting the word to move out. How could God want us to move when He had called us to Oldcotes, blessed us and our ministry, brought many to know Him? We were to learn yet again that God's ways are not our ways; it was now time to take responsibility again for our spiritual walk and move.

Although we were convinced this was the right decision it would not be easy to explain it to our friends and neighbours. Our aim was not to judge or condemn others in their spiritual walk, rather to emphasise what God was saying to us. Needless to say it was not fully understood by some, but we had to leave that with God. As a local preacher on the circuit I made an appointment to see Jess Besley, the Superintendent Minister who as always was gracious and understanding. He was personally saddened that we had come to this decision because of the effect it might have on the chapel and people of Oldcotes, but he realised that we must follow what God was saying to us. We maintained our fellowship and I served all my preaching appointments for the quarter.

At the beginning of 1980 we worshipped together as a family with Poplars Christian Fellowship on the second occasion that they met at the village hall in Carlton-in-Lindrick. Forty or so of us were in the timber-framed hall, built large enough for several badminton courts. What had we come to? The hall seemed enormous and the numbers seemed minuscule. Each week, we made a point of setting up the musical equipment and chairs in a different pattern so as not to be overpowered by the empty volume of the hall – we were like peas in a drum! This sense of smallness was not however going to last. Within a few years we were to see the hall filled to capacity in both our public meetings and our regular worship times.

CHAPTER SEVEN

NUMERICAL INCREASE

Our love for children led us into another phase of our lives that was to continue for the next twenty-five years. We earnestly prayed whether we should foster other people's children. Fostering, we were to learn over the years, can be described as the other face of permissive and prosperous Britain. Many have asked us why at the time, with three children of our own and a busy lifestyle, did we ever even consider fostering, with all its emotional upset, its effect on the family, its increased demands and its questionable community image. All we knew was that God had so blessed us as a couple with a strong loving relationship, a larger than average detached house, and a lovely family life that we felt we could not keep this to ourselves. We wanted to share what we had with those who were not so fortunate, secure or loved. This was, however, an unknown area of service for us and not one at the time that our Christian friends had had any experience of either. It was up to us to pioneer any kind of approach into this area of community service under the auspices of the local social services department, and all this prior to the organisational changes of the early 1970s. We duly made all enquiries, completed our applications, and waited.

Within weeks we were visited by social services personnel to view the kind of people we were, to check our motivation as well as to look at our home and its facilities. The requirements of the department were quite rigorous in order to discover the couple's real needs. It was the social worker's job to emphasise the negative points that needed to be considered in fostering: problems the children might exhibit, such as disturbed emotional behaviour, rejection and the possible effects of abuse. All these would add pressure on the foster parents' marriage and their family. Illness might be another problem, or pressure from existing children. As these hazards were recounted, Ann continued to complete her ironing, remaining undisturbed at the horrors described. The blacker the social worker painted the problem, the greater Ann's resolve to assist the desperate need of the children. We knew that God was greater than any problem and, together, we could overcome all these obstacles.

The social worker in question was very professional but was also a Christian as it turned out and she had no hesitation in recommending us. This inspection completed, the essential prerequisite seemed to be how many bedrooms and spare beds we had and whether there was any dust or fluff underneath them! Looking back, this initiation was a far cry from the later introductory course that foster carers were expected to take (and in which we often participated as experienced carers). It differed too from the stringent form filling and child protection checks thought essential today. Within no time at all, one Friday afternoon, we received the telephone call to welcome us as foster parents and, incidentally, would we take a two-year-old Down's syndrome child, the following day, for a week's care? Thrilled at our acceptance, Ann did, however, raise one problem; the following day we were going on our holidays – camping in Devon! Would this child be able to cope; would it be in order to subject him to the challenges of camping and what would his mother think? None of these questions appeared to insurmountable and Liam became our first foster child, experiencing going on his first holiday from home.

We coped amazingly with this additional needy and demanding, but happy child. Our lasting memories were of him hutching himself around the campsite on a plastic potty! It was also significant that we experienced personally for the first time some of the stigma parents of Down's or special needs children suffer at the hands of others. Discrimination was more evident then and although we did not have any direct altercations with other campers, some obviously had problems in accommodating a family composition with a special needs child. Ann's empathy for both the children and parents developed through this, our first of many fostering experiences. Liam came to visit us on a number of occasions until his untimely death through heart failure, a common problem of the Down's condition.

After only a few weeks of normality our home was invaded by an older child, Jack, who had been living with his frail grandparents in their small council bungalow in the next village, having been abandoned by his single parent mother. His grandparents were doing their best in his upbringing but at ten years old he was very demanding and was beginning to learn the tricks and scams of petty crime. Could we help? This would certainly be a challenge. We decided we would try.

Like so many others, Jack not only lacked direction in his life, he lacked the stability and security of love, of caring parents, and the discipline of a stable home life routine. He arrived at our home, with his social worker, a lady in her forties; we were introduced and he explored his new home. Social services had a series of criteria for the placing of children, who should as far as possible be of similar socio-backgrounds to carers, of similar gender when appropriate, and of younger age than the carers' oldest child and so on. Jack met none of these criteria; this was our first instance of realising how desperate the authority often became, breaking its own rules to place needy children. Looking back, the fact of Jack being older than our own children, our inexperience and the social services' Nelson's eye approach did not produce the best for all concerned. The time was tough but not without rewards and examples of God's faithfulness. Even in all the difficulties, we were able to maintain our trust in God and when, ultimately, Jack left us it was several years later.

All our fostered children enjoyed benefits from the system, which may have been the purchase of a bicycle, or help towards a holiday, new clothing or the funding of sports fees to appropriate children. For Jack, Christmas time with the receipt of special gifts plus the many more from our family, friends and relatives, created difficulties. His emotion welled up and he refused to open his presents along with our own children. Ann took him aside and sought to comfort him and ask why he was having problems receiving. Jack burst out crying saying, "My grandparents will have nothing – I can't have these." Feeling for him Ann said to Jack, "Let's pray about this and ask God to especially bless Grandma and Granddad today." Comforted by these words the two prayed together, and then returned to the festivities and joys of the children unwrapping their surprises.

A little while later there was a knock at the door and we welcomed a friend, Bill, a newly converted middle-aged widower, into the clamour of a Christmas morning at Charisma. He was also a driving instructor and, in his desperation and loneliness, had recently become a Christian as a result of the encouragment of one of his pupils. He was able to follow this through with the help of his Christian neighbour and committed his future to his Lord. Here he was this Christmas morning with a shopping bag in his hand and he explained his reason for coming. He had been invited to share Christmas with the family of a friend but had come to bring his own Christmas dinner – vegetables, meat and pudding, plus tins of this and that, crackers and sweets – to us for he "knew we would know what to do with it." Ann looked at Jack and said, "We know where that is going," and within minutes Jack was on his way to share these blessings with his grandparents and to explain how and why they had arrived. We were proving in real life that, "before you ask I will answer."

Fostering was for us a team effort. Family, children, community, church friends, school, social services each played a vital part in meeting the emotional, psychological, physical, spiritual, emotional and intellectual needs of the children – many damaged or abused, and many demonstrating behavioural problems that highlight previous experiences. Through our entire time of caring we owed a lot to all these groups or individuals who supplemented our input and in many instances provided what we could not do. Outstanding in this was the local primary school head teacher, Mr Crapper, who was understanding and a great help when disruptive behaviour or other misdemeanours occurred.

Jack's social worker has subsequently said what a favourable impression she received as she first visited. Ann, with all her children, her responsibilities and duties was busy but unflappable and the home somehow had an atmosphere of peace. In fact the reality over the years was that the social workers often visited to gain a listening ear from Ann, for they knew that in her they had someone who would give them time, even in the busyness of her own life.

Thanks too are due to our village neighbours who tolerated so much but also wanted the best for the children. I remember the time when a pensioner came to the door to talk. With hesitation he explained that the money for the milkman was regularly disappearing. Keeping a watch early morning it was soon discovered that Jack was helping himself to this as he delivered the morning newspapers. We agreed together to pay the milkman another way, prevention leading to cure. Years later, on re-carpeting our hall, we found a cache of coins, possibly the milk money of years before. Sadly as Jack grew older he became much stronger and used his strength to threaten the family with a knife. We had been left to rely on our own resources to such an extent that I had to notify social services of the danger threatening my own family and within days Jack was removed to a local assessment centre and then to the southern part of the country. Although we appeared to fail with Jack we showed a love and a stability that must have had a profound effect, for Jack now lives in the village, settled with a family of his own.

Just as I am writing this, a knock sounds on my office door. It opens and in walks a six-feet-tall twenty-eight-year-old man, carrying a black plastic bin liner, concealing a baseball bat. Not coming to "do my head in" – he assures me it's to protect him in case of likely trouble. He is Paul, obviously desperate to talk, desperate for someone to listen. Along with his half-brother Steve he came to our home for short-term fostering whilst we were still at Oldcotes. I told him what I was doing and he instantly went into reminiscent mode. "I remember the time," he said, "when I wouldn't get out of the social worker's car, bawling my head off in fear of this new home." Somehow and sometime later he made it. "I remember the cake with marzipan on the top," he said, licking his lips, "and do you remember the time at Christmas when my eyes were like saucers seeing all those presents . . . I've never had Christmas presents or birthday cards since then. I used to love sitting round the kitchen table," he continued, "I was really happy then, but I've got so much hurt and pain inside (he put his hand to his chest). At the end of the day I'm scared; is this what I'm going to be all my life? I've a big family, you know – but they don't want to know me. I'm twenty-eight and never had a job; I've two children and I've only got one chance to do something with my life, so they will be proud of me. I'm a very insecure person," he said, sweating profusely and wiping his forehead. "I've tried to cry and get it all out of me . . . it's all my mum's fault, turning up again when we were settled and then letting us down again and again. For her it was her life that came first."

Paul began to slur his speech and I asked whether he was on drugs. He assured me he wasn't since he'd only been out of prison a few days, hinting that both finance and opportunity were a current problem. I started to share with him the story of Luke chapter 15 and the prodigal's return – making it contemporary and relevant in the retelling. He listened and I asked if I could pray for him and we called upon God in our weakness knowing that "He is able to do far more than we could think or ask."

I cast my mind back to almost twenty years ago when Paul came to live with us. The social worker explained the brothers' situation to us and assured us of their intention to leave them with us for three weeks until the problems resolved themselves. Today's surprise meeting showed that even to date the problems are still outstanding.

Paul was a very disturbed, needy child, so wanting love from his mum but rejected time after time. Deep within, for five years, this urge to return to his mum seemed somehow to plague his life until at the age of fourteen he left us finally to be with her. Sadly, it lasted only a few months and Paul knew rejection again. His disturbed behaviour put a lot of pressure on our family – but neither Ann nor I had any regrets about what we had provided or attempted on his behalf. His half-brother Steve on the other hand, two years younger, was a street-wise juvenile with a smile from ear to ear; he could charm anyone by his winning ways. It never took Steve long to ingratiate his way into any situation, ending up within minutes being either the centre of attention or the proud user of the special toy or piece of equipment. Paul stayed with us for five years, whereas Steve stayed for nine – at the time this was called short-term fostering; today such a situation fortunately for the child's sake would not occur.

Other precious children would enter and leave our lives and our home, like the time two sisters and a brother came for Christmas whilst their single mum had a hospital visit and operation. Then there was Sarah, a girl from a nearby village, whose family were business people. She was the same age as Martin, and had two sisters and a brother of her own. Sadly, tragedy struck the family and father died. Mother remarried and her husband one day in a fit of frenzy killed mum in the family home. Sarah was there to see this happen. Their prosperity had not saved them from such a trauma. This tragic act of domestic violence led to much pain, caused the family to split up, and dramatically altered their once prosperous lifestyle. No longer could Sarah ride her pony at Hickstead each year, no longer was there the challenge of sibling rivalry. Sarah became a well-integrated member of our family for a number of years, but from time to time would rush into our bedroom in the middle of the night, suffering from nightmares. As soon as she left school Sarah moved to live with her older sister and at eighteen came into her legal inheritance and left the area.

Then there was Gary. He was a local boy with a single parent mother. He had Gilles de la Tourette syndrome. The symptoms of this complaint meant that he suffered from facial tics and made loud involuntary noises. Worst of all was a bizarre memory for swearing, with unpredictable, inappropriate and impulsive behaviour. On one occasion, whilst looking after Gary, we were in town shopping and he had one of his uncontrollable outbursts. He was obviously under pressure and I felt it the best solution to take him from the situation to return to our car. Unfortunately, this was parked on the other side of the High Street and it meant running the gauntlet of the crowds going about their legitimate business. I picked Gary up and walked towards the car park; all the time Gary was speaking loudly with expletives every other word. Very soon, and understandably, I sensed eyes directed towards me with looks of disgust, suggesting, "How on earth could that parent allow his child to swear so violently and why couldn't he be controlled?" The walk seemed endless and the embarrassment was keen, but that was the cost of compassion and I had no regrets.

On arrival at the car, Gary broke down in tears – he was genuinely sorry for the trouble he had caused. He sensed that he was guilty of something he couldn't control. "I'm sorry Uncle Norman, I'm sorry Uncle Norman," he sobbed and I loved him and held him close. I know this running of the gauntlet of a non-understanding crowd had created a bonding between us. It was one which was never lost, even when he was transferred to a medical placement in the south of the county with his condition coming under a more stable medical regime. Until this was put in place, however, we continued to care for him in our home as the need arose.

Fostering is not easy and understandably many have difficulties in merely contemplating the use of their home, never mind taking on board all the upset and emotions that the reality of the experience entails. It is also true to say that there are rewards too. These can be broken down into two main areas, financial and well-being. Finances are paid to foster parents by the social services department for the time, effort and expenses of parenting. It is however important to stress that these in no way fully compensate for the costs involved. As with lots of things in life, fostering costs, some say blood, sweat and tears, but definitely financially. It's a calling you enter with eyes wide open, but knowledge never nullifies experience, which is invariably much worse or more extreme than you naïvely assume.

The local authority provided the essential pieces of furniture, bunk beds, specialised equipment, bikes or toys, holiday and even travel expenses, but no account could be taken of larger vehicle costs, extra sundry costs and insurances but we realised this was all part of our ministry in the community. For a number of years we ran a VW caravette – the cheapest and simplest vehicle before the advent of the now popular people carriers – to cope with our extended family numbers. Inevitably breakages of household goods and thefts of items also occurred but we took all these setbacks in our stride, it was all part of the restorative care for those who had suffered. From time to time incidents happened that became a problem for our own children. Our ministry was also to love and care for them through such crises, which were not of their making. Needless to say the family gave a lot to enable this ministry to continue.

The other main reward was the achievement of little successes with and on behalf of those for whom we cared. Ann loved the children as her own and prayed much on how to get to know them, put them at ease, and help with their physical and emotional development. Reprimands and discipline were individually tailored to the children and encouragement and tears went hand in hand. Prayer became an invaluable tool in how best to help the children and how best to represent their interests to social services, family and community, which inevitably included schools and the neighbourhood. At one stage we actually had so many children (our own or fostered), that we seemed to attend more school parent evenings than members of staff. To be able to release a child back to parents after a stay was always rewarding when we knew that the child had benefited from being with us and was re-equipped to get back to normal life. Conversely it was painful to release one who you suspected would find reintegration difficult.

CHAPTER EIGHT

FURTHER ON

The name "Poplars" was derived from the house at Costhorpe which formed the base of the Christian fellowship and had no religious significance or affiliation. These were young Christians working out their faith as far as possible in line with their understanding of the Scriptures. One such practice, later to be discarded as couples married and moved into their own accommodation, was the sharing of all funding and financial resources, known as "koinonia". This enabled the joint mortgage to be paid monthly and financed the hospitality provided for all comers. The financial liabilities of the large Faith Group budget were supplemented too from this source, especially since many expenses paid by churches were often small and inadequate.

Apart from four exceptions, the average age of the fellowship members was in the twenties or early thirties. Derek and Mo Wilkinson were for years the only married couple whilst Pete and Ruth Hardy, married in 1980, had recently purchased a home in Worksop. In late 1979 and prior to our arrival, Alan and Audrey Fenton-Smith and family had committed themselves too. It really seemed that Christians were indeed coming together. Not surprisingly, because of its unusual composition, its numbers and its loud and forceful music and singing, Poplars became well known, on local CB radio at least, as a "commune" or the "clap and be happy set". It never was a centre of communal living in that sense, but people had obviously realised that this group was far from the average church. The numbers of young people and its quality of musical presentation, the emphasis on praise and worship, evangelism and hospitality, often provided a threat to other, not so strong, church groups, lacking the obvious dynamism.

What had we come to? As the weeks and months unfurled we knew we had come home. We, with our teenage children, were a few years older than most and our input was both to teenagers and twenties alike. For our children the possibility of meeting, sharing and spending time with others of their age was invaluable. Very quickly we embraced the work with the young people, which was a practical way of serving them, integrating our own children and involving the young people of Oldcotes. Not surprisingly, our larger than average lounge/dining room at Charisma soon seemed rather small as thirty-plus young people met each Friday evening. The young people attracted others and teenagers came from Retford and villages in the Trent Valley. We continued this work for a number of years, and it bore fruit that these youngsters testified later was foundational for their faith. We naturally thrived on this opportunity – meeting the needs of our own children, encouraging others in their faith, and directing young lives in a deeper faith with Jesus. We found that hospitality works especially well with young people: open the door, provide love and a warm welcome and lots of food and they will always respond.

We also discovered that obeying God's will, in this instance the demise of the Faith Group, was not a decision that was made lightly or without emotional repercussions. We had come as a couple and as a family into a group of people keen to obey God at whatever cost but who were hurting as a consequence. We were able to speak to individuals about their emotions and pain without any axe to grind and in so doing helped care and bring them through the wobbles and misgivings of that period. We were naturally expressing our gifting, using our home, our experiences and our ministry in up-building another part of the body of Christ. In helping individuals we got to know them and they too became secure in our non-judgemental approach.

Within weeks of our arrival we were providing hospitality for a single mother and child recommended to us from David and Jetta, now living and ministering in Copenhagen. When they had been with us for about two weeks we were blessed by the fellowship, who paid our flights to Denmark to personally return the family. There were no cheap flights at that time and the generosity of the people was outstanding. It was January, Denmark was wintery and cold and although we were only there a few days (whilst our parents looked after the children) we felt our input was beneficial. Returning to Manchester was memorable. Looking out of the aeroplane and seeing England's "green and pleasant land" bathed in winter sunshine was such a relief after Denmark's icy and grey landscape.

The demands on our time were extensive but somehow we managed to "keep all the balls in the air". Needs of children, foster children, careers, church, young people, friends, parents, house and garden, speaking engagements and personal counsel and support for others, plus of course maintaining an open-door policy on hospitality – miraculously, all these things were fitted in.

New friendships developed as we now encountered a whole new raft of contacts. Roy and Bev, who we had asked previously to help us at a GNC camp, were active members of Poplars so there was no difficulty in getting to know them further. At this time they were not yet married but this would not be many months away. We warmed too immediately to Pete and Ruth Hardy who shared themselves with us, which proved to be a constant reminder of the effectiveness of prayer years before at Worksop Evangelistic Fellowship – "please pray for Pete Hardy". Perhaps this history in God was the quality that led to our enduring friendship since that time to the present. We did not realise then that our lives would be so closely intertwined. The end of the Faith Group also provided a further phase in the life of Poplars. It was now time for personal relationships, marriages and the development of families, as well as time for the establishment of local church. The realisation that this was church, and fellowship was what was happening, took a number more years to outwork.

Our home at Oldcotes served us well and provided enough space for our children, foster children, our visitors and ourselves. The available space was pressurised even further when we took in Yvette. She was a teenage member of Poplars, one of three sisters, who had been traumatised emotionally through the breakdown of family life. Living with her father and younger sister did not work satisfactorily. Ann's heart went out to her, her mothering instinct kicked in and Ann knew that God could transform Yvette through love, counselling and consistent support. Using my architectural skills, the study soon was extended and this became a ground floor bed-sitting room – the house was now bulging and provided home for ten people. For several years the patient care and love, alongside occasional help from others, enabled Yvette's life experiences to be changed from constant nightmares, insecurities, self-mutilation and emotional highs and lows to those of a responsive, settled and secure young lady.

It was a difficult period of ministry alongside the emotional roller coaster rides often experienced by our foster children at the same time. Our children were brilliant and mostly took these things in their stride and as far as possible we protected them from most occurrences. We constantly had to make sure they were not overwhelmed or neglected and to do this we gave them time too, Ann discussing with non-communicating teenagers or me taking Martin to watch Sheffield Wednesday (even when they were in the third division – they too needed all the support they could get). Throughout this time as a homemaker Ann spent much time in prayer in order to be sensitive and know how to balance the legitimate needs of our children and the equally legitimate needs of the neglected and wounded of the society of which we were part. It was often said as a compliment that she had a "heart as big as a bucket".

In spite of some funding from the local authority our needs were always a matter of prayer and God always provided, oftentimes from unknown or unlikely sources. One such occasion was in 1973, the year of the local miners' strike. Solid fuel was hard to get and at that time, although we enjoyed the luxury of central heating, it was fired by coke and we had run out. Purchasing more was impossible. We prayed that God would meet our needs. He did; a sack full of coke was discovered in an otherwise empty coalhouse;

this was a real practical blessing and we never did discover where it came from. It was God's timing and provision and the solution to a very practical problem of how to meet the needs of warming our young family.

In our enthusiasm to do the will of God, we were, and me particularly, always wanting to get it right – perhaps an attempt to please God, not fully understanding that as Father He wants to bless His children, even when it has to be by grace, totally undeserved. There were however principles that we had learned which we always kept, not legalistically, but in faith. Such a tenet of faith was to give to God of our blessings, whether this be time, talents, or resources, including our finances. We sought to set aside a tithe of our income. Looking back now, a tithe is quite finite and we owe all we have to Him, but then it was a big faith step with so many demands upon our funding. Whatever the temptation Ann managed without raiding the tithe tin, a triumph she later publicly acknowledged was not merely a discipline but a gift of God. Over the years the priority of acknowledging God first has proved to be a blessing and we've never been able to out-give Him. We have had to learn to receive as others have given to our needs and us.

As the demands on our living space increased, we made our needs known to God. This was becoming a priority for us whilst at the same time we were aware that the house at Poplars was beginning to empty. More and more of the occupants were getting married and having their own homes. Since koinonia had ceased, meetings were being held elsewhere and what was at one time bulging through over use was now reverting to a large under used home. It seemed so logical to swap houses, us to go to Costhorpe to Poplars, Derek, Mo and their extended family to move to

Charisma in Oldcotes. Easier said than done, but we all knew it was right.

First the legalities had to be overcome, namely the matter of valuation and the Poplars Christian Fellowship Trust deeds. Slowly and meticulously this was achieved and at the August bank holiday weekend of 1982 a fleet of cars and vans moved furniture from one home to another (a matter of two miles each way). So many cars, so many helpers, that by Saturday afternoon, all walls, skirting boards and carpets had been vacuumed, all furniture moved and all boxes emptied and crockery, cutlery, pictures and effects unpacked, washed and stored. A miraculous achievement that I've never seen equalled. The opportunities, challenges, and ministries of Oldcotes were now a thing of the past and a new period of our lives was emerging, a time in which we would see equally challenging and successful events and changes we could not anticipate.

CHAPTER NINE

ALL CHANGE

No sooner had we settled at Poplars than we had to face how best this new home would meet the family's needs. What alterations were we to make, what essential repairs needed to be done and ultimately what decorations and colour schemes were we going to decide on? The normal decisions each purchaser of property has to face at some time! Poplars was not, however, normal! It was a larger than average dwelling; constructed in 1926, it had rooms of generous proportions and ceiling heights of nine feet six inches with plaster mouldings and friezes. Moulded skirting boards were twelve inches high. The kitchen and attached sculleries, though improved over the years, were inadequate; sanitary fittings were out of the ark and years of neglect meant window frames needed replacement. Added to this, flashing needed replacing, rewiring was essential, lead plumbing was unsatisfactory and plaster cracks and patches of damp needed urgent attention. The external structure of rosemary roof tiles and red engineering bricks to the front walls, with mixed common bricks to the rear, was sound, but the dwelling had seen better days and needed refurbishment. The challenge was how to do it, firstly economically and secondly in a practical way so that disturbance to family life was kept to a minimum.

These were the kind of problems I was working with day in, day out in my position at Doncaster. My post as chief housing architect was to run a section of the Chief Architects Division of Technical Services responsible for the Metropolitan Authority's house building programme. Since the late seventies government funding had been made available for public sector housing and Doncaster's demand was of high priority. The programme the council embarked upon was to erect some fifteen hundred new dwellings each year for three years, and a year later commenced existing council house refurbishments of approximately eleven hundred dwellings per year. The schemes, about a hundred in all, stretched the entire breadth of the Authority (one of the largest geographical authorities in the UK) with projects extending from single figures to those in the hundreds.

I led a team of twenty-five, including architects, assistants and clerks of works, with further input from quantity surveyors, engineers of various disciplines, and private professionals as needed. The work was frenetic, the responsibilities great, the teamwork was terrific but the pressures were unbelievable. Housing is always politically sensitive; clients, committees and prospective tenants are rarely wholly satisfied, but with little acclaim the department basically met all the targets in the time scales that had been set, thanks to the skills of construction contractors, the energy of the staff, the support of seniors and not too little prayer. Hours were long and the challenges were great; especially hard was the political cut and thrust, the petty but real departmental struggles and the nitty gritty of human relationships in the work situation, but I survived thanks to the grace of God. Looking back I wonder how we managed this achievement and I thank God for Ann's support and strength, for the teamwork we had learned in all the activities we touched.

Home, however, was often frenetic too, but in a different sense. We continued to keep up our busy lifestyle of service, for which we received not merely an alternative to the pressures of career but the satisfaction and blessing of obedience to the call of God. We gave much and spent many sleepless hours ministering to visitors and children, but we received far more in return. Our friends Keith and Gwen said that they recalled that our outstanding gift was hospitality. Ann was so warm and inviting, such that "to come to your door was to feel being drawn in." Ann's invitation – "You must stay" – was what they remembered. "It seemed to us that immediately we were family. Ann exuded warmth, initiative and eagerness, whilst you showed strength, and good sense."

We decided that we would tackle our own building problems by employing a number of contractors, suitable to their specialities, which would enable the work to progress more quickly. My skills enabled me to have the right contacts, knowing whom to choose and knowing the quality of work to be completed. Extensive repairs meant further loans, though obviously the value of the house reflected its condition, and these eventually came through, giving us the freedom to proceed.

To suit our programme we decided that the electrical rewiring should have priority, followed by the kitchen revamp. If Ann was to continue with her hospitality specialism, the kitchen needed urgent attention. The rewiring did however mean that a very important problem had to be faced. Each room and each circulation space and even the loft and garage would be disturbed, floor boards would need to be raised and areas of walls would be chased out, creating the penetrating plaster dust. Ceilings would also be disturbed and plaster work patching would need to be inserted. The "tranquillity" of a speedy, settled move would be short-lived. If we were going to have mess, why not have it all at once? I accepted a quotation from a local builder to replace the double bay windows to first and ground floor rooms (four in all), for the replacement of the other timber windows, plus the demolition of the rear room outside wall to provide a patio door. The window replacements were still to be timber to maintain a true character; they were, however, to be double-glazed.

Ann's brother John was continuing to use his skills in electrical contracting – he was, therefore, a "natural" to do the work and we were happy to brief him on our requirements, but his availability demanded he commence almost immediately. We did not, however, experience the full impact of the onslaught on our property. Onslaught is not too strong a word as subsequently the children were able to voice the immensity of the building operations they suffered whilst rewiring took place. Whilst they were being supervised by Yvette and Ann's mum, Ann and I plus Martin had conveniently left Costhorpe to travel to a previously arranged ministry visit to India! All things being equal, such a trip would not be planned to coincide with chaos in the family, but such was our lifestyle that we felt that this visit was important for us irrespective of the home front and we knew that, in spite of teenage hormones, builders' rubble, Nan's dilemmas and Yvette's needs, all would be well and the children (and home) would not suffer irreparable damage. Thankfully, this was the reality and, in spite of the daily problems of living on an active building site, the children came through unscathed. Those who made the India trip, however, returned somewhat more affected by their first experience of visiting the subcontinent.

CHAPTER TEN

FAR AFIELD

Lucas Jacometti, a New Zealander, had visited Poplars on a number of occasions when we had held events for our young people and singles. His passion was sharing the gospel, particularly to Indians, and inevitably he shared his experiences of doing just that. He was planning another trip in the autumn of 1982 and was looking for volunteers, support and prayer. As he spoke of responses to the work of the Holy Spirit and the gospel, he enthused us with his stories of healings and miracles and challenged us about the vast numbers of Indians who had yet to hear of Jesus. This touched chords with Ann and myself – perhaps this was part of our call and offer for mission work; we would see. The next step was to pray through the implications and we met several times to inform ourselves of the realities and implications of such a visit.

First of all there were the practicalities of taking leave from work for a trip, which needed to be of at least a three-week duration. It was not normal for personnel to take this length of leave at one time, especially at such a senior position. On feeling assured that we should be involved, I made my

application and received approval. The annual leave alloca-
tion I had left until April of the following year was three
weeks and one half day! Leaving the family under "normal"
conditions would be difficult emotionally for Ann, but at the
time in question we had to ask if we were being foolish, irre-
sponsible and selfish. Addressing these issues we felt no
guilt and felt a release to pursue things further.

Lucas was planning a large team visit, and his emphasis
was for a whole range of ages, experiences and abilities.
Martin rose to this challenge and suggested he might be
included. He was just short of sixteen, but what better way,
we reasoned, of exposing him to mission than to include him
as a team member? Enthusiasm is understandable but these
decisions, on top of all the costs of moving, now meant we
had to provide expenses for three members from our family.
Our faith for finances would be tested too.

As for Martin, he decided his animals should be sold. The
menagerie at this time included goats and ducks; the pigs
had already been fattened and had met their demise
at a local slaughterhouse. Gradually we managed to say
goodbye to the vestiges of the good life and, along with gifts
and donations from various quarters plus our own input, the
financial provisions were made. One advantage of selling
the animals was that we had no need to move them to
Poplars and no headache of wondering how they would be
protected, fed and watered in our absence. For Martin,
however, it was not an easy decision as these animals had
become family pets, but with maturity beyond his age, he
recognised that this was his way of funding his trip.

Lucas had provided each one of us with a breakdown of
information on Maharashtra, the state in India we were to
visit. These included such practical details as language,

culture, finances, climate, customs, health precautions, religious practices, dos and don'ts and so on. Whatever the planning, we were to learn on this trip, and later when organising trips for others, that the most essential qualities are flexibility, adaptability and sociability. Trips rarely turn out as planned, people rarely fall into nice neat categories and even seasons vary from year to year. In our preparations we were also introduced to a team from Watford and, along with ourselves and under Lucas' leadership, the complement was sixteen persons. As we planned our visit, so too did others from the church and these included Derek and Mo Wilkinson, Rosie Dunn, Teresa Lavin, a young Christian of Martin's age and from his school, and David Clayden, a former Church of England vicar who at the time was worshipping at Poplars. For most of us this was the biggest adventure we had been involved in.

October/November were considered the best conditions from a temperature and climate point of view, especially for us novice Europeans. It still proved hot and humid and we were advised on the equipment we were likely to need: malaria tablets were a must, first aid kits, light summer clothing, Bibles and notebooks, gifts and walking shoes etc. The list seemed endless – we did not however have to worry about mosquito nets, as these were to be collected in Bombay on our arrival.

With much prayer, tears and trepidation we left Costhorpe and made good time to Heathrow where we met the remainder of the group, all, except Lucas, being equally excited and petrified at the same time. We had chosen to fly Air Egypt, which at that time was the cheapest flight, but it was not direct. We had to call at Cairo and remain there for a least one hour. Simple enough, it seemed.

The flight was uneventful and surprisingly comfortable, nothing like we'd been led to expect. On arrival in Egypt we were all told to leave the plane and head for the terminal building. On exit it was obvious from the heat, the humidity, the dust and the noise that we were no longer in Europe. Neither did it improve in the terminal building. The concrete structure was encased in black and grey marble but since it was now late evening, the darkness inside was magnified by the darkness outside. We were pointed to a seated waiting area after it was demanded that we surrender our passports and tickets. These were duly piled on to the reception desk. Part of us disagreed with this practice but, since there was a proliferation of soldiers with AK47s, our objections seemed trivial. At this time such high profile security arrangements were unknown in the UK; guns were not a reality we had accounted for. We kept a constant eye on the passports, which came and went throughout our stay in Cairo. We could only guess what was happening to them and obviously in our trepidation we feared the worst. This visit was certainly an education; we realised we were only half way to India – what would arrival at Bombay be like?

Inevitably such waiting and nervousness meant visits to the toilets – but how to find them and what would they be like? Eventually we discovered a set in the basement; they seemed to be the original Victorian suite around which the airport had later been constructed. They were a kind of vestige of British colonialism.

Looking at our fellow travellers, also seated in the waiting area, it was interesting to notice the difference in culture and attitude between the Africans and Europeans. The majority of other travellers were either Arabs or Nubian types who were seated around quietly and submissively whilst the nervous Europeans talked and marched backwards and forwards. Minutes before we were due to leave on the second half of the flight, an official arrived with a huge pile of passports, placed them on the counter and invited us, as a company, to come and select our own. You can imagine the rush and mayhem. We managed to retrieve all our documents, but one first class passenger was heard to complain. He had been given an economy class ticket in place of the one he originally surrendered (his seat had apparently been allocated to someone else) and for the rest of the flight he was seated on the floor, near the escape hatch! We were beginning to realise that not everything that happens in life is fair or as planned. Having each other and also feeling responsible for Martin and Teresa enabled us to diffuse any tension we were experiencing and Ann in her outgoing manner was a catalyst of calm to the whole group, such that the flight from Cairo to Bombay quickly passed without further incident. The flight also gave each one of us an opportunity to get to know the other members of the group.

One of the stipulations of our trip was that whatever equipment we needed for our meetings we would have to take or hire whilst there, since the Indian church (and public) were too poor to subsidise anything. We were soon to discover just how poor, and what a gulf separated developed and undeveloped nations.

The sights and sounds from Bombay airport were too much to take in all at once. First palm trees in sunburnt road verges, traffic everywhere. Then there were taxis, rickshaws, elephants, donkeys, roaming cows, handcarts all seemingly every colour of the rainbow, signs and illuminations, smoke, scents, spices, and above it all the noise of traffic horns, insects and music. The effects of western, or British, influence were still recognisable, but there were signs also of the time that had elapsed since that influence made its mark. The buildings had somehow not changed, or been maintained – a glory of previous decades, a glory that *was* rather than existed now. It seemed too much to take in, and of course it was far too soon to make assessments or give opinions.

We headed for the YMCA. This would be our stopover for a couple of days in order to get ourselves acclimatised and catch up on the sleep we had already lost in the flight. Our rooms were spartan but clean and we did have an en-suite of a kind with a shower (leaking of course) and an eastern loo. The balcony overlooked the teeming back streets of the city and the beds were almost flat to the floor. From the ceiling a big fan hung, which took some skill to operate and which turned with a constant grating noise as if something was catching. Our cases were propped up against the wall and we flopped on to the beds – it was rest we needed, but sleep came slowly.

The beauty of such a place was that it was considered safe, hospitable and sympathetic towards a group such as ours. There were dining facilities available and it was cheap – all necessary requirements, but facilities that would not always be available when we left the city. Lucas was in his element and it was obvious that he thrived on the buzz the city provided. That evening he took us around the area to get a feel of that part of the city. The roads here seemed narrower than near the airport, but no less congested. Everywhere individuals were sleeping on footpaths, verges, under trees and there was the constant coming and going of crowds, ladies in saris of all colours and qualities, men in beards and turbans, many unshod, children playing, mostly dirty, some begging, all eking out a kind of living.

The buildings were moth-eaten and tatty on the whole; across the way was a house of ill repute and, everywhere, tea houses. Off the main streets were areas of shanty towns, where hundreds of families lived under hessian, cardboard or plastic sheets raised to form some kind of shelter between road and properties, where footpaths should have been. Outside, mothers were cooking on kerosene lamps whilst children sat or played in the streets. As we made our way gingerly past these hovels I experienced for the first time the loneliness of being an intruder in a different culture; if there was such a feeling of colour prejudice, I was feeling what it was. No one was violent or offensive, but I was the infiltrator. We quickly returned to our base, understanding and appreciating the need for a safe house.

The following morning, being Sunday, it was planned that a group of us visit a church in the slums whilst another group visited a church in another part of the city. This was an opportunity to share with our Indian brothers and sisters. We dressed casually and as best we could to suit the temperature and were soon driven to the meeting. The slums spread to the north of the city and it was estimated that a million people lived in a square mile. Houses similar to those on the pavements we had already seen proliferated everywhere; some were constructed out of old cars, others of tin sheets or timber and some even of concrete sewer pipes. Animals roamed freely, dogs were mangy and often limping, dust was soon blown up by cars or any kind of movement. Sewerage drained slowly down channels and, from time to time, the situation of latrine and toilet blocks became obvious because of the prevalence of organic smells accentu-

ated in the heat. Everywhere flies were irritatingly obvious
and as before the noise was deafening.

We arrived at the little tin tabernacle and were welcomed
by the caretaker and one or two others. Already notice of the
meeting was being given by a public address system situated on the roof of the building, operated from inside the hut
and directed towards the thousands in the immediate vicin-
ity. With admiration we saw that these Christians were eager
to share the gospel. We learned that the meeting was to be
relayed direct through the public address system to all who
would listen. After a while the congregation members and
also our translator arrived. He was dressed in an immaculate, finely creased, open-necked white suit, and very smart.
He was everything we were not; I looked around at our
group, a real ragamuffin bunch, shown up by a pristine slum
dweller. We were to learn later that he lived not far from the
church building in a home the size of a motor car, which he
shared with six others; there was one bed, which they slept
on in turn. Yet in spite of these physical limitations he was
well educated and one hundred per cent committed to his
Saviour. We praise God for these committed disciples.

We each shared our testimonies and Derek spoke – I think
maybe we were in shock or jet lag but we appreciated the
experience. Afterwards the church blessed each one of us
with a cool can of Limca (lime carbonated drink). We were
thankful, but humbled; it tasted terrific.

That evening we took the train to Sholapur for the next
set of meetings. Somehow the luggage seemed to have
increased and it took several taxis to carry it and us to the
station. Living on a shoestring, Lucas had booked an
overnight sleeper (third class), and we entered the station
and headed for our carriage. It was unlit and comprised

a series of chained boards hung from the ceiling acting as bunks! At the end of each wagon was an open eastern-type toilet. With less than enthusiasm we placed our cases and equipment into the dark sleeping areas – there were no corridors on either side of the carriage and throughout our stay people came and went to the toilet, or merely to inspect the group of Europeans. From the platform the sound of the tea trolley comforted our minds and Lucas did everything he could to assure us all would be well. Having warned us that thieves were about, he detailed some of us to keep watch over our valuables whilst others "slept". I don't think any of us slept, out of apprehension and because, however you settled, the bunk boards were not in the least comfortable.

The train eventually left the Victorian station and we made our way along the track. Since it was now dark we saw little of the scenery except for the junctions, level crossings and stations along the way. We passed through the hill post of Poona (famous for holiday ex-pats in the period of the Raj) and on to Sholapur – a textile city towards the heart of Maharashtra.

Lucas had done his planning well and along with the help of Indian nationals and European contacts had managed to rent a bungalow compound for us to use at Sholapur. The compound obviously dated back to the period of British rule and now formed staff accommodation for a local Christian school. We drove up to the building and stepped from the vehicle on to the veranda, which was sound but had seen better days. Soon we were exploring our accommodation; that is, after we had unloaded every piece of luggage and equipment.

Since we basically only had two large rooms and access to a kitchen and dining room, it was decided that we split into male and female groups, each of the large rooms becoming a dormitory. By now we had acquired a mosquito net each; these were cheap enough to buy, but Europeans tend to be taller than Indian nationals so we did find them quite limiting in length and often had to sleep in a foetal position to ensure no contact with the nets, which would create vulnerability to mosquito attack. We were also able to purchase lightweight white national dress, which was considerably more comfortable than our British summer gear.

The sleeping quarters were really comical. Mattresses were provided but it was place them where you could, alongside your case if possible; but we managed to catch up with our sleep. It wasn't easy to suspend our mosquito nets, so one tough guy slept without his, on the basis that camping in Scotland in the summer was a far greater hazard then Sholapur. Needless to say, he suffered no ill effects.

The ladies too found the accommodation testing but, again, somehow survived. I'm told that Ann was a great encouragement in this also, since years of hospital beds and nurses' quarters had given her the ability to overcome in conditions less than adequate. We managed to eat well, in spite of the large ants that seemed to live in the small scullery-cum-kitchen. We also managed to wash off our sweat and keep clean, either under the outside tap or whenever the shared bathroom was available.

It was recognised that if the visit was to be most effective and beneficial, then two purposes needed to be achieved. Firstly, it would assist the Indian church if leadership training and teaching sessions were held; and secondly, to serve the community at large, a straight proclamation of the gospel would be more relevant and effective. At the time of our arrival only the latter had been foreseen and the equipment we had guarded and brought from Bombay was for that purpose. The query we raised was how at such short notice were we to notify the local church leaders of the offer of training sessions? To our Indian friends this did not present a problem. Somehow their network managed to pass on the news so that within twenty-four hours about seventy pastors, their wives and small dependent children turned up from nowhere. This sudden arrival meant that all of these would need feeding and at our expense but this was little in comparison to the costs of travel so far.

Mornings, therefore, became teaching sessions for the church leaders whilst the ladies addressed the pastors' wives (and children) in another part of the compound. Ann had no difficulty in ministering spiritually and practically to these receptive and submissive ladies. A number of these contacts were to continue beyond this visit and for several years by letter. Derek and David shared the ministry to the pastors, whilst the rest of us men benefited from their teaching. The temperatures were high by British standards but it was not unusual for the Indians to wear woollen scarves, especially in the evening; a real mixture of cross-culture dressing.

The afternoons were generally free, although the pastors and their families camped in the compound, so they were never far away and conversations often continued through this period. The evening session commenced soon after sundown – which was approximately six o'clock. With little warning the sun seemed to drop quickly, the fruit bats (flying foxes) used to leave their perches for their night's feeding forages, whilst the flocks of smalls parakeets would settle in the trees and nightfall would be a cacophony of insect noises.

Our meetings were held some two hundred yards away from the compound. A high stage had been erected with a series of supports around it, from which we hung the fluorescent lights we had brought from Bombay. Trailing wires took an electrical supply from the bungalow. Certainly there was no finesse to the structure and its illumination, but in the autumn night it more than served its purpose.

The Indian pastors had done their advertising well and crowds of locals turned up to hear the Europeans, whose photographs and notices about the event had been spread around town. Lucas, Derek and David were to share the word throughout the week at that location. The rest of us were there to pray for those who responded for whatever reason. We sang a number of well known old Christian songs and choruses, accompanied by two hand-pumped keyboards situated on the stage and played by two young helpers. The pastors and their families sang a number of songs and both the ladies and the team together assisted with renditions of other current choruses. Since the ladies were of a superior singing quality they were invited to sing each evening. The messages were to be simple and appropriate, expressing the love of God, all in a similar format. The stage had somewhat of an aura about it from the bright fluorescent lights hung over the speakers. These in turn attracted hosts of moths and insects flying above their heads. Such proliferation of food also attracted the odd strategically placed praying mantis, which sat upon the public address equipment poised ready to spring.

The responses to the preaching were far greater than we could have expected and many came forward at the end of the meetings for prayer for salvation, healing and deliverance. Inevitably a number of the needs were beyond where we were in both our experience and abilities but we pressed on and saw many lives transformed. The persistence of the Indian pastors was amazing, especially those who, being English-speakers, advised us on how best to pray. It was our first contact with desperate people; it underlined the fact that the gospel must be in demonstration of power as well as in words. We were at the extreme limit of our faith and anointing but not at the limit of our aspirations.

In the afternoons, once the teaching sessions had ended, we had the opportunity to wander through the streets of Sholapur to get a flavour of the rest of the city. It heaved and teemed with people throughout, particularly in the market area. These expeditions provided an opportunity to purchase leather goods and selected textiles for presents for our family; all at what we thought were bargain prices.

The completion of the week's preaching meant we were to pass on to the next phase of the trip. The plans indicated that we were to leave the relative comfort of Sholapur and its compound for a number of unknown frontier areas under the leadership of several of the pastors whom we had served that week. We agreed to split into four groups; Ann and I took Rosie and Teresa with us and we headed with the help of Pastor Y. M. Dupte to the town of Parli-Vaijnath, to the east.

Parli-Vaijnath was a typical Indian town, teeming with people and full of small dwellings, multiple small shops and wandering animals; the poor or non-existent roads were congested with traffic made up of every kind of vehicle imaginable. The impression was of a successive stream of different people, colours, clothing, turbans, and there were noises of all descriptions, smells beyond belief and here and there Hindu shrines and temples. One of these shrines was historically significant and the town therefore had religious importance even though it was a backwater community. Visitors and pilgrims crowded the streets, providing a boost for the local economy and it was an ideal (though often dangerous) place to proclaim the good news of Jesus. This was Dupte's home town, which he used as a base for his work in the predominantly Hindu neighbourhood and beyond that in a number of smaller villages where younger pastors and their families ministered.

Dupte shared the ministry with his wife Pramilla and their family, then of five children, and with his brother Phrobidas and his wife, Camel. Their home was basic, their possessions were few, but white eyes and shining smiles lit up the shades of the room. He spoke good English and was a converted Hindu, now in his late thirties. His mother and father also lived with him. Nearby was the simple white-painted church building to which interested locals were invited and with whom we shared the gospel. In view of the size of his home and the number already sharing it we were to be given accommodation in the first-class hotel in the town. It was at that time perhaps the only hotel and its description a euphemism, probably meaning "far above average". It was to prove to be an experience we were never to forget.

After travelling for hours both by train and taxi we were relieved to finally arrive and to be shown to our base, which took some finding, down a back street. Eventually with Phrobidas' help we signed in, showed our passports and carried our cases up the steep concrete steps and down the narrow blue-painted corridors to two rooms at the end. We pushed open one of the brown slender doors to reveal a room which boasted little decoration except light green paint smeared over rough rendering. In the middle of the room were two single iron bedsteads with interwoven metal straps as springs. The floor covering was ceramic tiles and a very old wardrobe graced the other corner of the room. There was a window and semi-balcony overlooking an open area outside and projecting from one of the room's corners was an en-suite area with an eastern toilet, which was already "fragrant". Both rooms were identical; Rosie and Teresa took one, Ann and I the other. We hadn't expected luxury, and luxury is what we didn't get!

We set about helping Rosie and Teresa unpack and feel comfortable. The first problem was how to suspend the mosquito nets. It was essential we got these erected; the splattered blood marks on the walls indicated previous occupants of these rooms had also encountered problems. We had no string and neither did Phrobidas. This was the first time that poverty struck me – he had nothing, no resources and no cash to solve a purely simple practical problem! Somehow we had to stretch the mosquito tapes and add a shoelace or two, and with a bit of this and a bit of that we managed to hang all the nets. Locking our cases and our bedroom doors, we followed Phrobidas and came to Dupte's home for an evening meal. Sitting cross-legged on the floor we tucked into a plateful of rice and meat, eaten of course with our right hand and washed down with hot tea (or in my case coffee) in a small glass tumbler, heavily sweetened and with still-warm buffalo milk. Not exactly the Ritz – not exactly bottled water, but somehow we survived that meal and the others that were to follow with only the occasional essential rush to the toilet. Looking back this in itself was a miracle for which we thanked God.

It was soon time to return to the hotel to retire. We said our farewells to the girls and with much laughter and clumsiness settled down for a night's sleep. Night time posed a number of problems. The mosquitos were many and nothing we did seemed to deter them. Yes, we had nets, but these were merely mild deterrents for these determined insects. I was not, however, aware of the attacks that would result from another direction. The metal straps that formed the bedsprings, unknown to me, housed hosts of bed bugs. The warmth of my body attracted the bugs from below and the mosquitos from above. By the morning I felt as if I was almost eaten to death. I described my forehead as a lunar landscape and other parts of my anatomy were covered with blood and pinpricks. I have never been one for heat and insects – yet here we had both in abundance. Ann thrived on heat, and insects somehow did not seem to like her.

In the morning we had a good laugh, first at my expense and then at the girls' expense. As they awoke they went out on the balcony only to find that the open space in front of their room was like an open latrine. People were squatting wherever they could. Needless to say the balcony of their room was not used in future for enjoying the views of Parli. These problems did not prevent us from serving the church and the people of the town. We sang, spoke and testified at many meetings, whilst Ann and I shared on the family and relationship truths that we had learned first at Blaithwaite and then proved as we outworked our own marriage. The people enthusiastically received our input and the time soon passed. We wondered how the other groups were succeeding, including Martin who was under Derek's leadership.

We left Parli and headed to our next destination by train and our rendezvous with the other members of the group. Their experiences in the churches had been similar to ours, but they could not boast of a first-class hotel.

We travelled to Dhond, where a public evangelistic meeting was planned. We had been warned of likely problems from militant Muslims and it was touch and go whether we proceeded. In the end we continued with the meeting, treading a political/religious fine line and, in spite of one or two missiles, survived the threats. Ann and I were hosted by a Christian family and spent the night in a railway man's house (more of a pre-cast concrete garage construction). We occupied the home's cast iron bedstead, whilst the family slept outside the front door. Hospitality that put ours to shame! The one-roomed home had a small kitchen extension at the rear; there was no lighting and the lady of the house squatted on the floor to cook us chapatis and rice on a single kerosene lamp. The home had no furniture other than the bed and six leather suitcases piled one on top of the other for storage of clothes. On one wall was a shelf, which had a series of brass tins containing family needs, valuables and food. We left this Christian home humbled – we had been honoured and spoilt, an experience more than compensating for the tribulations of the accommodation at Parli.

The timetable was rushing by and we loaded up the equipment once again to leave for Bombay. We struggled to get it all together and Derek and I attempted to lift the metal chest that contained the public address equipment and fluorescent lighting. However we couldn't shift it; were we losing our strength? Just then we were saved further embarrassment when a small Indian porter came up, lifted the chest on to his head and proceeded to climb the bridge steps that went over the railway lines. With little hesitation he achieved the flight of steps, proceeded over the bridge, down the other steps and on to the train for Bombay. Every man to his trade! We were happy to pay what was in reality only a few pence for his exertions.

Back to Bombay meant back to the YMCA and luxury, bathrooms, clean water, comfortable beds, fans and air conditioning in the dining room. How we appreciated this respite. We had twenty-four hours to spare so we treated it as a day off and enjoyed this touch of luxury. First it was swimming in a private, former army open-air swimming pool, not far away – it was beautiful. After this it was off to view Elephant Island via the George V Gate. The cruise across the water and the views of Bombay were terrific and we enjoyed letting our hair down. In the evening we went out for a meal to a local European five-star hotel. Leaving the taxi, we encountered several of Bombay's deformed beggars, as we moved on and into the thickly carpeted hotel entrance. This contrast said it all – outside, poverty and desperate need; inside, a different world of opulence and self-centredness. How on earth could these two conditions of man be resolved? I suppose you could say we were continuing the status quo, but it was too big for us to tackle, especially there and then, the evening before we were to leave. For a relatively small sum we ate a good meal and returned back to the YMCA for a night's sleep prior to our flight home.

By now a number of the group were suffering from the demands of the trip: mosquito bites that had gone septic, sheer exhaustion, most emotionally bushed and others suffering from the condition euphemistically known as "Bombay belly". The return home could not come quickly enough. One problem still existed and that was leaving Bombay airport, which you would think would be straightforward. It was, with one exception! As we went through the many customs checks, each one of us was asked whether we had duty-free goods. None of us did, as most of us had spent all our money on the trip. This was unsatisfactory to one officer who suggested to one of our party that he might like to buy some whisky if he wanted to get on the plane. Although last in the line, he understood this veiled threat, ran back to Duty Free and purchased a bottle of whisky, which the customs officer gladly received before stamping his passport. In all my travels before and after, this was the most blatant of all customs officers I experienced. The flights were again uneventful but it was noticeable that our stop at Cairo had an entirely different feel; the sun was shining and the intimidation of the night, the black granite and the armed soldiers no longer existed.

We arrived home late Sunday evening to a tumultuous family welcome and a running commentary on the construction works that had turned the house upside down in our absence. It was getting late and other things were on my mind, however; it was almost time to return to work. Fortunately the timetable had been kept; I did not have the "runs", and I returned to the housing programme, recognisable, but somewhat slimmer than when I had left three weeks earlier.

Fortunately Ann was not committed to work but was thrown immediately back into the duties and responsibilities of wife, mother and homemaker (which also involved being tea lady and clerk of works for the building operations). In spite of all these calls on her time, in her typical unflappable way she more than coped. Her mum and Yvette had done a marvellous job of holding everything together and the teenage children, in spite of all the inconveniences and practical demands and female hormones, also managed to survive home and school in our absence.

The rewiring had upset the entire house and the demolition and window replacements had created further dust and draughts. Within a few more weeks this phase of the alterations was completed and we settled down to a lull in activity; that is, until I invited Pete Pilsworth to assist me in replacing other windows that had yet to be done. Pete was at first reluctant to be involved but felt obliged, I suppose, to give a hand, as we were previously both actively involved in similar works at his home when he acquired it and moved into Oldcotes. Perhaps the scale of the alterations was similar; the size of Poplars, however, was much larger. Pete and Chris still kept their membership on at Oldcotes Chapel after we left, working out how they themselves should proceed. Eventually both they and the Peels left to attend Poplars, but continued to reside in their home in Oldcotes.

CHAPTER ELEVEN

SETTLING IN

For a number of years whilst we lived at Charisma we had an entire wall decorated in wallpaper with regency carriage motifs. It proved a useful topic of conversation and different visitors spent a vast time counting the carriages. It was a sad day when this wallpaper had to be stripped. Decorations are a very personal matter and the decorations at Poplars were something different. We felt no pangs of conscience in stripping the tartan wallpaper in the dining room, or taking out the cupboards and the call system for the servants. Doing a house swap meant that we already knew the property and had consciously or subconsciously addressed a number of the property needs and how best the changes would suit our family. We could only take this so far however, because as the family grew and changed so did our needs, and some of those initial alterations were changed again so as to make the house more suitable to our ever developing requirements. I suppose being in the construction industry meant that alterations were easier for me to consider and execute than for most people.

We set ourselves a programme and concentrated that winter period on internal renovation works. What had been the master bedroom was soon divided into two rooms, together with built-in wardrobes, all done by brother John, whilst I was able to do enough decorating in both reception rooms and bedrooms to ensure that everything was ship-shape for the Christmas holidays. Most things seemed to need attention and everything was bigger than average, but with dogged persistence, economies of purchase and endless patience the changes seemed worthwhile. The ten of us settled into our new routine and into the former "clap and be happy" building which now became our home.

The exterior only had a respite because of the time of year, but that did not escape for long. New gates were added, a new rainwater system, further drainage connections, and I managed a complete pointing of the rear elevation by myself, in March of all times, with no ill effects due to frost. It was a cold operation and taught me much about the role of a bricklayer (and labourer) but I remain pleased that even architects can turn their skills to practical building. We also owed a lot to willing helpers, not least one of my former bricklaying clerks of work from Doncaster, who would visit at weekends and was responsible for fireplace constructions and many other miscellaneous jobs. Ann was always friendly to each of our visiting tradesmen and the buzz of family life seemed an attractive welcome.

Fitting into the new neighbourhood was not as easy as it had been at Oldcotes. We were in the former colliery manager's house, set in its own grounds, and distanced on all boundaries from adjacent properties. To the front was the main A60 arterial road with a drive plus verge and footpath, whilst to the rear was a hedge and fence, with the local cricket field beyond. Our strategy had, therefore, to be different. We took every opportunity, however, to get to know whom we could but the intimacy of Oldcotes, plus the fact of having younger children then, made our previous efforts seem easier.

The season soon came for developing the garden and through trial and error Martin and I discovered that it was excellent for certain vegetables, fruit and flowers, but less suitable to many more. Just short of an acre in total, it was generally far more exposed to the elements (particularly chilling winds), so that whatever was set had to be hardy. Only later as we managed to sell off some of the land and the size became smaller and more protected did many of the plants excel. We had discovered that onions and leeks thrived. For months, year upon year, we never seemed to run out of them whatever the season! A major planting programme for shrubs, saplings and fruit trees was embarked upon. Existing apple and pear trees had erratic types of harvest, so we supplemented these with further eating apple varieties and additional Victoria plum trees. I cut back much of the overgrown privet and added willow and a proliferation of flowering shrubs, and gradually we stamped our own identity upon the garden.

We did not attempt, however, to change the "lawn" – or should I say the grassed area? Tenderly manicured by the colliery gardener for years, this vast area had, since the colliery closure, been sadly neglected and was now the home of daisy, plantain and other broad-leafed weeds, which were very well established. Since it provided a natural play area both for our family and our visitors, and in view of the expense of laying and relaying turf or grass seed for such a vast area, it remained untreated for the whole of our stay.

The one exception was when I lifted the turf in the centre to provide an area for a family bonfire. Wildlife proliferated too, which was a great delight to watch, squirrels and birds particularly; but less desirable for my vegetable garden were the visits of mice, rats and rabbits, which inevitably made you think of the characters from Beatrix Potter, such as Peter Rabbit – with me being Mr McGregor.

In one area particularly Poplars was better situated than Charisma. Oldcotes suffered from its situation around a crossroad of the A60 and A631. Walking anywhere inevitably meant crossing one or more of these roads. In the times before the emphasis upon conservation and preservation, greedy farmers had ploughed up the historical footpaths and the local rights of way. To attempt to take in the surrounding beauty of the village on foot was not easy and incurred the wrath of farmers. Poplars, however, did not have these limitations. To the south and west of the property was a public footpath, leading alongside the cricket field and from there beyond into the Langold Country Park.

Years before, much of this area had been the colliery property, with buildings and railway sidings. The lake had been an amenity as well as an asset for the mine and its workers. The colliery had closed in the mid-sixties and the majority of the buildings had been demolished and the railway sidings removed. Self-set saplings and bushes had now taken over and thanks to an injection of cash the Local Council had landscaped much of the area so that it became an ideal spot to walk, play and gravitate to for countless activities. For us it provided a very convenient area for taking walks with our many visitors, and for our countless children it was a place where they could let off steam – as well as being a centre for bird watching, life-saving swimming and angling.

I managed to be involved in the bird watching, assisted in the angling (which to me, apart from the maggots and constant casting and recasting of lines, was like watching paint dry) but I never took part in life-saving swimming.

Family life continued as busy as ever, with the children entering their teenage years and deciding to some extent their preferences at school and the likely direction their careers or education would or should take. At the same time our fostering activities meant that much of our attention was directed elsewhere in partnership with social workers, to deal with the deep emotional needs our charges often exhibited. There always seemed to be regular turnover of social services staff due to career promotions or internal restructuring, but our continuity enabled us to get involved with many professionals, a number of parents and other foster carers.

Our involvement with the community grew and on several occasions we were invited to offer our perspective on fostering at day or evening courses. Over the years the fostering scheme became far more professional and demanding, with stricter entry requirements and increased expectations. Inevitably, owing to the increase in the national abortion rate and the use of contraception, the birth rate declined and it became unusual to have babies available for adoption. At the same time the increase in family breakdown led to a greater stress upon single parents and children. It became far more usual for older children, even teenagers, to be needing fostering places, and this, together with the trend for fostering of several siblings, put extra pressures on the system, the staff and on carers in particular.

A further advantage of our move to Poplars was that it was still in the same school catchment area as Oldcotes, so apart from the children needing to get a new school bus (all children in this catchment were bussed six miles up to the local Portland Comprehensive School in Worksop) it was "business as usual" for them, retaining their existing friendships. This too was a great stabiliser for our foster children, whether of secondary or primary age, as the primary school was situated at Langold, midway between Costhorpe and Oldcotes.

From time to time we would still get a late Friday afternoon request to take another child for fostering, particularly when the department was desperate, since it was realised that we were active in several spheres. Officers were aware too that the children under our care had emotional needs that required very careful handling. Nor was it only the children who would exhibit problems. Ann's mum, although she was extremely generous and caring and tried to accommodate our different lifestyle and extended family, had moments of self-pity, even jealousy, that we had to deal with as best we could. We agreed that she visited us alternate weekends, which helped us on many occasions from a supervision point of view, but meantime we had often to consider how best to encourage her through her moods. Gradually we became aware of the patterns or causes of her depression. Ann particularly had to deal with the guilt that her mum would want to pass to her and on many occasions I had to confront this in a firm but loving way.

Similarly, Yvette also had her moments, tears and tantrums and Ann prayed much with her, challenging, cajoling and ministering against fear, negativism and depression. Consistency, forgiveness and practical love won through in the end, but it was not without much emotion, loss of sleep and prayer. Fortunately in all this, both in demands and support, the church was terrific and many individuals came alongside Yvette, Ann's mum, the individual foster children and our own teenagers. The church carried our burdens, recognising our call to these hands-on, pioneering ventures. In similar ways we too were able to come alongside others who in their own or extended families were suffering from caring at all costs.

By now the Poplars Christian Fellowship was beginning to expand. This was a natural outworking from the demise of the Faith Group and the concentration of time and effort in the Carlton area. The worship sessions were vibrant and had attracted many from the villages and farther afield. At the same time a number of the fellowship had married, settled in their own homes and were influencing their neighbours. Over the years of the ministry of the Faith Group, relationships had been made throughout the country and from time to time visitors would descend upon the church, some of whom would come with their families and needed additional hospitality. Saturday evening or midweek meetings would result and this provided yet another catalyst to include others in our activities. The village hall was no longer too large for us and Sunday meetings became more regular in seating arrangements, to maximise numbers.

During the mid-eighties we held a series of monthly Saturday evening sessions – "Going Forward with God" – and invited a number of national speakers – Gerald Coates, David Pawson, Derek Brown, John Hutchinson, just to mention a few. This served the body of Christ in the area and became instrumental in many from other churches progressing in their faith. It also meant that Poplars attracted a number of transfer-growth members.

Wherever and whenever possible we tried to be involved in the local community activities. One of Ann's inspirations was to hold a Craft Fayre at Carlton Village Hall very soon after the introduction of the early May bank holiday. No fixed event had cornered the market by then and so our event proved overwhelmingly successful. The weather was brilliant and literally busloads of visitors turned up. Those providing refreshments never stopped all day, whilst stall-holders recorded resounding sales and successes. One friend was invited to offer insurance services and that day obtained as many as eight good new clients – for him an extremely beneficial day. It was an opportunity to provide a service to the community and to show that loving Jesus was not a solemn experience. We made sure that we didn't get into the traditional mould of making an annual event of this success. Actually, we never did repeat it.

Community, of course, is made up of individuals and it was to individuals that we sought to relate. One of them was Ann Jackson, who later wrote:

> I first met Ann on a bus in the eighties. She sat by me and, by the time we had arrived at the bus stop where I was to get off, we were friends! That's how she was with everyone she knew; you became friends instantly! I had just become a Christian, but Ann soon had me involved in praying with her for others. It was a real learning curve and Ann knew it! In spite of this, she always made you feel special. She was a spiritual visionary who could see how something could be done and how to bring it into being. I often hear her voice in my mind saying to me, "Go on Ann, you can do it."

CHAPTER TWELVE

GOOD NEWS, BAD NEWS

We enjoyed being involved in ministry through the church, our home, our careers and in the community. All seemed to be going well and in spite of the emotional times we knew we had resources in Christ to deal with the vicissitudes of our lifestyle. It was in the thick of life that Ann did not feel too well, but such was her strength and drive that she thought little of this and carried on as normal, until one day she shared with friend Ann Jackson about her pains and her doubts as to whether it was something or nothing. After talking and praying together Ann advised her at least to see the doctor, as this would be the advice she would give to others.

Having no legitimate excuse not to, she made an appointment with our GP, a small, genial Asian who specialised in paediatrics and gynaecology. He asked Ann whether she wanted to be treated privately or on the National Health Service. Ann replied in a blasé way that the NHS would be more than adequate, and was staggered by his response. "Are you available to see the consultant this afternoon?"

"Yes," she said, realising that this must be more than it appeared if a consultation would take place so quickly. She notified me at work of the outcome of her visit and kept the appointment with the consultant. Within the week, samples having been taken and results received, she had been diagnosed with ovarian cancer and was to be admitted to hospital within the next few days, or weeks. It actually took five weeks in all from the decision to visit the doctor to her entry for surgery.

This was a bolt out of the blue; without warning she had been diagnosed with cancer. Naturally we shared the diagnosis with the family and church as best we could. The children were tremendous and had grace to accept this unknown. Sadly, some of their secondary school teachers were unaware of what the children were going through and were unsympathetic at the time to them and to their unknown plight. Perhaps we should have forewarned them. Today I am aware that staff are briefed on the needs of children as they and their families go through personal traumas. It was also somewhat of an unknown for me at work. The responsibilities of the job meant I had to give my undivided attention to the programmes, my staff and committee meetings. It was going to be hard to support Ann and keep going. My senior colleagues, however, understood and in a remarkable way the family's needs, the challenge of work and above all Ann's needs were all satisfied. Even in these stresses and pressures God enabled us to overcome.

This situation did mean that for the first time we had to face some very fundamental problems. Cancer was a potential killer we could not ignore. Lurking around the corner was an unknown future. We had to find God for our family and ourselves in this serious situation. God's people were as always faithful in prayer and support. One day as Ann prepared herself by reading her Bible, she was impressed by the following passage from Luke 21:18–19. She read, "Not a hair of your head shall perish and by your endurance you will gain your lives" (NASB). What was the relevance of this to her situation? Ann's nursing experience had shown her that usually, as part of the treatment of cancer, chemo- or radiotherapy is used and this often results in nausea and hair loss. She felt God was saying to her, "You will not need chemotherapy treatment; trust me, you will not lose your hair – your crowning glory!" This was a real encouragement – it would still be the surgery route, but there would be a way out.

In due course Ann was allocated her time to visit the former Victoria Hospital in the centre of Worksop, with her operation scheduled for the following day. Her professional experience and knowledge of the routines of surgical nursing enabled her to settle down and sleep through the night until she was woken early by the staff and given her "pre-med". She was to be first on the list due to start about 8.30. Feeling the effects of her preparation, Ann was approached sometime later by one of the senior staff. For some reason all but one of the anaesthetists were away at a conference and the one scheduled for the day's operations had just telephoned in sick!

There would be no operation that day – possibly tomorrow. It was appreciated by the staff that the hospital was to blame for this poor performance. Coping with cancer was bad enough – but coping with an on-off operating system was far from satisfactory. The staff were so concerned they suggested we had every legal right to claim compensation from the hospital for distress. We never did. It was a surprise to me on my visit later to discover Ann sitting up in bed relating her experiences. We laughed at the situation.

As we talked I was called out of the ward by a registrar who had noticed that there had been no contact by the hospital with any of Ann's relatives, and particularly myself as spouse. They had failed to alert me to the gravity of the diagnosis and surgery. There and then he went through the consequences of such an operation and its aftermath. I thanked the doctor for this approach. It's not the easiest of topics to raise with a patient's family at any time. I assured him that since Ann was a nurse we were aware of the implications of the disease (I would later say that this awareness was theoretical, rather than experiential, which are miles apart). I also pointed out that we were Christians, that we had faced the possible outcomes, and that we were confident in our faith that all would be well. I returned to Ann and shortly after further prayers and embraces said my farewell to her. She had been informed that the chief anaesthetist would attend the operation the following morning; a kind of compensation for the day's debacle.

Ann knew that immediately after her operation she would have tubes everywhere and the effects of the anaesthetic would mean she would not really be conscious and certainly no attraction to be viewed. In spite of these warnings to the contrary I was not deterred from visiting. Arriving as early as I could that night I soon saw that Ann's assessment was right; tubes were everywhere and her consciousness seemed to come and go. No sentence seemed to be finished… it was, however, brilliant to see her, to hold her hand and to praise God she had come through at least the first part of the treatment.

The next day couldn't go fast enough for us all, for I had little news to share and of course the telephone never stopped ringing. It was midsummer and it happened to be warm and sunny at that time. As soon as I could get home from work I visited the hospital and hastened into the ward, but there was no Ann! Up and down I walked until a nurse came in view; I asked where Ann might be. The answer staggered me. She was outside on a paved courtyard area, sunbathing! She showed me the direction and I made my way outside. There was Ann taking in the sun, and now with only one tube in place. Surprised, I asked what she was doing. She knew that so long as she kept infection at bay, moving about could only be beneficial to her circulation and healing. Although movement wasn't easy and she had to walk doubled up, the experience of being able to sunbathe had invigorated her. Such was Ann's spirit that she was determined to recover; staying in bed as a patient was not a concept she looked forward to.

Within a few days, she was allowed to recuperate further at home. Her nursing knowledge always seemed to help at times like this; the staff had confidence in her to do only what was necessary. This was of course another one of those times when our support services thankfully kicked in, with countless friends assisting and Ann's mum taking practical responsibility, along with the girls, for laundry, ironing and cleaning, with Martin assisting me in the garden maintenance.

We had always taught the children to be industrious and to learn the age-old skills of domesticity and hard work. At Oldcotes most of the children had delivered newspapers around the village at some time – the rewards were always helpful but the work experience far more of an investment. As the girls grew they learned the necessary homemaking skills of cooking, baking, needlework, even knitting, and countless thousand others, whilst DIY and gardening were passed on to the boys. Its sounds less than PC now, but these were essential skills we felt we must pass on to our children in preparation for the time when they too would be parents. Subsequently we benefited from these slow, often frustrating and tedious lessons on practicalities when the children were able to demonstrate their skills to their friends and family. Saturday employment became the norm as the girls grew, jobs being passed on from sister to sister as one left home for higher education – but more of that later.

This year (1993) was the first time in our marriage that we had determined to take a holiday that didn't involve camping and we had booked a stay in a guesthouse in Sandown, Isle of Wight. Ann had been there previously, when younger, and had fond memories; I had never been so I was looking forward to new experiences. We had booked earlier in the year; not knowing that hospitalisation would be necessary. Since the children would be at a series of camps, we would be free to spoil ourselves. We had, however, also planned to take with us two of the unmarried young ladies, Heather and Rosie, from the fellowship. There was obviously a period of doubt as to whether, in view of Ann's operation, our holiday plans would be fulfilled. The timing could not have been better. Five weeks after her return home, after having come through the effects of the anaesthetic and having had time to resolve the pressing issues of home and family, we were able to keep to our diary dates and off we travelled for a holiday where Ann was not the generator but the recipient of hospitality. It was years later before we pre-booked another holiday. God's timing was immaculate once again.

The holiday proved ideal and Ann benefited from the rest from responsibilities. Heather and Rosie were tremendous companions and we saw as much of the island as we could. As in any time together, conversations eventually came around to relationships and for both the girls this was a tender area. Now in their mid-twenties, they had been active members of the fellowship; Rosie particularly had devoted years to singing with the Faith Group and this giving of themselves had meant neglecting their personal aspirations, especially in respect of relationships with members of the opposite sex. All the eligible men seemed to have been spoken for. We made this issue one of prayer and Ann suggested that as a priority they should list the qualities they were looking for in a mate. Nothing was to be overlooked since God was interested in their well-being. By the end of the week both had their lists, comprehensive down to hair colour, temperament, abilities and, above all, spirituality. This was going to be a challenge, finding two likely candidates; it was also going to be the first of Ann's matchmaking exercises. The holiday had truly been beneficial but it was now time for Ann to get back into some kind of normal routine – normal, that is, for us since we realised our routine did not represent normality for most.

The summer quickly passed; demands were always less at this time of year with people being away. September, however, was always considered as the start of the fellowship year, very much like the new school year, when theoretically all were reinvigorated after a summer break. Since several of the members were actually schoolteachers this fitted in well with their timetables too. The autumn programme took off with monthly public meetings, to which we now included invitations to friends from Watford, including those we had ministered to in India. As expected there were amongst them several young single males and females – but eventually nothing materialised from all our efforts on the marital front. Lucas visited our home on a number of occasions and when eventually we felt success was near we discovered he was much younger than surmised and the likely ladies much older. Somehow the chemistry question faltered on the age issue.

However the November bonfire outreach was far more successful. In view of the large garden at Poplars, regular bonfires were held on the vegetable area either side of the lawn. This year we invited whom we could and this included a contingent from Ruth's church in London. Forrest and his friend Bob, from the Southend area (Forrest formerly went to Ruth's church in Cricklewood prior to his move to Southend), somehow fitted most of the criteria of Heather and Rosie's lists. With encouragement, relationships developed and visits north and south persisted. Accommodation was always available at Poplars, especially for such important trysts and, after months of serious courting, wedding plans and arrangements were in hand.

We were now an introduction/marriage agency and took much stick from other Christians over the years when we made the needs of our unmarried girls known publicly. We did not arrange marriages as in the culture of the Old Testament but we did hear the hearts of the ladies who wanted to marry and yet felt inhibited on introductions. Over the years several other couples were brought together and left to outwork their relationships; all of these have remained strong and the couples have been in church leadership for years. God had answered our prayers in these foundational practical areas too.

Month by month it was necessary for Ann to visit the hospital as a follow-up to her operation. Post-surgical analysis had confirmed the diagnosis of cancer and as far as the surgeons were concerned the growth had been removed successfully. It was however essential that she attend clinics. Each month the question was mused over by the specialist as to whether the treatment would include chemotherapy. Ann was not looking forward to this and made it a real matter of personal prayer, especially in view of the word she had received about the hairs of her head being numbered, which she interpreted as meaning chemotherapy would not be necessary and no hair loss would result. Month after month the surgeon was happy with Ann's result and healing, such that eventually it was decided that no chemotherapy would be needed. We were blessed that we could now get on with life. This episode was behind us.

CHAPTER THIRTEEN

MID-LIFE CRISIS

Our children continued to mature and 1984 saw Martin complete his secondary education and leave school to take up horticultural studies. His initial emphasis had been upon animal husbandry but he realised very soon that success in that field would only result if he were to marry a rich farmer's daughter. Since this was highly unlikely he resorted to horticulture. The course meant a year's practical placement prior to three years' study at Askham Bryan Agricultural College near York. For the first year, therefore, he took up employment with Bassetlaw District Council, being based at Retford. Each day he cycled the ten miles or so each way down the country lanes. This particular year, however there was yet another national strike affecting fuel deliveries to power stations and since Bassetlaw boundary is the River Trent, four large power stations on the east of the district were daily problem areas with picket lines. Only once was he forced off the road into the verge and hedge, fortunately unhurt, by a twelve-ton lorry running the gauntlet of the pickets. By the time this practical training finished,

Martin and Jenny were married and the first of our children left the nest and the daily trips to York were no longer our responsibility. Since they settled in Langold, about a mile from us, we were able to continue to help them as necessary, especially in the refurbishment and decoration of their home.

The year 1985 was significant in two specific ways. The first was in respect of my career. Ever since our transfer to Poplars, our input into the lives of individuals in the fellowship had been growing. Initially we were helping members to overcome the emotion of change, but then this extended to helping individuals and families in a pastoral way. Alongside this, we would seek to spread the word of God, encourage and train the young people and lead and maintain home groups, all in and around the district. As the numbers increased so too did the responsibilities until it became obvious that I could no longer continue to keep up the pace of maintaining two occupations. Something would have to give.

The church eldership prayed about our future. Two years previously Derek had given up his post to work full time for the fellowship – but his ministry was mainly prophetic leadership and the people needed practical pastoring. The question came to us to consider: would I be prepared to care for the church, not in a part-time capacity as I had previously done, but to leave my post at Doncaster in order to serve full time? By that time I had been in post for almost twelve years. I had been able to get the position owing to an Act of Parliament that brought in Local Government Reorganisation on 1 April 1974. Becoming Chief Housing Architect at the age of thirty meant that I had progressed my career in a speedy and dramatic way. Now it was time to consider my future. In order to determine to what extent we were to support Derek financially when he left his employment, we decided as a leadership to ensure he had the average salary of those in the eldership. In a similar way I submitted our needs, bearing in mind the size of our family and the likely loss of income, and my remuneration was agreed.

After much prayer together and a confidence of the certainty of the decision, I gave in my notice to leave the Architectural Division. The seniority of the post meant a three-month working notice. To some of my colleagues, my decision was a shock, to others less of a surprise. I had always let others know of my faith, produced the goods for my employers and attempted to maintain my integrity in spite of the often very delicate political sensitivities of a Metropolitan Authority. By mid-May I had terminated my employment at Doncaster. Yet again our obedience to God's word meant I was now available to throw my energies wholeheartedly into the significant event of the year.

It had been announced that Billy Graham had accepted the invitation of the churches of Sheffield to hold a mission there in June, based at the Sheffield United football ground. Such a high profile series of meetings inevitably takes a lot of preparation and churches from the Sheffield area were invited to participate. Many churches had reservations about the "American approach" or the "mass evangelism" format, and so too did individuals. Peter Fenwick and others did not have these reservations and neither did we and as a result of this backing we as a fellowship got behind the preparations. The fellowship could only benefit from the training sessions and the opportunity to take others to hear the gospel. Ann, full of enthusiasm for the event, bearing in mind her own historical connections with Billy's ministry at

Wembley in 1954, attended the initial Worksop planning meeting as our representative.

To her amazement the planning meeting was successful except for two local areas: Whitwell and Creswell, from which no representatives attended. No local churches felt they could rise to the challenge of these tough mining villages. Ann knew that our own village had representatives from about six churches, yet here were two entire communities left out in the cold. Without hesitation, on her return, she shared about this gap with the eldership. After prayer we decided to accept Ann's recommendation that we ourselves should take up the challenge of these areas. Carlton-in-Lindrick was well served; we would concentrate elsewhere. We informed headquarters of our intention and took responsibility for these two communities some twelve miles away.

Responsibility meant prayer, advertising, door knocking, arranging for transport to and from the mission, financial involvement, counselling, visiting and follow-up. Poplars members enrolled en mass as counsellors and for follow-up – only the large Sheffield churches could match the volunteer numbers from Poplars.

So it was that we selected the Model Village at Creswell to be our first place to canvas and invite the residents to the mission. Creswell was known to be a tough place and the Model was the centre of this toughness. The two-storey houses were large and built in two concentric circular patterns around a central grassed open area. Not knowing the village we commenced door knocking at the first terrace block we came to on our left, with the view of completing the circle. We were surprised by the reaction of the residents. Expecting to encounter resistance, we found in fact that the name of Billy Graham obviously rang bells and very little negative reaction resulted. One resident gave me the normal banter about not needing to go to church to worship God and so on, but it was stimulating to be able to respond, defend our faith and present the gospel. If this one were to come it would have to be a work of the Spirit. That evening proved successful; we didn't manage too many of the hundreds of properties but we did get twelve people who wanted to attend the mission – success beyond our wildest dreams, for we were "cold canvassing" amongst people we didn't know at all.

Our visit to Sheffield went without a hitch and of the people we took a number responded and went forward on the football pitch for literature. Alongside this, as participating churches, we were given names of other local people who had visited and shown an interest. The biggest surprise of all for me was the news I received as soon as I did the follow-up at the Model Village. The person who had given me all the banter had visited the mission privately with a friend and he had been soundly converted! He was somewhat embarrassed when I saw him! Our later follow-up meetings were to be held in his home once the mission was completed.

The mission made quite an impact locally, even though distances travelled were in the region of twenty miles each way. Ann's foresight had proved correct; there was a definite need in the area for a gospel presentation even though some places and individuals appeared to be the most unlikely. The enquirers who went forward each night at Sheffield completed a few personal details, which were then passed to a central office network and allocated to supporting churches near to where the enquirer lived. Several local enquirers' details were forwarded to Poplars and I took it upon myself to visit those who were spread around the

Creswell and Whitwell area. As a result of these contacts, it was not long before a number of them were happy to attend weekly meetings. These inevitably grew as other family members came along to see what was happening. One miner escorted his wife to make sure we were not after her money. On later discovering that that was not our motive, he himself responded to the gospel and continues to this date as a faithful disciple and congregational leader.

Pete Hardy and I worked together on the weekly follow-up meetings at Creswell. Allowing for the fact that this assembled group was "unchurched", we were astounded at what happened. They were completely at home and very personable. There were two teenagers; Paul and his wife Marion; our hosts, Janet and her husband, Eddie, and a couple more of the neighbours. We introduced ourselves, started with prayer and explained the purpose of the meeting and made sure that we all were comfortable (since the seating arrangements were limited) before we launched into the teaching/communication mode.

We had not gone many minutes into our discourse, allowing for questions and answers, when one of the group lit a cigarette but continued to listen. It was obvious that this was a different culture; smoking was normal and no rudeness was meant. We did not feel at liberty to reprimand or challenge this in any way and felt that if it was to be called to a halt, it would be the conviction of the Holy Spirit that would bring it about, not our rules or regulations. We proceeded for another few minutes, when our hosts suggested that we all took a break for refreshments! Several others lit up too and then out came the sandwiches, cakes and pots of tea. This was not going to be a dry, lifeless type of meeting; this was a social occasion.

With further stops and starts the meeting came to its natural end. We had managed to present Bible truths in understandable ways – albeit in short concentration spans and through the occasional cloud of smoke and the ubiquitous cup of tea. The meetings continued weekly for months and numbers came and went. Several others responded to the gospel and – surprise, surprise – most of the smokers no longer smoked, not because we told them not to, but because they heard God for themselves. The hospitality never did diminish and even after the meetings ended and some of our initial members moved on, people continued to be lavish and generous in their sharing from their own homes. Whenever possible Ann would love to attend these down-to-earth sessions and she became a mentor for a number of the ladies who responded positively to her counsel, love and wisdom. These were bizarre sessions, but built relationships that, because of our commitment, regular visitation and prayer continue still today.

CHAPTER FOURTEEN

INTRODUCING RESPITE

As head of fostering in Bassetlaw, David Robinson was a great help in ensuring that the system accommodated change, so that our personal needs were met and our suggestions listened to. It was in response to David's invitation that both Ann and myself became advisers to other prospective foster carers. At his request and insistence our caring also took two further additional emphases. The first of these was to pioneer respite care and the second was caring for young single mothers and babies.

The move to Poplars meant we now had further space and were able to consider, alongside the care of Steve and Paul, the county's new venture into respite care, the branch of fostering in Nottinghamshire called "Home from Home". Respite care, so much part of social services' provision and parlance today, was in the eighties quite forward looking. Respite care provided opportunities for specialist fostering, especially of special needs children, whose parents were thus enabled to spend time with their other children and in normal, often mundane, activities. Such things as shopping, visiting the hairdresser, leisure activities, holidays or even work could be indulged in without guilt. Since this was unknown at the time, parents had to be secure to allow their children to be cared for by others and they had to overcome personal problems of shame or failure. After years of caring for the particular and individual needs of a child, parents often did not realise that others could relieve them of this duty. Very often, these children were also wheelchair users.

Ann's enthusiasm for this additional service provision was unbounded and when it was initially introduced in the Bassetlaw District of Nottinghamshire we and one other family were chosen to pilot the scheme. Ann's nursing skills, her adult training centre knowledge plus her large heart caused her spirit to rise to a challenge that ultimately made the scheme and our continued involvement in it a success over many years.

Enthusiasm and feelings were never enough, and although in her gifting Ann excelled naturally, her aim was always to be one step ahead so that what she knew and what we shared was of top quality. In order to find out more and be able to present the best possible care she took part, in 1988, in the Open University Patterns for Living course for what, prior to PC language, was termed "mental handicap". This enabled her both to speak the language and understand the current theories and practices on caring for those with special needs. This investment of time was to prove beneficial for the work that was later to develop, not only in the provision of respite care in Nottinghamshire, but also in the nineties in Eastern Europe.

Generally Down's syndrome children and young people have a very happy disposition and Christine was no exception when she came to stay with us. As a teenager she was a big girl physically, but she endeared herself to our family, going everywhere we went when she was with us. What a delight it was to care for her, to alleviate the pressure on her family and introduce our own children to special needs and how to overcome fears and misapprehensions. Thankfully, all our children took our fostering and respite caring in their stride and we always believed they benefited as individuals by having experienced a much richer family life than most.

Eventually Christine left visiting us to go to college, but we continued to have contact with the family. Other children would come and share our home for periods, but notification always seeming to be Friday afternoons about four o'clock. Our next respite care child was Mary who initially came for the odd weekend but for whom we cared up to the age of sixteen. Mary suffered from cerebral palsy and had little eye contact or verbal skills but we soon lovingly cared for her as our own. We did begin to notice as she grew older and bigger how much more difficult it became to lift her and move her around, later in a wheelchair rather than a buggy. Once again we were coming to know the difficulties which the parents of those with special needs experienced on a daily basis. We were shocked to hear that Mary's mother had contracted cancer and within months had died. Her father, having a very responsible post at a local independent school, looked for our help to continue and once again we were able to assist; this later developed to include respite care for two or more weeks at a time as he went on trips or on holiday.

Foster care is directed towards the most vulnerable in society, our children. Sadly, research points to the fact that those abused become the abusers and the victims become the perpetrators. Ann firmly believed that this cycle, through the love of God, could be broken, and committed her time to ending this pattern. Exploitation of the vulnerable is, however, widespread and our next venture in care was to have single mothers and their babies in our home, so that Ann, both as mother and nurse, could assist these young teenagers (as they turned out to be) by teaching them the basics of child rearing and parenting. When I say "in our home", I mean as part of our family, as much as they wanted to be, but living in our granny flat bed-sit complete with sink unit and cupboard, furniture, en-suite shower and toilet, all with a separate entrance. Ann spent hours advising on bathing, feeding, dressing, caring for babies and sorting out finances and benefits; and, when necessary, contacting agencies, visiting parents and doing the thousand and one other small but vital jobs that arose. David Robinson was aware that we not only had space, but also vision to see this specialist care become a reality.

Each situation was different, as too were the abilities, understanding and willingness of the teenagers, but for several desperate families our open home provided a sanctuary in which to work through the stresses of change, shame, reconciliation with family and growing up. Since we only had room for one family at a time our input in this way was somewhat limited, irrespective of demand. It proved to be, however, a benefit for those who were in need, and who were cared for rather than condemned. Those little children have now grown up and recently one returned, this time with her father, to say thank you.

It was whilst we were at Poplars that there occurred what were perhaps two of our most difficult and certainly our most emotional incidents in fostering. The first was the arrival in 1984 of Peter at the age of almost three. He lived close by with his mother who was quite a vulnerable person, and unable to read or write; she was mother to other children and she had suffered domestic violence at the hands of Peter's father. Peter too had similarly suffered much abuse and eventually his father was imprisoned for actual bodily harm directed towards him. The aim of social services was for Ann to work with mother and child for restoration and rehabilitation. For a number of months she patiently pursued this, in private and group meetings, at case conferences and the like, but with little success since mum was only just coping with the other siblings, who eventually had to be taken into care and were ultimately adopted. Much effort went into assisting mum, and contact between siblings was often arranged.

Peter, however, had many nightmares, disturbed sleep patterns, unusual behaviour and swore profusely. It was a long, slow process to lead him into some kind of secure, stable state. Sadly, the violence and neglect he had been sub-jected to (often left in his cot for hours, or days, day or night, without food, contact or even light) led to Peter suffering intellectually, which was compounded by his mother's inability to stimulate his development. His normal speech and behaviour progress also was a long, hard slog.

In view of mum's other responsibilities and other liaisons she soon withdrew from the scene, happy in the knowledge that Peter was benefiting from foster care at our home. As with other children, schoolteachers were tremendous in their support, but his character was aggressive and this created many problems, such that on at least one occasion a personality clash between him and his teacher was obvious. What were we to do? Seeking advice was always helpful but the outworking of this was always personally demanding. We sought to get Peter educationally statemented in order to obtain the help that he needed; however, Nottinghamshire did not (and still does not) give too much credence to this method and has the smallest percentage of statemented children of any county in England. It was obvious that Peter needed help so we committed our time and money to pursuing it for him.

We brought in a friend of ours, a primary school teacher, who assisted him in reading and when she could come no more we enrolled him with the Dyslexia Society for weekly sessions. All this helped to some degree, especially in the confirmatory diagnosis that he had a very short memory retention and was underdeveloped in other areas. We looked also for a change of school, visiting other local ones in South Yorkshire since being close to three county boundaries these distances were minimal. A report by a county educational psychologist also highlighted his need but the most the school could offer was special assistance for so many hours per week, shared with all those others in the school (who turned out to be in double figures) similarly needing special input. The demand and the inadequate supply was stacking up against him.

In spite all these negatives we loved Peter a lot and somehow he seemed not to be a priority for social services' attention. Mum had moved to the south of England, he was settled and we felt any further disturbance would lead to damage. We felt it right to apply for adoption but because of our age (we were both in our forties) were not optimistic of success. The adoption procedure dragged on and on until all admitted that it would be to his disadvantage if our application was disallowed, and so in our late forties we became the proud parents of a ten-year-old – celebrating the fact with family and social worker at a local restaurant. Ann's patience and concern had succeeded.

Peter also, with the help of his social worker, produced a scrap book of photographs, letters and other items – called his life story book – which in time would be a reminder in adulthood, should he need it, of his roots, family, siblings and life. This kind of material is a known help in facing the realities, even the hurt and pain, of the past, and also serves to record for personal posterity the people and events prior to adoption.

The second difficult and emotional incident was when David Robinson contacted Ann with a request that had never been made of us before. Would we take a baby ourselves? Now it's not unknown for couples to become parents in their forties, but for us this would be a challenge – having a baby as a foster child was a totally new experience and would prove demanding on top of our other foster commitment, the respite care and both Ann's and my own employment. However, with some prayer and with a touch of bravado we decided that this was the right thing to do.

The baby was yet to be born but was due at any time to a single girl in Retford, just ten miles away. Ann's brief was to make a relationship with mum, if possible, before the birth and then afterwards to give help in parenting skills with the ultimate goal of mum bringing up baby herself. As expected, Ann rose to this new challenge and commenced contact initially with the aid of the social worker. Mum was currently in a failing relationship with a middle-eastern man and, in spite of the best intentions, problems of abuse were foreseen.

Within days the baby was born. He was a beautiful healthy baby, light swarthy skin, dark eyes and dark hair and within weeks he was resident at the Daniels household. As he demanded regular nightly feeds, I often woke (for we always took turns) and mused on how difficult it now was to get up in the night and feed the baby. We had both done this for years when our children needed attention, but we were younger then. How I rejoiced that we had chosen to have our children when we were younger. Life beginning at forty might sound good but, with early mornings and baby feeding, I was not convinced. In spite of all these minor sleep deprivations it was very rewarding having Simon, who grew and developed into a stunning child. Taking him out in his pram and later his pushchair was always a head-turning moment as he was the source of many a conversation. Ann's work with his mother began to increase but she was not the easiest of personalities and at times her language and attitude were choice to say the least. This never deterred Ann from her determination to fulfil her mandate.

In discussions with the social workers, it became clearer that Simon would not be returning to his mum, but would be placed for adoption at her request. For a number of reasons there never seemed to be babies available locally or nationally for adoption. Simon was one of the exceptions. There would be few problems in securing loving parents for him. It was the duty of social services to ensure, however, that any parents should be of similar ethnic background, so that, once Simon grew, his ethnic heritage would be maintained. No local couple of Arabic and British backgrounds was available but the national computer records indicated that a possible suitable couple, wanting to adopt, lived in the North East.

After all the necessary meetings and discussions had taken place with Simon's mum, the social worker made contact with this couple and informed us of them wanting to visit to meet Simon. In a day or two they duly phoned us and Ann invited them for a meal the following weekend and, "Would they like to stay overnight?"

We made our preparations and all went well. The meal was to be a roast – but would they like pork? Were they Muslims? All the kinds of things we needed to know and not make mistakes! With a little trepidation we opened our home to this couple. We didn't need to worry; as always God had gone before. We got on with the two of them straight away, he being very outgoing and she quieter and down to earth. Yes, they did eat pork – they were not Muslims; the husband was of displaced Palestinian descent, of a family of former Christian priests, now living in Jordan.

Not surprisingly, they took to Simon immediately and we did as much as we could together to get them familiar with him, his routine and his likes and dislikes. They were smitten. The time together had been not merely an icebreaker but a real introduction to their newest family member.

We reported back to social services, who again made contact in order to discover the family feelings at first hand. Without a doubt everyone's blessing was given to further contacts and to putting all legalities in motion. We decided that the next visit to our home would best be made when we were out. We had arranged a family get-together at Center Parcs, so we suggested that the prospective new parents use our home as their base whilst we were away. This went without a hitch and enabled the bonding to get even deeper.

Although the process had to go through all the panels and legal procedures, which inevitably took months, the time eventually came when we said goodbye to our little baby Simon and waved him off to a new future. Of all the children who had come and gone in our lives whilst fostering, releasing Simon was our most difficult experience. He had been the son of our old age – a "Benjamin" baby – and I had some personal inkling of what it cost Abraham (as recorded in

Genesis chapter 22) to give up Isaac at God's request. It surely must have tested his faith and tugged at his humanity. We commended Simon to God, blessed the family and dared to believe he would be a key in God's hand to open up the gospel to his own people. We continued to keep contact with the family and often shared notes and experiences.

Steve, who had come in 1981, along with his half-brother Paul, had now been with us nine years and he asked if he could go to live with his father. After discussions with social services, this was agreed and off went this young man to find his way in the world without our protection. Although it didn't quite work out as he expected, Steve did not suffer the emotional roller coaster that brother Paul experienced. Within a little while he was able to get work and a home of his own to rent. Steve was quick to pick up skills as he observed adults and practised whenever he could. One typical example of this was his ability to drive, even when under age. We might never have known this had it not been for a conversation with the parent of a school friend of Steve who lived nearby. She asked whether we knew of Steve's night time activities. We said that we didn't and she explained that recently, in the early hours of the morning, Steve would arrive at their home in a car, call for her son with a pre-arranged signal, and off they would scoot together into town, enjoying a night ride and spree together. They had only got to know this from their son when he failed to get the school bus one morning.

We confronted Steve with all of this, and he confided to us the modus operandi that he'd been employing for several weeks. Apparently, after the household had gone to sleep he would get up, pick up the keys to Kate's car which was parked in the drive, open the window and shin down the rainwater pipe, push the car down the drive with the hand brake off and then start it up away from the house. Off he would go and pick up his friend and enjoy Worksop and district at night. At home no one heard him and no one suspected the activity. Fortunately, no one was hurt and the car was never damaged. Had there been problems, I shudder to contemplate who would have sorted out this legal nightmare of responsibility. He was able later to use his driving skills whilst living with his father, sadly, again not always for legitimate purposes. Since then he's settled down somewhat and is far more responsible, having left the area for one where his record of car crime has not preceded him.

CHAPTER FIFTEEN

PUSHING BOUNDARIES

Ann had attended a number of conferences led by Eileen Vincent. Eileen and her husband Alan had been working in India for years and had returned to the UK to take up leadership of a number of churches, at one of which Ruth, Ann's school friend, was a member. Eileen had started to write books and her current one at the time was on the work of Dr Cho in Seoul, South Korea.

This relationship proved helpful and on Ann's recommendation Eileen was invited to lead a ladies' conference at Worksop on the subject, "The Place of Women in the Church". Perhaps, today, this appears quite tame, but at this time it was not only thought provoking, it meant that Eileen herself had to think out the issues well in advance of her sharing.

Looking through the shelves of the Christian bookshops, Ann noticed that there were few books on fostering. Those available tended to be North American in origin and culturally different, in most aspects, from the current British practice. Ann felt that there was a niche market available for a good publication, which would inform about good practice, legalities and procedures, as well as highlighting many of our experiences of the children we had fostered – but of course changing names to protect confidentiality. She set out to write such a book, taking as examples some of our characters and supplementing their stories with current fostering information. Prior to starting she liaised with Eileen on how best to produce such a volume, about printers, fees and practical details. The project took some time, but did not prove as difficult as expected since our experiences over the years were full of anecdotal incidents, alongside factual details supplied by our local social services department. On completion she was able to offer the text to a number of Christian publishers, who all replied with the "I regret to inform you" letter. Fostering was not a likely moneymaker and so long as publications remained unavailable it would continue to be so.

Further prayer, letters and telephone calls did, however, raise one hopeful possibility. Dr Anne Townsend was compiling a series on life issues, and fostering and adoption was one of those listed subjects. "Could Ann amend her text to fit into this library of pre-planned subjects?" For a number of months a dialogue continued between compiler and author until, at last, all was complete and acceptable and Ann received her first fee on approval for her contribution and hard work. Liaising again with Eileen, Ann was encouraged that this initial fee was a generous one and we thanked God for our good fortune. At last, a forward-looking publisher was available to edit a whole raft of books on practical life subjects that would benefit Christians.

The first books were issued, but then all went quiet. We enquired why and were shocked to hear that the publisher had been diagnosed with cancer and the series had had to be stopped. Sadly, the book never did get printed and neither did a parallel version written for children (and illustrated by me); but the pre-printing royalties did make up the shortfall in our budget so that we were able to have a holiday in Austria with Peter and Ruth. It was a holiday on which all the children (except Martin and Jenny) decided to accompany us because of the attractive destination. This break became in reality the last of our family holidays – the teenagers would make for their own destinations in future.

Since we were travelling to Austria through Germany, we decided that we would call in and register for the Fire Conference (hosted by Reinhard Bonnke and his team), which happened to be taking place in Frankfurt as we were passing through. The meetings were well attended and of excellent quality. At the end of the last meeting Reinhard asked everyone to stand to pray for the reunification of Germany – a matter close to the hearts of the German people. This we did, but I remember thinking, "I don't have faith for this – but I'll stand with you in your prayers." Later I reflected on this many times, realising that what God wants to do does not depend on my faith.

Harldstadt in summer proved to be an ideal destination. Peter and Ruth had visited years before and seemed to know all there was to know about this beauty spot. From there we travelled south-west to the Tyrol, basking again in the sunshine of the beautiful Austrian mountains near Innsbruck. All too soon the idyllic location had to be left and we had to head back home.

We were towing caravans. We had acquired a Montego 1600 and, together with awnings and small tents, we managed to cram all our essentials plus bodies into the car and caravan. Fortunately, we were also able to overflow into Pete's car so all bodies and equipment were accommodated. Early morning saw us dismantle and prepare for our return. As we came to the campsite entrance, however, we were stopped and informed that the road ahead was impassable, for through the night there had been a storm in the mountains resulting in a flash flood down the valley. Sections of the road had been swept away; the torrent was still raging and boulders, trees and debris had been washed down. The whole valley was now an emergency area. We had been totally unaware of this and, though late to bed, our sleep had not been interrupted. We decided to park upon the adjacent area of tarmac and wait with a view to leaving as soon as practicable. The day saw helicopter after helicopter flying up and down the valley on mercy missions. This was a real eye-opener and later conversations with the campsite owner proved that this had been a tragedy for the area.

Our conversations highlighted the fate of four teenagers who had spent the evening on the campsite speaking to our daughters and who had returned home about midnight only to be impacted by the flood in full spate. The car they were driving plunged into the torrent at a section of the road washed away by the force of water. All four were lost, presumed dead. This was a real shock, one we kept from the girls until we had returned home ourselves. The next twenty-four hours were a mixture of emotions, sadness for those who had lost their lives and their homes, thankfulness for our own safety and apprehension for our return home. We had planned to leave Zeebrugge for Dover, allowing ourselves two days to travel back through Austria, Germany, Luxemburg and Belgium. We had no idea when we would be allowed to leave; would we miss the ferry and, worse still, would we get another one and how would we finance it anyway?

At regular intervals we enquired as to the progress of the emergency services and especially the clearance of the valley road, all for hours without success until finally, late afternoon, we were told that it was hoped by the following morning some access would be available. It meant a further day on the site or at least on the car park. Apart from all the excitement of the distant comings and goings of the helicopters, it meant that we had an extra day to use up so we pooled all our existing food supplies and feasted on what was available.

Early next morning we enquired about the condition of the road and were given clearance, at least to attempt to depart. The expedition to Austria with ten of us, two cars and two caravans was in itself at the limits of our resources; now our return home was to test them even further. Like some geographical expedition, we tentatively set forth into the unknown.

The signs of devastation were everywhere; trees wedged under bridges, boulders the size of cars littering the roadside and debris of all descriptions in heaps all along our way. Clay and silt covered most vegetation and grassed areas were flattened. Damaged vehicles and houses along the route indicated the force of the flooding. Slowly, we edged forward, this way and that, until at last we said farewell to the valley and left the residents to continue to deal with their traumas and losses. We had planned a route through Austria to enable us to take a "leisurely" drive home, but now the situation had changed; we had less than a day to get to the ferry to be sure of our bookings. Looking at the map we chose the shortest route possible, omitting to realise that the shortest route in Austria is not necessarily a straight line. We had not allowed for the Tyrol Mountains or the fact that we were travelling with maximum weight of equipment and personnel. This became obvious as we headed up the road bypassing Innsbruck. In our ignorance we took the road that went over the peaks, and was clearly signposted "not for caravans". Clearly, that is, *in German*, which none of us spoke! We pressed on, but the weight and the incline began to have its effect until, gradually, the car came to a halt. We were stuck "halfway up and neither up nor down" – like a latter day "Grand old Duke of York"! Zeebrugge seemed even farther away. We had only one option, to pray, and we did.

Our prayers were answered in a way we didn't expect. Just then a milk lorry stopped and the driver asked, we presumed, if he could help. We communicated by sign language and I managed to persuade him to tow us up the mountain by the aid of our tow rope. Leaving a couple of the children we set off slowly up the mountainside. Milk lorry, car and caravan – what a sight! It was scary and I spoke in tongues all the way, so as to build myself up. The road soon led into a series of hairpin bends, which we negotiated amazingly well, but to my utter surprise Austrian drivers were overtaking us on these bends as we ascended.

The journey seemed one of the longest in my life and I was perspiring everywhere, but quickly the milk lorry pulled into a lay-by almost on the brow of the mountain. We pulled up, applied the handbrake and jumped out, relieved and thankful. I approached the driver, overflowing with appreciation, but begging him to return down the hill to collect Peter and Ruth and the rest of the children. We were obviously asking a lot of this volunteer, who must have had his own schedule to keep. He willingly agreed and returned, but not before I had given him our tow rope and a further one I had with me for emergencies.

By now Ann had entered the caravan, rescued the portable gas stove and was brewing up a cup of tea! We waited for the others, not knowing what their needs were. After leaving the campsite we had swapped children, so no car had a complete family and, to top it all, our passports were separated too, so in the eventuality of us splitting up we had incomplete documentation! Safety, however, was far more vital than contemplating such bureaucratic nightmares.

As the kettle boiled, the milk truck appeared, plus car and caravan and the rest of the children. What a relief; we had all arrived safely – at least to the brow of the hill. Everyone jumped out of the vehicle, ecstatic at our reunion. We profusely thanked the driver and offered him a drink, but he had his timetable to keep. Pete went on to explain in detail how their trip up the mountainside had proceeded. This it transpired was even scarier than ours since after a little while the tow rope had snapped and only a quick application of the handbrake averted disaster. The spare tow rope saved the day and enabled the vehicles to resume their slow ascent. The brew was a welcome relief for all. Once again, with her inexhaustible supply of tea, Ann had supplied much needed comfort.

As we were drinking, a small saloon drew up and out jumped a couple of young men who, communicating in broken English, asked if they could help since they were motor mechanics. This was yet another godsend. We explained our adventure and, with meticulous care, they gave the car engines a visual check before leaving, assuring us that mechanically all was well. By the time we had finished our refreshments, the cars had cooled and we set off for the ferry. The few hundred yards over the brow of the hill proved not to be a problem. We looked back as we reached the peak, only to see a sign above the road: "Caravans forbidden!" The phrase "ignorance is bliss" came to mind. In the luxury of our safe return we thought much on this incident, which assured us that God does answer prayer, especially "help!". But we were convinced that this milk lorry driver was angelic too – and if he was, this angel had a handlebar moustache!

The journey through Germany and the Low Countries was long and wet, and with very few stops we arrived at Zeebrugge in thirteen hours, relieved to arrive in time for our appointed ferry without further incident. On arrival, we were stewarded into the parking area by an attendant who informed us that there was a delay and "would we mind waiting?" We had arrived days after the tragic sinking of the *Herald of Free Enterprise* and the ferry company were now ensuring a correct safety procedure, which was resulting in delays to the established timetable. We were happy to comply, having come through what seemed like "flood, fire and tempest"; a little wait was nothing. Our last family holiday proved to be one to remember.

For two years in the early seventies Ann also worked as a part-time staff nurse on the Paediatric Ward at Kilton Hospital in Worksop under, would you believe it, Sister Daniels. Her duties on the night shift were the full responsibility for the ward – patients and junior and auxiliary staff – in liaison with medical professionals. Again, this meant that we could work as a team, me babysitting as necessary. It meant however, that Ann's sleep was minimal, but that was always a hazard of the nursing profession. On one occasion as she worked, yet another emergency child case was brought into the ward. It turned out to be our daughter Kate; it always reminded us of Jochebed, the mother of Moses, paid to look after her own child.

Not long after obtaining the necessary Family Planning Certificate, Ann decided to pursue the City and Guilds Further Education Teacher's Certificate. This normally took two years to complete, but Ann was able, with her previous qualifications, to compress it into one and many hours of writing and presentation were given to her submission. In June 1976 she qualified and this enabled her to pursue the health education route seriously in her career. For eight years she lectured, initially part time, and then full time, at the Rother Valley College of Further Education.

Her duties there included Link Courses with secondary schools, teaching first aid and health care subjects and O-level human biology. She was also a member of the team responsible for training nursery nurses for their NNEB qual-ifications. Anne Beer, herself a trained nurse and leader of the department, said that "Ann was a natural communica-tor and outstanding in her work, extremely friendly with staff and students alike and yet professional at all times." She went on to add that "Students were happy in her classes, had considerable respect for her and especially enjoyed family planning sessions, which were hilarious. Some time ago I met a former student of Ann's. She was pushing a pram and had a whole retinue of toddlers with her. 'Eh, Miss,' she said to me, 'I right enjoyed that Mrs Daniels' lessons – 'specially the ones on birth control!' "

The demands of family, church responsibilities and home led Ann to ultimately leave the college and the pressures of career, choosing not to be ruled by the "system" which demanded more and more. In spite of her resignation, she maintained relationships with her former colleagues, who continued to value her input by letter or telephone call.

A number of years passed before Ann sought regular employment again. Feeling freed of some family responsibilities as the children grew, she again lectured in a part-time capacity, which gave far more flexibility. This time it was at the North Derbyshire College of Further Education at Clowne where she taught health care subjects to pre-nursing and City and Guilds students. Alongside this, she also spent nearly three years working part time in Worksop at the Nottinghamshire Regional Society for Autistic Children and Adults. Her duties were to teach basic literacy and numeracy, especially to young adults. Autism presented a whole series of problems, especially in communication, and Ann really appreciated this time of getting to know individual students and learning how best to get them to reach their potential.

Ann thrived on meeting people and her work experiences provided many opportunities to pray for them as well as share her faith. Above all they were opportunities for her to serve the community, extend her professional knowledge and contribute to the needs of the family. Little did we realise at the time how all these exposures to the needs of individuals would form platforms for our later work abroad.

CHAPTER SIXTEEN

LOCATION, LOCATION

As the children grew into young adults they inevitably extended their friendships and, together, would visit Sheffield and get involved with young people of their own age. These included Pete and Rita Fenwick's children, the children of Geoff and Pauline Williams (now resident in Sheffield after years in India) as well as those of David and Shirley Whitehouse who had by now moved to Sheffield. Such were the relationships that on many occasions our home was a place of rest to many not normally resident at Poplars. Each weekend Drewie and John Russon were sleeping somewhere in the house; it was a good time for all.

Contact with Pauline and Geoff, initially through the CLC, their family and the church, was also an important milestone in our lives. Geoff, with a radiant smile and a deep love for the Lord, was a real encourager, especially for mission. Much more experienced than us and knowing (or so it seemed) every person on mission in Asia, he encouraged us to look at mission in many ways – one being that of using our homes for visiting foreign nationals. This we were happy to do, so in 1988 we made contact with Joan Seager of Ollerton, a local representative of the British Council and from then on at regular intervals our doors opened to visitors from India, Ghana, China, Mexico, Japan, Hong Kong, Belgium, USA, Canada, Russia, Malawi, Malaysia, Nigeria, Romania, Germany, Peru, Denmark, Thailand, Brazil and Korea. At all times we hosted our guests, involving them in all our normal activities so as to highlight what a British Christian family was really like.

The late 1980s saw many changes in the family. Martin and Jenny were married in 1986; Kate left home to study occupational therapy at St Loyes College in Exeter; Yvette married another friend of a friend from the London area; Paul returned home to be with his mother and Liz left school to commence nursing at Newark. One by one the children were leaving the nest. These changes released us in many ways, but in others provided further responsibilities. Fortunately, the five-hundred-mile round trip to Exeter only usually happened twice each term.

Paul's return to his mother took a lot of pressure from us all. Since he suffered deeply from rejection, his aim was to rekindle contact and affection. Sadly, his approaches were often rejected and his life was one big roller coaster of emotions. He longed for her involvement in his life, but she, however, craved a life of her own without the demands of children. He exhibited many signs of deep emotional need but this meant single-mindedness on his part to the exclusion of all others. His departure was not one we looked forward to for, in spite of all his problems, we had come to love him. Because of his age, social services were obliged to listen and act upon his requests. We made our farewells and promised to keep contact. He had been with us, not for three weeks as originally stated, but five years. We foresaw that his return would prove to be a fantasy and not the solution to his problems.

And so it was; within months of his return Paul was again rejected by his mother and a life of further emotional needs continued — ultimately resulting in a lifestyle of petty crime. His brother, the more sensitive and younger of the two, also shed tears along with ourselves, but he was to stay with us for a further four years. We aimed to ensure contact between brothers and/or mother as much as possible. Perhaps the overriding emotion we experienced at this time was one of relief – Paul's demands were extensive and however much we seemed to try, his behaviour became a drain on the family.

Change, however much needed or desired, does bring with it a sense of loss for what has been. Our family life was changing. We had brought up our children (and many others' children too) always aware that our main role was to love them, make them secure and release them when appropriate. We rejoiced in the children's spreading of their wings – but for Ann especially it was not without emotion too. She did not brood, but faced her feelings of loss by committing them to the Lord.

Irrespective of the children we had for long-stay and respite care, we always had an open door policy towards those in need and especially to the church. This meant too that we spent time with church families who also had needs, and helped in personal counselling as problems arose. Weekends, especially Sundays meant that invariably we had several extras for lunch and possibly for tea. Ann worked on the principle that, if we were having visitors, the more the merrier so long as we had enough seats to accommodate everyone. Her cooking was never cordon bleu – more a matter of "throw it all in" – but always tasty and never with any left over. "Seconds" were the order of the day. Cooking for large numbers never fazed her.

Following our visit in 1980, India had never been out of our blood. We had a yearning to return. It was, however, not easy owing to the demands of the family and church. Over the years, we had received regular prayer letters and updates, indicating that other members of the team had been able to return. Finally, in 1988, Ann suggested that I return myself and I persuaded Jenny's father to accompany me. Building upon the previous experience, we again left in October, made our trip for approximately three weeks and liaised with Dupte in respect of all the details for contacts, meetings and activities.

This time we flew Air India direct to Bombay. This was far less hassle and much more luxurious. Staying again at the YMCA and the Methodist Home, Bombay, at least for me, was not the shock it had been before. Soon we were off to Parli and there we again stayed in a first-class hotel. It was an improvement on before – the balcony was usable, so too the fan and the en-suite, but the accommodation would not reach any European star ratings whatsoever. On the walls we had one or two geckos and around the base of the wall was a regular path for a column of ants, which we found went about their business as long as we did not disturb them. The mosquito problem was minimal and, fortunately, we did not suffer bed bugs.

The town had altered – it seemed to be bigger, with more housing and even more people. Nearby the hotel was a small Hindu temple, having a bell which was rung by every devotee as they visited and prayed, but far worse was the shrine, which we managed to visit. Decked with garlands of flowers was a phallic stone column to which the Hindu visitors prayed. I quickly retreated; the atmosphere struck me as oppressive. At our pre-arranged meetings we were well received by the pastors and the churches. There was still a lot of travelling to be done, however, and my memories are that the driving tended to be down the centre of the road wherever we were and whichever way you faced. Only at the last minute did our drivers pull over to the sides, which, being unkerbed, were in a poor state of repair. The three weeks passed quickly and we returned home to a wonderful welcome from our families.

Our contact with Eileen Vincent led also the church's contribution to the book, *Ten Worshipping Churches*, edited by Graham Kendrick and published by Marc Europe. Eileen had been impressed by the worship at the ladies' conference and recommended to the publishers that we fill the vacant slot. We were contacted out of the blue and within days (so as to meet the publisher's deadline) Pete Hardy wrote a chapter on the church's origin, ourselves, our worship, the place of music, singing, discipline and the way forward. Pete wrote, "Over the next few years, we see a need to develop a strong, healthy church body in Carlton, worshipping in an even greater revelation of that which Jesus spoke of – Spirit and Truth. To carry the work forward in Whitwell and amongst the group of people in Worksop who are currently worshipping with us, we need to develop and recognise new leadership."

These words were to prove prophetic, for the late eighties was a very emotional period in the history of Poplars. The eldership had reduced, for various reasons, to five. It was at this time that we felt it right to face the issue of leadership in the church and realised that, owing to limited opportunities, it was likely that we, the eldership, could become blockages (like corks in bottles), preventing the growth of others through our insistence and need to minister. We discussed the meaning of this for some time until, finally, there was a split in the eldership on the future we should pursue. Unfortunately, this became an issue and over weeks and months a polarity emerged in the church. In order to prevent acrimony and so as to know the way forward we invited Derek Brown from King's Church, Aldershot and Peter Fenwick from Sheffield House Church to judge our hearts and the way forward. Over the years we had come to respect Derek Brown's prophetic ministry. We had attended conferences organised by King's Church and Poplars was associated with his ministry. As an eldership we shared with the church about our motivation to release others and that if these two men of God judged both our motives and manner to be wrong we would resign our positions, which meant for Derek and myself a return to other employment.

Ultimately, it was judged that we had acted correctly and our motivation was to do what was best for the church. We were exonerated. This meant that others had no alternative but to repent or find a more suitable church. Sadly, a number of the members chose the latter option and overnight the church lost many previously committed people. These were personal friends and supporters. Everyone was now in a sense of grief and loss. Emotions were high and pain was evident. This event took years to heal. We all felt their departure, but God had given several prophetic pictures, which helped explain that even in this tragedy He was in control.

The first had happened months before at one of our worship times. Ian Clague, a member with a prophetic gift, came to the microphone to share a word and he demonstrated that God was going to "take the carpet from underneath us." So as to illustrate this, he removed a rug, which had been placed over the PA wires at the front of the meeting for safety. As he did this the whole apparatus of microphones, cables and PA system seemed to come apart and hit the floor. The devastation was far in excess of his intention. We later saw this as a prophetic glimpse of what was about to happen.

The second picture we had was that of a flower seed head – a poppy or similar – full of seed, which then went on to explode, sending its seeds into the wind and beyond its immediate area. Tragic though it appeared, this explosion was to ensure reproduction, but over a wider area. These words did not make the pain of departure less but did explain that behind it all God had a purpose. As we worked this out we were complimented as a church, for our loss was others' gain, and one emerging new church, where many of our members had gravitated, stated that we must have been doing something properly, since these newcomers were all leadership quality!

On reflection, Poplars had lost many long-time members, most of its singers and musicians and a good proportion of its serious financial supporters. The remainder of us continued to meet in spite of all the pain and loss but the experience threw us all on the Lord. Again, it became necessary to use our home as a refuge, especially for the singles or single parents, to ensure that we all came through this trauma stronger and still trusting Jesus. For some members, however, this process took a long time, during which others also left.

As this was progressing we continued to host our visitors and during 1987 one of them shared on his experiences of visiting Romania. He spoke of the plight of the national church and how Christians eked out a living to physically survive. Romania was part of the Warsaw Pact and its leader Nicolae Ceausescu was somewhat of a political maverick, receiving favours from the West whilst being at the same time a committed communist. He and his wife Elena ruled the country as dictators at the expense of the ordinary citizens. We heard that wintertime in the Carpathian Mountains was particularly difficult. Many families existed on what they could harvest. Fruit and vegetables were bottled for the long cold winter. Summertime gave a break but food, fuel and basics were in short supply.

We listened to these tales of woe and put the plight of Romanians back on our prayer lists. Ever since the mid-sixties we had been aware of the cruelty and torture of the Ceausescu regime through the writing and talks of Pastor Wumbrandt, who had spent years in solitary confinement in Romanian prisons. Ransomed by the West, he outlined his experiences at the hands of the security police. How on earth could we help these needy brothers and sisters other than by praying? We supported our friend as he continued to arrange clandestine meetings to have contact with the needy. Secrecy was vital since it was illegal for Romanians to have contact with westerners. Politically, things were slowly changing in Eastern Europe – first in Poland, and then in the USSR when President Gorbachev introduced *glasnost* and *perestroika*. Changes were introduced and we had the velvet revolution in Czechoslovakia

Gradually, each state of the Warsaw Pact felt the pressure for freedom. On 9 November 1989 the unthinkable happened; just over two years since we prayed in Frankfurt, the Berlin Wall came down. In an article in *The Daily Telegraph*

Daniel Johnson said of this incident that "the night the wall came down was the most important date in post-war history." We watched with intense interest as the dominoes began to fall and in December 1989 changes became apparent in Romania. Even then we were not aware that these changes would affect our lives forever

CHAPTER SEVENTEEN

FIRST-HAND EXPERIENCE

Timisoara, a city of about 325,000 people situated astride the small river Bega to the west of Romania and whose population included a high proportion of ethnic Hungarians, was the actual place where the Romanian revolution/coup d'état began on 15 December 1989. Initially, members of Pastor Laslo Tokes' Reformed Church committed themselves to pray with and for him outside his manse near the centre of the city. He had received pressure again and again from the Securitate (the Romanian secret police) who were against his ministry and had chosen that day to evict him. It was illegal and, therefore, unknown for crowds to assemble on the streets as they did on this occasion. In view of the numbers the police resisted taking action. Encouraged by this open defiance, others were attracted until the crowd size grew.

Somehow a momentum was established and the crowds began to move into the centre of the city, ultimately stopping outside the Romanian Orthodox Cathedral. Speeches were made and a popular demonstration had begun. Throughout the week in the afternoons, especially after work finished, the people continued to assemble. Numbers grew daily until the whole of the square was filled. The police failed to respond adequately and the military were instructed to take over. It soon became apparent that things had gone too far and they refused to be involved. At this, a chant from the crowd spread like wildfire: "The Army is with us." Shooting occurred, with random firing in all directions, resulting in some being killed. Their bodies were taken to the hospital along with the wounded. Ultimately, bodies were reportedly taken in unmarked ambulances to Bucharest for cremation so as to hide the evidence of the anti-government feeling. Still today missing persons have not been accounted for and hospital staff were known to have reported that the Securitate entered wards and killed a number of the wounded.

In spite of all these crowds, the danger and the atrocities, no action or uprising occurred in other cities in Romania until 21/22 December when the feelings of anger erupted elsewhere across the country. Not surprisingly, in this move-ment for personal freedom and freedom of expression, the Christian influence was evident such that one of the chants of the crowd was, "God is coming; God is coming." These Christian men and women took huge personal risks; risks that were taken also by the populace and ultimately taken up by politicians opposed to the regime of Ceausescu. The memorial today in the square at Timisoara is one of a cross under pressure, symbolic of the struggle as it began.

Televised footage of Ceausescu in Bucharest, speaking to crowds and promising a host of changes in benefits and food, graphically showed the fear in his eyes at prerecorded boos from the PA system plus the angry voices of the crowd. This was the end of the beginning; the President and his wife were whisked away by helicopter from the capital. Within three days photographs of their bodies were shown around the world. They had been tried, found guilty and duly executed. Some kind of freedom had at last come to Romania. Communism had failed, but the legacy of the regime had yet to be revealed.

Braşov, an industrial city of 400,000 people in 1989, was mediaeval in origin but boasting many new apartment blocks for the imported Moldavian peasant workers. Situated at the base of the Carpathian Mountains, which sweep like a horseshoe through Romania and northwards into the Ukraine, its location was in the centre of the country north of Bucharest. Fourteen kilometres higher up in the mountains, beyond Braşov, was the latest of the country's skiing resorts, Poiana Braşov, often hosting westerners on affordable skiing holidays.

As the recriminations and resistance spread through the country, so did the fighting and the death toll. Braşov was no exception; crowds were invited to attend meetings in the square, only to be fired on by persons unknown. Some thirty people were killed – predominantly students. Today, their memorials are within yards of where they fell. No one was found guilty of these crimes.

The chaotic situation was still unresolved when Ann suggested I visit Romania weeks later in March 1990. We discussed this with the church leadership and Bob Evens, from the Worksop congregation, agreed to accompany me. Our contacts had told us the procedure for obtaining visas, how best to visit and who to see when we arrived. Not knowing what to expect, we set off by TAROM (Romanian Air Transport) on a package holiday to stay at Poiana Braşov and we made the Hotel Ciucas our base.

The plane journey was most peculiar, rather how I pictured a Boy Scout outing. Romanian nationals (obviously with all the right contacts) had visited Britain and were returning home. It seemed that each carried several pieces of hand luggage, which by the look of their packages were microwave ovens, ghetto blasters and all things electrical. At the rear of the plane a number of seats were out of use, but each was filled with luggage tied to the seating with string! The quality of the plane (an early British BAC111) was much worse than on our previous flight to India via Egypt, with some obviously broken seats and missing safety belts, just to name two irregularities.

We arrived safely and went to collect our cases in the time-honoured way. There was only one luggage carousel. It stopped and started the whole of the extended time we were waiting. After an hour and a half we passengers had exhausted our patience and I made my way into the cellar to retrieve my case. The waiting area had been dim – we counted only twelve fluorescent lights. The cellar was like a black hole; there were just two forty-watt lamps throughout. Unfortunately, our cases were black. We hunted for some time to find our black cases in a black cellar. Eventually, we were successful and our courier, with two others, a man and his daughter, took us to an old minibus, which was our transfer transport to Poiana!

We eventually left the airport car park but not before our courier hopped off, and that was the last we saw of him. All our queries would remain unanswered. Fortunately, I had brought drinks and snacks and we shared these on the journey. There was to be no stopping for toilets or refreshments on the less than comfortable three-hour journey to the hotel.

Our rooms were basic but comfortable enough. We had arrived in the last week of the season, which was not busy at all. The snow was generally melting, although on the mountains skiing was still possible; Poiana Braşov was beautiful in the snow. We were not there to ski; we had come to make contact with those in need, to find out what the situation really was like and to see where we could help. The package included our meals, which were paid for on a voucher basis, the vouchers also being interchangeable in the city below. To our amusement we would order the same breakfast of eggs, rolls and jam or similar only to find that each day they would be charged at different rates. No two meals cost the same!

As soon as possible we made contact by telephone with Stelian who was to be our guide for the week. Stelian spoke excellent English (as many others also did, we later discovered) and proved an invaluable translator in difficult situations. Our first visit was to the Paediatric Hospital where we were instantly shown into the Director's office. Representatives of Médecins Sans Frontières were there checking their latest consignment of drugs. Naïvely I introduced us as representatives of the churches in England who had come to see how we could help. I subsequently realised that in translation this had conveyed the impression that I represented the Church of England.

However, I pressed on and we were given a list of essential items, which were immediately needed. It was headed by, first of all, a paediatric surgeon. It actually took five years for me to fulfil this request but we were able, on our return, to meet all the other needs and our later visits became opportunities to bring these essential items in our luggage (which always exceeded our allowance by about half a ton!). After all the formalities and the mandatory cup of black coffee, we were given white smocks and shown around the hospital in a military fashion as if we were medical professionals.

The hospital was opened in 1985 but in many places was unfinished and even dangerous. Holes in the linoleum flooring were everywhere, ceramic tiles were off the wall and lighting was inadequate. All wards were the same drab off-white colour and there were no pictures, signs or posters. Each room had prison-like metal cots, or low metal beds for the older children. These were all chipped and the bedding grey through washing with poor or no detergents. There was no noise, no children crying, laughing or talking; a dull hush pervaded everywhere. What a contrast to the British hospitals; we couldn't believe what we saw. The children were subdued and staff few in number. Equipment was poor or non-existent. Many mattresses were wet and the smell of urine was apparent. The younger children wore tight swaddling-type nappies of the same grey material, fastened at the front, not with pins, but by knots.

We went from cot to cot and we stopped at one. It contained a little girl, Monica, who appeared to be about five years old. She had recently been admitted to the hospital. Out of the two hundred and fifty children we had seen, I felt an urge to pray for her. I laid my hands on her and prayed as we would at home. The staff seemed surprised but did not react and we passed to another ward. Eventually, we left the hospital with our shopping list of needed items, saying farewell to all those we had met. Three weeks later I learned that Monica had been admitted to the hospital because she had two stomachs and was not keeping her food down. From the time I prayed she started to improve and retain her food and by my next trip she was ready for discharge.

Stelian showed us around Braşov: the City Hall, his own apartment and anything we wanted to see. He explained to us that on 22 December he was one of the crowd in the city square and was fired at. He suffered a bullet wound to his left arm, which was still healing. His muscles and bones had been affected and he was now classed as disabled. He also took us to his former place of work at a local tool factory. Its condition and environment reminded me of Sheffield in the 1950s when I used to visit my grandparents; it was almost literally a "dark satanic mill."

The thrill of the trip for both Bob and myself was the opportunity we had whilst visiting Stelian's home to share about our faith and our love for Jesus. Stelian drank in all that we said and in a little while openly repented and gave his life to the Lord. Unknown to us at the time there was much in his background for Stelian to outwork and put right; sadly his walk did not always match his talk until, years later, he fled to the UK. We felt at the time that his response was genuine; follow-up had to be left to our visits, but was chiefly between him and the Lord. The Romania we had come to was still in chaos, a people scared of informers, of each other, of the security police. This was going to take a lot to remove and remodel.

We also spent a day on an excursion to St Gheorghia, north of Braşov, to visit the home of Eniko Nady. A few weeks earlier Eniko, an ethnic Hungarian, had visited Worksop and stayed in Whitwell. She was a slightly built young lady who had managed to leave Romania after the revolution. She was the first Romanian contact in Britain with whom we were able to discuss the conditions in the country at first hand. The village turned out to be the typical poor rural Romanian village – a mixture of communist concrete apartments and traditional East European dwellings. Roads were generally unmade and the village dusty and dilapidated. Eniko's family were welcoming and embraced us profusely. Our visits included contact with the local priest, who proudly showed us his church building – renovated and endowed earlier by former British Royal Family members in view of its association with Queen Mary, who by birth was a princess of Teck.

It was all an eye-opener to real conditions, especially when we visited the local store and were shown the available commodities. There was no meat, milk, bread or basic foodstuffs. What was apparent were some pickled gherkins, some flour in a barrel and a few bonbons. As a memento of our visit we were presented with a simple wooden spoon – the only other article available. We couldn't believe that these people seemed to exist as if on nothing. Years later, I was to meet Eniko again. She had remained in Britain, put on a little weight, completed her studies and had taken up a post with Casa Sperantei (The House of Hope), a hospice charity with bases in Braşov and in the south of England and working on behalf of the dying and their families . . . a small world!

This situation was, however, typical; wherever you looked there was no sense of happiness or contentment – more a sense of hopelessness. Everywhere seemed grey; no one looked you in the eyes; fear seemed to stalk you; the population were surviving the best they could. Nowhere was this more obvious than when we visited the local orphanage. Externally, the building looked better than most, with a beautiful title over its door: The Crib. It was, however, in reality more of a workhouse, except it was for children up to three years old. Stelian was able to get us an introduction to meet the Director, a medical practitioner and communist party member who was definitely in control, but bemused at the interest of personnel from the West. We were able to offer gifts of food and toys and, after the obligatory cup of black Turkish coffee, we were shown around the facility. It had previously been the paediatric hospital and was a two-storied building around a pleasant courtyard. Internally, however, it proved to be clean but lacking spirit and life; everywhere there were the same drab, often dark, colours and a few non-uniformed, compliant staff. All was quiet; babies slept, but toddlers lay in metal cots, lifeless, unstimulated and motionless except for those rocking to and fro, the movement of boredom and institutionalisation.

I entered a second-floor section where two members of staff were talking on the landing: seeing my camera they quickly placed themselves in the centre of the two adjacent wards, ready to have their photograph taken. The cots virtually touched each other – just two little walkways allowed staff to get to the far corners. The two small wards contained fifty-seven cots between them, supervised by two adults as they saw fit. I will never forget this or other sights we saw. I was to see worse sights later, especially of children with special needs, but these images were the ones exposed by the media. The world was shocked to realise that in Europe, over forty years after the Second World War, such conditions were allowed to exist. It was later discovered that over 100,000 children had been abandoned in Romania, many merely for economic reasons. What had we come to? What could we do to help? In a small way, over the years since then we have been regular visitors to this place of need, giving ourselves, our love and our skills as well as toys, foodstuffs and concern.

The visit to Braşov, however, seemed to end so quickly and we returned to Bucharest in the same worn out minibus, down the hairpin bends of the mountains, up and down the next range, across the plains, through the Romanian oil fields at Ploesti and on to Otopeni airport and home. Emotionally drained at what we'd seen and experienced, we shared every detail with our families and the church.

This time it was Ann's turn to visit Romania and along with Bev Turner and Liz Williams, two other church members, she left two weeks after our return. We had heard that HIV/AIDS could be a problem, so they took five hundred AIDS testing kits, plus countless foodstuffs, bandages, toys and assorted goods. Ann took half of the kits to the Blood Transfusion Centre where the Director received her with open arms. Up to this point testing for HIV was primitive – purely visual, and with the results being sent to Bucharest for checking. Without exception, the results all returned negative. The gap between truth and deception in this area took years to bridge. The reason for the incidence of HIV was classic. Some workers were paid for donating their blood and given a meal and a day off work; and screening was poor. Infection soon entered the system and was passed on when the blood was used medically. Constanţa, being a port on the Black Sea, had visiting sailors from around the world and these were blamed for HIV infection entering Romania.

Sadly, it was this same infection route that led to the high incidence of HIV amongst Romanian children. The European Centre for the Epidemiological Monitoring of AIDS indicated that, of all the paediatric cases in Europe by December 1990, fifty-two per cent were in Romania.

The ladies' first call was to visit the Paediatric Hospital as a follow-up to our visit, once again handing over a number of goods on the shopping list as requested by the Director. Ann had also taken with her some samples of Milton sterilising fluid. Since she discovered that there was no disinfectant in the entire hospital, she was able to weaken this solution and spent two days, along with her colleagues, scrubbing floors, walls and surfaces with the weak solution. It was unknown for a professional to perform such tasks, but her serving the community in this way, together with her personable character, won the hearts of doctors, nurses and patients alike.

In their work they seemed to gravitate to the dystrophy (or malnourished) ward where already a number of British couples were present with a view to selecting likely children for adoption. Ann was surprised to see these couples and so many children in the ward. Most of the children present were there for one of two reasons: firstly, they could have come from the local orphanage with a complaint compounded by their malnourishment. In these instances, they were kept in hospital for as long as possible to strengthen them. Alternatively, the children were those failing to thrive, and in these cases HIV infection was a real factor. Malnourishment, HIV and TB seemed to go hand in hand. These symptoms sparked Ann's curiosity, which she pursued to discover the causes.

As well as the sterilising fluid, she had brought with her leaflets for foster parents, giving details on aspects of HIV, especially its causes and incidence. These leaflets proved invaluable, first of all as a reference and then as a document of some authority for the British couples, and also as a springboard for the introduction of AIDS awareness teaching to the hospital professionals. Some thirty-five children had been singled out for adoption by the hospital authorities, but from her experience Ann knew that the British Government would not allow many of these to enter the country because of their medical health records. She was able to reduce these numbers down to single figures, which was an education for the naïve couples, but would prevent some of the emotional roller coaster ride that many others later experienced elsewhere.

Abandoned children in the orphanage or hospital ward were not necessarily available for adoption. Even when health records proved adequate, legally the signatures of both parents needed to be obtained. For many couples, finding parents and obtaining their signatures became difficult and their experiences were often recounted as horror stories of corruption by the media or in anecdotal evidence. Of these original couples, eventually four were able to adopt a child of their choice. Most of them expressed their thanks for Ann's help and intervention when they needed it most.

Using some of the AIDS testing kits the hospital staff were able to establish that a number of the children (this later turned out to be thirty) were in fact infected. Having her literature to hand, Ann was able to assist in nursing procedures and basic AIDS awareness for the staff. Soon this information spread and before long AIDS awareness was being presented to both doctors and nurses alike. The week's workload was expanding and at home I received a telephone call to inform me that the ladies could not possibly leave and would stay for a further week. Fortunately, Stelian managed to change their air tickets and this became possible.

The media were always looking for interesting stories and soon Ann was on local TV answering questions, explaining the reasons for coming to Braşov and indicating likely developments. She was also able to meet the Mayor of the city at that time. Mayors, we discovered later, were only in post for a few months at a time in view of all the chaos, change, political upheavals and infighting. This man offered the ladies a whole hotel, known as Hotel Timpa and used formerly by the Securitate, as a base for their operations. He said that it was free of charge – ours to do with as we wished. Ann addressed the issue of the abandoned children in the hospital, to which the Mayor replied that there were none! Having seen them, Ann explained that there were in the region of thirty-five. The Mayor stuck to his guns, denying any abandoned children. Ann slowly began to get the message. There were two answers: the public response and the truth. Communist deception and lies still prevented acknowledgement of the real situation, however unpalatable it was. Normality, rather than the whole truth, took many years to surface.

Not only were the days full with hospital, orphanage, public appearance and church visits; the ladies were also able to meet individual Romanians at their place of work or in their homes – individuals who were able, slowly at first and then increasingly over the years, to come to terms with experiences, emotions and losses imposed upon them by the previous regime.

The fortnight was full, exciting, challenging, tiring and soon over, but Ann knew this would be, for her, just the first of many trips that would show compassion to the needy and give help to the struggling, training to the professional and hope to the hopeless.

Our visits seemed not only to create a stir in Braşov, but also at home in Bassetlaw. There was widespread interest, obviously fuelled by the media coverage and the ever continuing shock revelations and exposures of what the

Ceausescu regime had perpetrated. We became local specialists and many of our friends wanted to be involved in our activities. We had in fact discovered the procedure for getting to Romania. We had made contacts who would be useful as translators, or for transportation and we had seen at first hand some of the needs. We had also made ourselves vulnerable to the vulnerable and resourceless, including many professionals. The outworking of our faith in all these situations had won the hearts of many and it was the beginning of relationships that we felt we could not ignore. Somehow we managed to make trips at regular intervals in spite of the extreme communication difficulties and each time we returned with a deeper love for the people and a greater awareness of their needs.

It was, however, time to take stock. What direction were we to take; how often could we financially, or for the sake of our families, afford to visit? We were aware of so much needing to be done and how few resources we had to tackle this enormous need.

All those of us who had already been to Romania under the auspices of BFOR (British Friends of Romania) met to discuss the way forward. Ann's medical expertise had broken into areas of need and specialisation far greater than originally expected. She saw that much could be achieved by voluntary aid workers and a wide range of skills, and this would mean extending opportunities for those beyond our immediate neighbourhood. Others saw the future in developing another registered charity, centred on the work in Romania and bringing in expertise from other interested parties around the country. We did not see this as the immediate way forward ourselves, bearing in mind that our work thus far, as well as the thrust of the church, came out of relationships. Introducing others, whatever their skills, would work against the closeness we had enjoyed to date. We also felt it unnecessary and time consuming to establish another charity, as we already had one in Poplars. We wanted to remain under the umbrella of Poplars and the work in Romania to continue to be part of its ministry.

The other members of the group did not agree, and decided to form their own charity. Since the openings and contacts to date had been predominantly in the medical field, and since Ann was the only qualified person of the group, they decided that education would be their emphasis in future. From that time onwards, Poplars Church (Romania) was born and the work nestled under the authority of the church leadership – an arrangement that in the providence of God protected both the work and us in the years to come.

My second visit to the Paediatric Hospital was again memorable for me in another way – but equally challenging. Ann had reported to me the stir caused in the hospital by the news of baby Monica's improvement as a result of prayer. In fact Ann had been told that "You do not need medicines to heal, prayer will do," as the story of my visit was recounted to her. No names were mentioned so it was not until we compared notes some days after her return that I realised God had indeed answered my prayers. Monica was duly discharged from the ward, eating normally. The doctor had not forgotten this incident and so, on my second visit, quickly explained to me the prognosis of another case they had and, "Would I come to pray for him?"

Ile was eleven years old and was suffering from lead poisoning, which the doctors attributed to contact with lead-based paint; he was in intensive care and had been given just twenty-four hours to live. Now the term "intensive care" conjures up a room with monitors, wires and highly technical means of diagnosis, treatment and care, plus sufficient staff, gowned up and in constant attendance. This intensive care room was merely an isolation room with one bed, bedside cabinet, glass observation screen, no equipment and no extra staff. In fact, the only professional was the consultant who took me into the room and introduced me to her patient.

I felt under pressure, recognising that the miracle performed before was by God; now I was expected to come up with the goods again. The consultant left me on my own and I desperately sought God for healing for Ile, admitting that I could do nothing and if there were going to be a change it would have to be of God. I prayed for about ten minutes and left Ile and returned to the staff. There appeared to be no visible change, but on my next visit six weeks later I met Ile sitting on the side of his bed, ready to be discharged. Not only was I happy to see such a recovery, I was relieved and thankful that God had once again used me – the phrase "man's extremity is God's opportunity" immediately came to mind.

CHAPTER EIGHTEEN

BACKWARDS AND FORWARDS

Our trips to Romania became yet further additional activities to fit in our busy lifestyle. How we managed to keep all these balls up in the air, I'll never know, other than by teamwork and God's blessing and grace.

Month by month our visitor list seemed to enlarge, with people from all over the globe, but now the numbers from Romania in particular increased. In fact, we had twenty-two Romanians come and stay in the next seventeen months. These were some with whom we had made contact – translators, doctors, lawyers, drivers, parents, teachers and students. As with most of our visitors, we aimed to show them our British way of life and local beauty spots, and to introduce them to our friends, family and the church.

A number of funny and memorable incidents arose on some of these visits. We hosted a doctor and his wife who arrived on their first visit abroad, exhausted but elated. On retiring to bed they opened their case and screamed. They discovered that they had collected the wrong case and had one belonging to a priest, containing full ecclesiastical clothing. I immediately rang Heathrow to find out what to do next. The answer was to contact our nearest airport and wait for the outcome. By a little persuasion, I managed to get the telephone number of someone else who had made a similar enquiry. A call to these people proved successful. They were a Christian couple hosting a Romanian Orthodox priest. He checked his case and his loss too. We arranged to meet on the M1 at Leicester Forest East to exchange suitcases the following day. This we did; identical cases swapped with very few words. In retrospect, it was like some spy movie with clandestine activity at a service centre. It brought great comfort to two very pleased guests.

One other incident that stands out occured when we hosted an elderly couple from Constanţa who were being accompanied by friends from Braşov. On one of their train journeys, the husband needed to go to the toilet, which he found without any problems. Unfortunately, to flush the loo he pulled the emergency cord and the train came to a halt. He was totally unaware of the trouble caused and our Braşov friends were highly embarrassed. When it was explained that this was done in ignorance, since he was unable to read English, and not with any malicious intent, the fine for improper use was waived.

During this period, in the early days after the revolution, travel out of Romania became a right and many people scraped together all the cash they could to fulfil this dream. As time passed it became more and more difficult and expensive to do so. The number of Romanian visitors fell dramatically by the end of 1991. The economic realities of the demise of communism, the effects of competition with the West and the poor balance of payments of the country began to bite.

As Ann travelled to and fro she became known to a wide circle of friends in Braşov. These included parents of special needs children and she attended and spoke at the monthly meeting of the Braşov Parents of Mentally Handicapped Children. This had been established immediately before our visits to the city and became an ideal platform from which to share our own knowledge and experience. Liaising with Colin Beacock of the Royal College of Nursing, Ann was able to invite three members of the support group over to the UK in May 1991. These included two parents and one teacher and, along with friends from Uckfield in Sussex, they were given exposure to local schools so as to understand the British way of treating and educating those with special needs. The parents particularly found this very enlightening and were hopeful that some of these facilities would now be made available in their country. A year later three men also visited at the invitation of the RCN and ourselves. This group, again, included two parents and a teacher; they too were suitably impressed. Sadly, the high hopes they had of the introduction of these methods and this equipment never materialised.

Colin also asked us to contribute to his and Bob Gates' book on learning disability and comparative care for those with special needs, as demonstrated through our work in Romania. The idea was to highlight the care in Sweden, the UK and Romania. Four of our volunteers and I produced the article for submission and after what seemed an interminable wait, *Dimensions of Learning Disability* was finally published by Baillière Tindall/RCN in 1997. It is still used as a textbook for nurse training.

Perhaps it was because of our profile in this book, or because by now students were asking to come with us to

Romania more and more for medical electives, that we were contacted by Renée Adomat of Birmingham University and asked if we would contribute a chapter for a book she was editing for use by medical students, to be entitled *Overseas Clinical Elective – a Survival Guide for Health Care Workers*. The deadline was tight but this we believed was another opportunity to put into print a record of what we had learned in serving the needs of the people of Romania whilst at the same time providing worthwhile information for prospective electives. After intense work and in reality little alteration, the chapter was completed and the volume published in 1997 by Blackwell Science Publications. It was another one of those God incidents that placed us in the right place at the right time.

I suppose, like many other ministries, the majority of our work was accomplished initially at home at the kitchen table. In fact, there was a period of our lives when the kitchen table became the centre of our ministry. This would be talking to people, listening, meeting their needs and, where necessary, introducing them to Jesus and the Holy Spirit. Discussions eye-to-eye with a cup of tea or coffee were much less threatening and, of course, it didn't just remain as one cup; Ann thrived on weak tea without milk or sugar.

The involvement in Romania, therefore, created even more work and soon there was a shift in emphasis; we just had to deal with all the correspondence and action the needs of volunteers and Romanians alike. The Poplars office was the obvious place to do this but since so many volunteers were only able to contact us in the evenings and since evening was the best time to get through to Romania on the telephone, we began to expand our evening work. We were conscious of family needs and had to keep a tight hold on this, so that as the work expanded we had to take every vestige of the charity's administration away from home to maintain our family's well-being. This meant that sanity returned to our home – perhaps in our enthusiasm we had let out our telephone number too easily.

Poplars Church office history was quite interesting. Initially in a home, it was restricted by space so later it moved to an annex of another's home. The annex had previously been a slaughterhouse. After several more years it moved to another home, then into an unused retail shop area – but all these were temporary bases. The breakthrough came at last when, involved as we were in local community activities, a member of the Local Authority Estates Department asked if we would like to rent the Development Office of an area the council had financed for small businesses. We looked at the property and jumped at the offer.

Canal Terrace was not the most salubrious address in town but it had, in estate agent terms, "character with amenities". As the name suggests, the property had seen former glory in a previous industrial era but the two-up-and-two-down provided more floor space than we had enjoyed thus far. Apart from having an internal toilet it was also carpeted throughout and had ample car parking space. It was into this that we moved our files, exhibition boards, desks and equipment. Canal Terrace became "home" to the Poplars Church (Romania) work for several years. The large upstairs room, light and airy, was ideal for the work and the necessary induction days and we soon filled the wall with displays of photographs or posters. In a funny way Canal Terrace was known to us previously. Prior to the council's redevelopment it had been, for several years, the home of two of our foster children. Each time we drove over the canal bridge our eyes would be directed sideways; our charges would longingly recall, "That's where we used to live!" Years later, as we pass, we think to ourselves, "That's where we used to work!"

It was obvious after a couple of years that the one-time enormous office was in fact cramped and, for us, past its sell-by date, but how were we to move from there and how were we going to finance such a move? For years now the church had had two full-time workers, Derek and myself, with Jude Henderson as administrator, so there were three salaries as well as office rent to find. The departure, years before, of many Poplars' members had certainly depleted the church's income. We obviously made this a matter of prayer but nothing seemed to come up until Ann kept on about a property in Watson Road in the town centre.

This Edwardian house was situated on the main one-way system of Worksop. It was three storeys high and had a basement, yard and garage. Internally, there were two reception rooms and a large kitchen, two bedrooms, one with en-suite, a large bathroom on the first floor and a large attic on the third floor. For some reason it was not selling. That reason was obviously not its accommodation or even its price; it was its location. Watson Road was the bed-sit area of the town and had a reputation for housing not only the needy but elements of the undesirables of Worksop. What better place to have a centre of the gospel, Ann argued, as she prayed through how best to proceed. Since the property was not selling, she drew to the attention of the leadership that this would make an ideal location for all the church's activities, including the administration for Romania.

In response, we prayed, visited, proceeded, negotiated and eventually we moved in in 1992. The property had been renovated, decorated and was carpeted; it seemed like a palace. Fortunately, we took the precaution of putting bars on all windows (insisted on by our insurer) and later received a renovation grant to customise it for our needs. What had seemed impossible became possible and was completed – God had provided a new base for our ministry.

CHAPTER NINETEEN

LEAVING THE NEST

By 1988 Kate had finished her occupational therapy course
and qualified, but sought, rather than go straight into a job,
to complete a Discipleship Training scheme with YWAM
(Youth with a Mission). She decided that she would do this
in Los Angeles. We encouraged her all we could and said
goodbye to another one. The day she left, our first grandchild
Jonathan was born to Martin and Jenny at Rotherham
Hospital. Jenny had qualified as a nurse at Rotherham so the
birth for her was like going home. Jonathan had been born in
Yorkshire – he too could qualify for the County Cricket Team!

Kate's stay was soon over and the experience for her was
tremendous. As part of the course she worked in Mexico –
the first of the children had started to be a globetrotter like
her parents. After completion of the placement in Mexico,
Kate returned home but was to participate in a prayer vigil
around France. We were asked whether we too would like
to be involved. All costs would be small because of the
numbers involved and the journey around France was to be
by train. We jumped at the opportunity.

From Paris we moved on eastwards, then southwards to Marseilles, westwards to Bordeaux and northwards again to Paris, staying on the route at convenient YWAM bases. The accommodation was basic and clean; the hospitality was first class and the fellowship and prayer times remarkable. Two weeks and it was all over and we returned back home, but not before we had made contact with John-Nat Foulquier and his family who operated Radio Harmonie in Bordeaux. Ann and I were able to share our testimonies on air and get to briefly know the Foulquier family. As a result of this we made two further visits to Bordeaux involved with the radio ministry and sharing in the local church.

Alongside our heart for mission abroad we were enthusiastic for mission locally. This included the nearby villages. Ann had become aware of a property in the village of Bawtry situated on the former London to Edinburgh A1 road.

Bawtry Hall near Doncaster is now the base for Action Partners (formerly Sudan United Mission) as well as for several other Christian mission groups. Previously the hall had had a varied history, being originally built in 1779 for a Wakefield mill owner (Pemberton Milnes) and added to in 1905 by the then owner. Eventually, it became the RAF No 1 Bomber Command Headquarters and its last effective operation was to send Vulcan bombers to the Falkland Islands conflict in 1982. Defence cutbacks, however, led to the Ministry of Defence closing the operations and putting the building and adjacent land and billets up for sale by auction. The building was vacated and remained empty from 1984 to 1988.

Ann had in mind that this property would have a new strategic role in the area, not this time as a base for destruction and war, but as a base for reconstruction and peace. She invited a number of church members to accompany her to pray and claim the premises for the Lord and Christian purposes. This was done with enthusiasm – but with few contacts and even less prospect of cash.

Months later the property came up for sale, cut down into a series of lots, the majority up for executive-type housing, whilst the hall, a listed building, was to be sold separately. Unknown to us, Action Partners had surveyed the property, in their desire to move northwards and thus be wiser stewards of the money donated to them. They proved successful in its purchase. For the organisation the move was traumatic, a number of their staff deciding to stay in the south of England, whilst for others it meant selling their own properties and going through a personal upheaval alongside the upheaval of the organisation.

As soon as we became aware of this answer to our prayers, we again visited to welcome our Christian friends to Bawtry and to the area. It was on one such visit that I was introduced to the Deputy Director of Action Partners, Colin Smith, who had just purchased a property in Worksop. I suggested that he might try out Poplars as a likely church family. A few weeks later Colin and his wife Barbara managed to visit and we invited them and their three sons to a meal with us at Poplars.

Although entirely different from the normal Baptist services that they were used to, Poplars did have an attraction for the Smiths who grew to appreciate us and become members of the family. We made it clear that our aims were to serve them and offer a retreat from their busy schedules. We recognised their primary call was to the mission and to Africa; Poplars was to be merely a base from which they could fulfil this primary call. The whole family turned up for the meal, plus Duncan's current girl friend, and the dining room at Poplars was full as usual. Little did we realise then that the family was to become so close to ours as time went by.

Our holidays in the summer of 1988 were again spent with Pete and Ruth and their children Mark and Laura in the Gironde in France. We had decided to hire a gite but had left it too late. The owner of the agency we had telephoned did say that he had just purchased a chateau, which he intended to lease. "Would we like to rent it for two weeks in August?" We jumped at the idea – five or six of us in a real French chateau!

The night we arrived it was dark and raining and it took some time to find the mains electrical switch; it was like some Hollywood set for a period film. Eventually we fitted into the chateau ambience – stone walls, uneven steps, large rooms, whistling wind and lightning – and we enjoyed every minute. Fortunately, the weather improved, although one evening we had an electric storm, like some natural firework display, for five hours. The owner made his own wine and his barn had vats fermenting the previous year's grape harvest. This was the same year that the young people too had decided to holiday in Bordeaux, not too far away, so we spent some time together. Kate, Liz and Jo, Duncan and Russ Smith, Martin and Jenny and baby Jonathan camped, windsurfed, sailed and had a good time together. Kate and Duncan were becoming an item, whilst Jo and Russ were yet to start their "on-off" relationship.

Being so close we also made ourselves known again in Bordeaux to the Foulquier family and took the opportunity to share on Radio Harmonie and renew our friendships with the church in their home. It was surprising that one of the first contacts we made in the summer of 1990, whilst in

Braşov, was one of the Foulquier family working with YWAM and performing in the main square. What a reunion and what a small world it is for Christians.

By 1989 Jo had entered her final year at school. We had never chosen to push our children academically for we realised that their abilities were more practical. We also believed that their well-being and happiness was far more crucial than their achievements. It was something of a surprise in the summer when Ann shared with me that she believed Jo was to be head girl during the next school year. We kept this to ourselves, but committed it to prayer. It was then a few weeks later that Jo came home at the beginning of term to announce that at a sixth-form election she had been chosen to be head girl. We were pleased for her and pleased that God had revealed his will to us in advance.

Jo's final year was special in many ways. As well as representing the school publicly, she was the last of four siblings, plus a host of foster children, all at the same school. Jo had decided to set her sights on becoming an architect (a chip off the old block), but for some reason she failed to obtain the A-level grades that had been predicted for her and went off to Sweden to complete a drama and mime course for nine months. This had previously been planned as a gap year filler; now it became a life-saver.

Kate and Duncan were soon married and decided to live initially in Langold within sight of the home Martin and Jenny had first set up. Langold was the village established for the colliers of Firbeck Colliery. The homes were large and well built and most had been improved to modern standards. Kate continued her career as occupational therapist whilst Duncan joined the police force – for which at six foot four he was ideally suited. After a training period near

Nottingham he was stationed at Worksop and gained much experience on a whole range of policing. After three years' commitment they both felt it was time to move on. Restless, initially he was employed by his grandfather's farm in Grove near Oxford. He then went to Cirencester Agricultural College, gaining a distinction in Management Studies and leaving college with an immaculate record. Sadly, the family farm found it difficult to employ such a modern whiz kid and he sought a post elsewhere. Feeling the call of God on their lives, they joined the Oxford Community Church, of which Duncan had been a member as a student and where he now served as an assistant pastor.

It was at that time that I had a word for Duncan from Isaiah 28:20: "The bed is too short on which to stretch out, and the blanket is too small to wrap oneself in" (NASB). I knew that it was for him – but I didn't know how it would work out. A few months later on a visit to Toronto he was personally head-hunted and invited by John Arnott to become Executive Director of the Airport Christian Fellowship. The training, the refusals, the service had all been worth it; a new chapter for Duncan and the family was beginning.

Having completed his studies at Askham Bryan Agricultural College, Martin set up his own business and continued to do well, particularly through the network of Christian contacts, plus his skill and qualifications. No project was too daunting. I remember producing his first promotional leaflet for clients. I entitled it, "A thing of beauty is a joy forever", a quote from poet John Keats – perhaps not the normal landscaping brochure!

By the early nineties, Martin and Jenny had three healthy children: Jonathan, Rebekah and Joel; but they also had the desire to serve overseas. This meant investigating possibilities of where, when and how. They eventually settled for Brazil, serving with WEC (Worldwide Evangelisation Crusade, founded by C. T. Studd). They would need to be orientated first at WEC headquarters at Gerrards Cross, near London, and then Martin would work in his capacity as landscaper at the Bible College at Montes Claros near Bela Horizante. Eventually, the orientation came to a close and the tearful time came to say goodbye to them all and off they flew to Rio de Janeiro. We missed their presence, especially the grandchildren, but we knew that this desire to serve the Lord was in their genes. We were pleased for their commitment. This area of Brazil was ideal for three growing children, with a warm climate, freedom from restrictions and a host of young Bible students to play with and look up to. Jonathan soon learned the Brazilian Portuguese language, whilst Martin and Jenny were well able to communicate, but not as fluently as the children.

The family served at Montes Claros for two and a half years, working in their spare time with local churches and on church projects, especially with street children. The venture was a demonstration of love in action – providing essential food from a centre five mornings a week. This was to prove invaluable for them on their return, for one year later Martin was able to lead a Tear Fund team to Rio and fit in a quick visit to the college and friends.

Ann and I never managed to visit Brazil owing to our work commitments and our involvement in Romania. Our children, however, did visit and Jo and Russ, and Kate and Duncan enjoyed some of the best of the sights of Brazil, albeit after miles and miles of journeying on Brazilian buses. On their return to the UK the family found the British climate very cold and the first thing we gave them were new sweaters and warm clothing.

During Jo's time in Sweden the school organised a trip to schools and colleges in Eastern Europe and they joined us in the spring of 1991 in Braşov, presenting drama and mime to a number of churches, schools and colleges there. Later both Kate and Liz were also to act as volunteers for a week or two in Braşov, bringing their skills and compassion to the needy, in the hospitals and in the community.

CHAPTER TWENTY

FIXING PRIORITIES

The work in Romania continued to expand and so too the demands on our time. Ann in particular had to plan well ahead in order to be available to go to Romania or alternatively we restricted her visits to out of term times. Caring for family and foster children and performing responsible occupations still had to be done. She was, however, a hundred per cent committed to these openings and was a significant influence in the development of the work to include volunteers. We decided early to restrict our activities to one centre (Braşov) and, although there were limitless needs, to expand only into areas where we knew we could fulfil a necessary task. We had also learned never to be ambiguous in what we said we could do and to promise only those things we could perform.

The work, therefore, expanded on several fronts; firstly volunteers contacted us from several quarters, particularly by recommendation of friends. We then found that there was a desperate need to promote better standards in health education. We knew that the work amongst those with disabilities was an area to which we could make a contribution and we could assist Christians by teaching and by providing impetus for summer camps. Ann was also conscious of the need for AIDS awareness training for professionals and she made this her top priority on her return to Britain from her first visit.

She wrote to a number of organisations explaining the needs and suggesting ways in which through co-operation these could be met. Only one charity responded but this was enough. ACET (AIDS Care, Education and Training), based in London, had just recently been formed by Dr Patrick Dixon and specialised in a Christian approach to AIDS and its implications. ACET expressed a wish to be involved in Romania, to have an input into informing professionals, and we agreed to work together. Patrick explained on our visit to his office that he was willing to put the resources of ACET at our disposal. It was not long, therefore, before Ann again visited Braşov, having organised the first ACET conference there, supported and funded by UNICEF.

Our previous contact with the medical professionals in Braşov enabled us to publicise a conference, arrange a venue and obtain translators and accommodation; no mean feat for so early after the revolution, and it was all approved by the local Health Authority and subsidised by UNICEF. We had been donated cartons of biscuits by British manufacturers and made these available for conference break-times. Delegates had never seen such luxuries for years and the biscuits soon vanished. Tea and coffee were brewed on a one-ring portable camp stove, primitive but effective.

Looking back, the conference, in its content and method of communication, was totally radical for those present. British personnel lectured on various topics and alongside Kate

Bristow of ACET, Ann took a considerable portion of the presentation. By now Ann had a relationship with many professionals – nurses, doctors, teachers and social workers being present who had heard of many tragic and traumatic events that delegates had suffered during the long, fearful former regime. In her session on grief, the translator broke down, realising for the first time that she was free to express the feelings of loss she experienced after an aborted pregnancy, and the pain of being intensely questioned and traumatised by the Securitate to ascertain whether this was self-inflicted.

The daily double journey of moving materials and equipment from the hotel to the conference venue soon came to an end, but this was not to be the last such conference in Romania. The representatives of UNICEF recognised that this was an essential investment for the benefit of the families and children there. Soon more conferences were planned and usually with little notice Ann was invited to participate. The Romanian government also put their weight behind this venture and conferences were held in Bucharest, Cluj, Iasi, Constanţa Craiova and Botosani, amongst other places. Invariably they were well received, given much publicity, filmed for TV and as a result had a large influence professionally.

Ann recounted that at Botosani in the north of Romania it was so cold in March when the conference was held that everyone had to wear their overcoats, gloves and scarves to keep warm, even when lecturing. The economies were such that the heating system was switched off on 1 March. Ann laughed as she remembered how comical each one of the visiting ACET members looked and behaved.

Ann owed a lot to the regular input of translators Malina Dumitrescu and Ana Ureche and through exposure to ACET was blessed by getting to know many hard-working, devoted Christians, including Kate Bristow and Maureen Campbell who years later would continue to visit and be involved in our lives. The work and influence of ACET began to expand, both in the UK and beyond to countries such as Uganda and Thailand as well as Romania. In July 1992 we were invited as guests of ACET and the Wellcome Foundation to the launch of ACET International at which Ann met personally for the first time its patron and her former heart-throb, Cliff Richard. Needless to say, she was not fazed by speaking to him or getting his autograph and introducing Ana Ureche to him.

It was at this time that others in Romania became aware of our activities. At one meeting Dr Adelhaid Maschek made contact with Ann, explaining that she had come on the train, some six-hour journey, to ask that we visit the coal mining town of Petrosani, in the county of Hunedoara. She graphically explained her needs, as director of a special orphanage, and Ann was attracted to her warmth, her sincerity and her love for the children. Again, we discussed this enquiry, prayed about it and decided to respond positively.

Since by now we were getting lots of enquiries about voluntary work from medically trained people, we felt that we could place a number together in Petrosani, working in the orphanage and hospital as needed. Thankfully, we had some lovely committed Christian workers who were willing to rise to this challenge and over the years we had input as expected, as well as in AIDS awareness training, parenting and child care. Petrosani was a very political town and obtaining approval was always difficult. Coming ourselves from a coal producing area we had an understanding and sympathy for the miners and their families. However, to see the conditions in the city was quite shocking; fourteen pits were in the valley, but safety standards and conditions were poor. As a result the miners, though well paid by Romanian standards, drank their earnings to soften the harshness of their situation. The streets of Petrosani reflected the hopelessness of coal mining in this area. Despite this, we were to discover lovely people and lovely Christians too. Even a group of Americans had been attracted to the town; a number had married Romanian girls and Calvary Chapel was running a local mission in the poorest part of town.

Over some eight years, with thanks to volunteers Zita Calkin, Deb and Toni Iordache, Jenny Bye and Julie Boffy in particular, and many others (including our niece Nicki) from Canada, we made a credible contribution to the poorest part of Petrosani. Once Deb and Toni left, it was clear that our humanitarian contribution to this desperate coalfield area was over. We would concentrate again exclusively on the work through our base at Braşov.

Braşov was also an administrative county as well as a city and some of our work extended to the villages beyond the city centre, particularly those where there were medical establishments or where we already had relationships with individuals. We were, therefore, able to work in Rasnov, Zarnesti, Cristian and Bran. At Rasnov we held our first children's camps, whereas Zarnesti and Bran had hospitals into which we were able to place volunteers over considerable periods.

Bran was considered a more prosperous village, being a tourism centre because of its castle, one of several connected with the former ruler known colloquially as Vlad the Impaler – the character upon which Bram Stoker based his novel *Dracula*. For our input in providing central heating and volunteers for the four-storey hospital, I was made an honorary citizen of Bran at a public ceremony in the summer of 1993.

Ann first met Graham Perolls on one of her trips to Romania and she started up a conversation with him on his journey to Braşov. Graham explained that he had made contact with a child at the Paediatric Hospital and he and his wife Caroline were in the throes of adoption. He also explained that, although his occupation was in the motor trade, his heart was in developing hospice care, especially for children. Ann had an immediate affinity with Graham and recognised how much our two visions were complementary. They exchanged addresses and on her return she made contact again. The upshot of this was Graham's vision to see a conference held in Romania on palliative care and the hospice movement. In view of our regular visits to Braşov and my contacts in the tourist industry there, I was able to set up a conference for up to two hundred people at the Hotel Sport, Poiana Braşov, in 1992. This became the first of several such conferences. Speakers came from the UK and included Dr Mary Baines, Pru Clench, Graham, Carol Stone, Adrian Moruzi and Dr Constantine Voinicu, whilst Ann led a question and answer session and Malina Dumitrescu translated.

The event was filmed and became the basis of Casa Sperantei's (the House of Hope) first video, tracing the development of the work in Braşov. News of the conference spread to the community, and amongst others we came to know and love the Blaga family, including Emilian Blaga who in his teens had been diagnosed with sarcoma of the knee. Our initial attempt to make contact proved futile as no one was at home, but this was quickly remedied and by early May we had arranged for Emilian and his mum, Viorica, to come and visit us at Poplars and receive treatment at Sheffield Children's Hospital. Every invitation of Romanians to Britain meant that we had to contact the Immigration Department, indicate our reasons for the invitation, and confirm that the charity would cover our costs for accommodation, subsistence, travel and treatment. We also needed to spell out details of medical care and expected periods of treatment, recuperation and return.

We were able to accompany Emilian to Sheffield for his examination. The waiting was lengthy and the outcome was not what we expected. The prognosis was poor since the disease had done its worst and we had to convey to Emilian and Viorica the news that amputation of his leg was essential. In much emotion they made the decision to proceed and Emilian and his mum spent weeks at the hospital whilst he recovered from the effects of the operation. Thanks to support from the hospital and Sheffield friends and the help of Paul and Maureen Gray, his recovery was good. Within several months they returned to Braşov with, of course, a purpose-made prosthesis – a piece of personally measured equipment hardly available in Romania.

Emilian became something of a local celebrity, first in the UK and then in Braşov on his return. As he grew it became necessary for his prosthesis to be replaced and once again mother and son returned to Sheffield for treatment. It was during the examinations for a new prosthesis that a chest X-ray revealed secondaries on Emilian's lungs. Again, it was my duty to share with the family the consultant's diagnosis and his suggestion that they return home and maximise fulfilment in the time he had left. This was not what the family or we had expected. For the next months Emilian survived remarkably well, having a girlfriend and a normal teenage lifestyle until he became weaker and weaker. I was able to visit the family again in June 1995 and had a tremendous time with Emilian who, weak in body, radiated an inner joy. He knew he was getting weaker but he also knew where he was going. Within four weeks he died but the family's contact with us all had won him several additional years of full life for which we were all thankful.

No sooner had we dealt with the immediate needs of Emilian than we became aware of the needs of Nicu Dutea. Nicu too was a teenager with cancer – this time carcinoma of the right knee. It had been necessary again to contact the Home Office Immigration Department to get approval of our invitation. Once this had been cleared, Nicu made his way first to Worksop and was then taken to Sheffield for investigation. In view of the rare condition he was recommended to go to Birmingham for treatment where he was accompanied first by Maureen Gray and then by Marius and Nicola Darcia.

Ann had made contact with Marius at the Paediatric Hospital in Braşov on her first visit in 1990 and Nicola, one of our early volunteers, later became his wife. They had taken up residence in Birmingham. Thanks to further support by the Birmingham Lions (especially Frank Fowler), Veronica Bradley and Philip and Barbara Viney, Nicu had regular visits. It was necessary for him then to move to Birmingham Queen Elizabeth Hospital since the tumour proved to be too extensive. After a series of operations, Nicu stayed with Ellen Royston at Maltby for a further eight months and was able to learn English. His return home was not as successful as expected and he soon returned to the UK; sadly, this time for the amputation of his leg. The emotional problems were great for Nicu but consistent support helped him through. The postscript to his medical treatment was that in spite of chemotherapy treatment, which usually renders a person sterile, he later became the father of a little boy, Marius, having married in 1998.

Ann and I took the responsibility for volunteers for the hospice work in Braşov and for two years I acted as Casa Sperantei's President. Eventually, I had to resign as the demands of travelling to Dartford for meetings, as well as the needs of the Poplars work in Romania, meant I could not perform these two duties adequately. I left, but not before recommending Malina Dumitrescu for Director of the Braşov Hospice – a job which today she excels at and for which she has received international recognition. The work and influence of Casa Sperantei has increased beyond all expectations, thanks to the invaluable contributions of so many, and is in itself a testimony to the energy of Graham, its council and its dedicated workers.

Initially, we were pleased to take volunteers with us when we visited Romania but as the demand increased we recognised that more organisation was necessary. This was to give us a greater degree of control, but also the situation in Romania itself seemed to alter constantly. At first we were welcomed with open arms; we could go anywhere and do almost anything. We were aware, however, that we were often watched and followed, presumably by the police or their agents, so our behaviour was circumspect in every way. This suspicion became a certainty when the hotel receptionist let slip that she knew where Ann had been and what she was doing. We had to put our trust in God and in keeping the matter to ourselves so as not to create panic amongst our workers. However, Ann later received a dressing-down from one volunteer who subsequently learned of the surveillance and insisted that it was her right to know. Leadership is never easy!

A good example of the changes was the issue of accommodation. This was provided free of charge for voluntary aid workers in Braşov and we had rooms first at Hotel Timpa and then Hotel Capital. Initially, food was provided – basic scrambled egg, bread and coffee or tea, often not available at weekends. Next, we were given accommodation, but not food and then later neither accommodation nor food. We had to find our own, which was not too much of a problem since we had many contacts who were happy to supplement their income, although the food supply was never consistent owing to political uncertainties and bad planning.

It was at this time that we used several homes for accommodation, some of them in the centre of town. Flight times often meant arrival in the city after dark and on one such occasion four middle-aged volunteers arrived at their abode early in the morning. On knocking up the owners, they made themselves at home and the owners gave up their beds for their visitors. It was only next morning that they realised that they had been delivered to the wrong address. These dear people had vacated their beds without a murmur, which underlines either the generosity of the Romanians, their naïvety or their submission to similar goings on under the former regime.

Ann received one of her strangest enquiries at home from a prospective volunteer. She was a seventy-two-year-old Roman Catholic nun from Ireland who had spent most of her life on mission in Africa. She enquired if she could visit Romania under our auspices and work with the children. Ann hesitated as she had not contemplated such an enquiry and, in a matter of fact way, responded by saying that the lady should see her doctor and get his advice as to whether she was fully fit for what she had in mind. Within hours she telephoned again confirming that she had seen her doctor, obtained his OK and could she go? Ann had met her match and responded positively. For six weeks Sister Xavier looked after six children in the Paediatric Hospital early morning to late at night, walking everywhere and climbing the hill to the hotel every time, no taxi rides for her. She was one of our hardest working volunteers of all time.

It soon became apparent to us that volunteers needed to be reliable and hard-working and these qualities did not come through qualifications alone. Similarly, a profession of faith did not mean automatic acceptance; we were looking for people who would work hard and play hard, people who would help us keep our good reputation in the eyes of the authorities. It was when non-Poplars volunteers were using our name to gain entry to hospitals that we introduced our own personalised letter of authority, each with a photograph and details. These later also became essential identification documents when we were stopped by police and not carrying passports.

It was not too long before we felt it essential to keep our volunteers, supporters and friends updated on our activities, achievements and changes. Initially, for the first few copies this was merely a typed sheet, two or three pages long. We soon realised that we must improve the standard of both reporting and presentation so, by copy five, we had expanded into a four-page, double-colour (green and black on white paper) format. These updates were, however, produced on a shoestring and looking back were not initially of the highest quality – but we had realistically to produce what we could afford since most of our funding came direct from individual donations, small amounts that added up in quantity. The exceptions were donations from schools when amounts would rise to hundreds and even thousands. We were grateful for everyone's generosity – and God's provision from whatever source.

As the work expanded so did our trips to further promote the work. These came about through the recommendation of our volunteers or through our church contacts, one of which resulted in an invitation by Mike and Jeanne Sigler to visit Texas and speak at the Last Days Ministry YWAM base at Lindale, near Tyler. Mike and Jeanne had been on staff at YWAM in Los Angeles, met Kate and had visited us in Worksop. Excited by the work, they invited us as their guests to the base at which they were now working.

East Texas was hot, but surprisingly like Britain in appearance, except for driving on the right, the white palisade fences and the timber homes. Those at the base came from around the States and a number were on DTS (Discipleship Training School) programmes, whilst others were actively involved in the Last Days Ministry work of printing and publishing. LDM had been formed by singer Keith Green and his wife Melody. Sadly, Keith and two of his children had died years before when his private plane had crashed. His legacy of songs and publications was continuing to be produced at the base. In 1991 the base had become integrated with YWAM.

We arranged to take Peter along, knowing that he would benefit from the trip and our supervision. We also decided to make contact with the civic authorities of the nearby suburb of Dallas, Farmers' Branch, which was twinned with Worksop, and our Local Council members were happy for us to make ourselves known. We spent a number of exciting hours in Farmers' Branch and received a certificate, signed by the then mayor Dave Blair, to announce that we were honorary citizens of the town. Once again our work had led us to people we could never have hoped to have met otherwise, some of whom later became volunteers for Romania or visitors to our home.

Ann always had the capacity to pick up real needs in people's conversations and would store that knowledge, or pick up on it as appropriate. She would take things from her memory bank and with sensitivity and good timing introduce a word, or a little act of kindness, which would show that she cared. This gift had the touch of gold about it that endeared her to those who confided or asked for help. She was also blessed with a visionary flair for initiating ideas and being able to translate them into relevant action. She was a spiritual entrepreneur – not always successful in everything, but fully enthused and able to see an idea, a project, a need and the way of fulfilment.

A typical example of this came from our visit to Texas. We were introduced to a family who lived in their own home on the edge of the ministry grounds. They had decided that it was time to leave and move on and in typical American fashion were holding a yard sale of their goods. Memorabilia, furniture, paintings and fabrics were all displayed and available for offers. They were travelling to the West Coast and would set up home again over there. They did not intend to take surplus baggage, which would cost dollars to move, even if they hired a trailer. Ann mused on this and came forward with the idea that something similar could be done locally in Worksop as a means of fundraising on behalf of Romania. We returned with a printed yard sale sign and

Ann promoted her idea enthusiastically with Derek, who immediately put his energy and resourcefulness behind it. For most of our Christian lives we had been against jumble sales to support church, but this was a different twist. The yard sale would support the humanitarian work for Romania and in so doing would also serve the needy of Worksop.

With Derek's flair for selling and the church's backing and provision of bric-a-brac, the yard sale entered Worksop folk-lore. Since its inception it has raised many thousands of pounds for the needs of Romania, created work opportunities for countless volunteers and provided a social forum which has drawn several people not merely to church meetings but to a personal knowledge of Jesus. It has become a ministry in its own right.

We were soon to introduce procedures, files, handouts, literature – information packs – Romanian language tapes (later CDs) and books (thanks to Christine Hogg), and ultimately the provision of induction days. These were held as regularly as possible and updated to accommodate changes in procedure both in Romania and the UK. Induction days were a joint effort and we involved as many volunteers as possible. Numbers vary according to the time of the year – our largest being fifty-two and our smallest in single figures. Today, these are held generally in Worksop and Northern Ireland – but have been held at individual centres and churches around the country to suit demand. Venues have included various colleges of further education, nurses' training schools, universities and churches, and audiences have been made up of both skilled and unskilled persons, believers and non-believers.

The induction days seek to inform prospective volunteers of all they need to know. We soon developed a programme, which included sessions on Romanian culture and language, health issues and administration, plus videos, slides and power point presentations on possible placements. A group interview was a means of getting to know the motivation of each individual. An excellent lunch and copious refreshments help to build relationships. We often say to volunteers that the danger of bombarding them with information is that they emerge "punch drunk". The main qualities we seek in a volunteer are sociability (able to get on with the rest of the group), adaptability (able to cope with alternatives) and flexibility (willing to accept that things will vary). In spite of all our preparations and discourse, placements rarely turn out to be predictable. The individual's own expectations are perhaps the greatest hindrance, and flexibility will allow for a reality of lesser intensity.

As the numbers of volunteers increased, so did our selection process and criteria and Ann was never afraid to suggest that individuals were not yet ready to visit people in need. Invariably those who wished to visit were eventually able to do so and over the years only a handful out of well over two thousand volunteers have created any kind of problems. These were directed to return home – but otherwise the contribution made both to Petrosani and Braşov, to hospital, orphanage, kindergartens, the churches and to the community, has been of a high quality. Most have had such a worthwhile experience that many return again and again. One advantage of the system we hold is that we do not restrict volunteers to one project and they can, therefore, visit according to our mutually agreed timetable throughout the year.

Our visits to Romania became more frequent and the requests for help more urgent. We concentrated on the needs that were apparent to ourselves. Initially, we discovered that the children in the Paediatric Hospital were suffering from a lack of stimulation. We therefore encouraged our volunteers to hold the babies and young children and where appropriate to take them out of their cots and play on the floor. Ann remarked, the first time this was done, that it attracted the doctors and nurses themselves, keen to see toys of western quality such as Fisher Price, since nothing like them was at that time available even for their own children.

The young children had been left to prop feed themselves and had little tactile contact and they also found it difficult to stand on the floor, being used only to standing on mattresses. For many it took some time and persistence to adapt. We then brought small tables and chairs, and cutlery and plastic crockery in order to teach them to feed. This again was a development stage many had not yet encountered and many hours were spent encouraging the little ones to feed themselves.

We carefully introduced the principle of play therapy as a means of development and this was something new for most professionals; but it was not unknown, for we had discussed it with Horiclaria, an educational psychologist in the Braşov Orphanage. She had tried to bring in the use of developmental stimulation by play, only to be disciplined by the former authorities. Here now, years later, we were introducing these concepts into the dystrophy ward for the malnourished. We were able to do this for several months with help from our volunteers, but the situation for the whole hospital was enlarged when the London-based charity Comedy Store, with their much greater resources, introduced the concept of play therapy for every ward and provided the funding for trained play therapists. Once these specialists were in post on the wards our role became one of support, and being an extra pair of hands for the remarkable job they were doing.

Since politically things were changing and at the same time volunteers seemed to be increasing in number, we decided that we needed to either rent or buy accommodation in Braşov. Purchasing property – even though some became available – was not legally possible so we had to resort to renting. We needed somewhere large enough to house all our activities and provide sufficient bed spaces for several volunteers.

Anne Lemm, a former nursery nurse from Sheffield, was our co-ordinator at the time. Anne was a bright, happy person, mature and very understanding and caring. One day as we communicated she broke the news that she had been offered a property to rent, towards the centre of town on Str Iancu Ianu, but the cost was $600 per month and we would have to give our response immediately. "What is it like?" I asked. It had a basement, a large entrance hall, WC, large dining/kitchen and lounge and upstairs were three bedrooms and a bathroom. Outside was a fenced garden – fully private. It also had an international telephone, hot and cold water, gas heating – for Romania, all mod cons! But where would we get the money? We decided, on Anne's recommendation, to take the plunge and commit ourselves. To recoup the costs we would need to charge volunteers for accommodation.

Anne's decision was excellent. Iancu Ianu, as it became affectionately known, served us and our volunteers for about five years, providing all we needed and never once suffering power or supply cuts like other areas of the city. At a time when local people did not have telephones or even reliable water supplies, we had every need met. God had richly blessed us beyond our wildest dreams. We were able to use the owner's furniture too and with extras that we bought it soon became a temporary home to many volunteers over those years.

Another of our short-term volunteers who decided to stay longer than originally anticipated was Rachel Jacklin from Scunthorpe. Initially working with Anne Lemm, she would stand in as co-ordinator when Anne visited the UK in accordance with our instruction not to be away from home for too long. Eventually, Anne decided to leave, having worked for five hard years and feeling that her input had come to an end. She gave so much to Romania and her work. We valued her greatly and knew it would be a challenge for a successor to match her achievement. Rachel then took over the co-ordinating duties in Anne's place. Rachel was in her early twenties, jovial and well able to communicate both with our young and older volunteers alike. She was excellent in her way with Romanians.

Since all our work seemed to be based on the twin emphases of relationships and skill, it was good that our co-ordinators could maintain good working relationships with professionals from several disciplines. Regular visits to placements and continuing discussion on needs meant that we were providing help that was appropriate. In view of the constantly changing policies and the minimal funding available, directors of various institutions were keen to obtain free, reliable assistance.

One of Rachel's regular visits was to a family in Braşov with two teenage children, Lydi and Cippi Maroschi who suffered from Werring Hoffman syndrome – a muscular wasting disease. The family lived in a first-floor flat with their single parent mum. Rachel would encourage the children and teach them both English. Ultimately, as the children grew and after Rachel left Romania herself, this work was continued by other volunteers. Both children were adept and quick learners. Marilyn Robinson was able to get them electrically operated wheelchairs and for the first time they became mobile in their own home without their mother's assistance. As they grew, volunteers, many of similar ages, would transport them from their apartment and drive them to the park or the cinema for outings. They both enjoyed their new freedom, which sadly was not expected to last much longer.

As the legal regulations relaxed on the purchase of property, we were advised by Graham Perrolls of a house for sale in Sanpetru, five kilometres from Braşov. Sanpetru was a rural village originally settled by German farmers – hence the Lutheran church building dominating the main street. Later, ethnic Romanians moved into another part of the village, whilst immediately after the Second World War another district became inhabited by Romanians working in Braşov. The village was situated on a flat plain from which rose a series of hills, partially covered by forest. These were the first hills after the Carpathian Mountains. In view of the terrain the hills were used primarily for hang-gliding and a small hangar on the edge of the village housed one or two small planes belonging to the local gliding club.

The house had been offered to Casa Sperantei but was not suitable for them. It belonged to a Christian family, the Tofners, who, like so many of German extraction, were taking up their opportunity to return to Germany to live. We tentatively surveyed the property. It was a single-storey premise with three sections of accommodation in an

L-shaped block, with a large wooden gate to the street opening to a three-sided courtyard. It also had a series of dilapidated pigsties, cow byres, a hay loft and a garage. The former barn wall and floor remained, the barn itself having been demolished years before. Beyond this was a plot of ground of about an acre.

We were advised that the purchase cost of the property would be in the region of £16,000, which of course excluded the cost of any alterations we might choose to make. Once again our level of faith was being tested. Trusting for the rent for the property at Str Iancu Ianu had been a big step forward – this was even bigger! We shared the information back home with the church and the trustees of the Poplars charity. It was agreed unanimously that we proceed with the purchase and plans for the renovations.

On the last day of March 1995, after hours of waiting in the bowels of the law courts in Braşov, after sweet talk to lawyers, notaries and officials, Ken Russon and Pete Hardy, as Poplars trustees, signed all the necessary documentation. Every document was notarised and legalised and Str Republicii Nr 153 Sanpetru became our property. We continued to rent the accommodation at Str Iancu Ianu until the owner needed its return for his daughter after her marriage. Although the renovations dragged on (typical of builders everywhere), the quality of work was excellent. We had employed a local architect, the sister-in-law of Stelian our first Romanian translator, to complete the plans and submissions whilst I acted as client. Ileana and her husband Raul had visited Worksop at the end of 1990 so that Ileana could give birth to her baby. The family stayed at Whitwell with Paul and Maureen Gray.

Paul and Maureen had been with us to Romania several times. It was on one of these visits that Maureen, a midwife, learned that Ileana's pregnancy was subject to complications and suggested her coming to the UK. This proved wise counsel and the Fintina family rejoiced in the safe birth of baby Ioanna at Chesterfield Hospital. Maureen was an avid linguist and their stay helped her in learning more Romanian, which she continues to share at our induction days for volunteers. Later Paul and Maureen were to become the organising force behind the annual surgical team visit that centred upon the Paediatric Hospital in Braşov. It became Ann's job to assist Maureen to ensure the vision for these visits was maintained.

CHAPTER TWENTY ONE

NEW CHALLENGES

From time to time we were able to take Peter along with us to Romania if we all visited together, one of us spending time with him as the other performed some prearranged activity or visit. As Peter grew, this became more and more difficult, especially because of his schooling needs. He was in fact having difficulties in the state sector and we ultimately resolved this when the time came for him to go to secondary school by introducing him to Bethany School, a small Christian establishment in Sheffield. This had the advantage of providing one-to-one attention and the school was more intimate and less likely to put Peter under pressure both academically and socially. The disadvantages were obvious; it would cost us financially, even though fees were in no way exorbitant, and it would mean ensuring that transport to and from school was available twice a day. This would be costly in time and money since the distance was a thirty-mile round trip each time. We knew this was essential and embarked upon it in faith, both for the money and the commitment.

The commitment did mean, however, that our regular trips to Romania, especially Ann's, would be more restricted as she would devote more of her time to Peter's needs and education. For a number of years, therefore, our days were juggled around twice-daily visits to Sheffield and, on special occasions, to open days and parent meetings. Inevitably, because we were the kind of people we were, Ann did some teaching at the school on a weekly basis whilst I served as a governor for a number of years.

Ann's priority for family meant, therefore, that I would be the one visiting Romania regularly. We continued to work together and our office for years included two desks. We always liaised and put lots of available hours into the work. For most of this time Ann worked as a volunteer, but as the workload increased I insisted she be remunerated. Ann never felt comfortable with this and, as soon as she could, withdrew from paid employment with Poplars (Romania) and looked elsewhere to supplement our income (especially to pay Peter's fees). She was also feeling that it was time for a personal change; she needed further stimulation. At no time did she give up the Romania work; she did, however, add another charity to her workload.

In spite of all the activities we were involved in, our home was a place of enjoyment and laughter. Again and again visitors recalled what a wonderful gift of hospitality Ann had. Numbers were never limited and the philosophy seemed to be "the more the merrier"! Ann was one for a party and a laugh even when it was at her expense.

One such incident occurred when we went to see the film *Titanic* in a local multiplex cinema. We had taken our seats and enjoyed quite a portion of the film when Ann asked to be excused to go to the toilet. I was a bit apprehensive, wondering whether in the dark she would find her way back. My misgivings were not unfounded for she seemed to be away ages – only eventually returning, groping in the dark to her seat. She couldn't contain herself, so out popped the explanation for her delay. She had walked into the adjacent screen area – but unable to find her seat had wandered out again, having to go to reception to ask for help. Sympathetically, they seemed to understand, for *Titanic* was showing that night on two screens – Ann of course had initially "returned" to the wrong one!

It was in 1994 that Ann turned her attention to the needs of the aged in Worksop and district. On two occasions the Reverend Geoff Dougill, the Superintendent Minister of the Worksop Methodist Circuit, had advertised, on behalf of a new committee he had convened, for a co-ordinator for the Worksop Live at Home Scheme. The scheme was a befriending organisation set up to encourage the elderly to live in their own homes, rather than in registered aged persons' homes, and to have volunteers visit them, enhancing their lives socially.

No suitable applicant was found at the first interviews, but as soon as Ann applied, he knew that she was the right candidate. Starting from an empty office adjacent to the entrance hall of the church building, the establishing of the work was no easy task – in fact one of the first comments she received from a church member was, "Not another voluntary organisation in Worksop? You will never get anyone to help!" This was the kind of impossibility Ann thrived upon, for soon resources were found, desks and equipment did materialise, contacts were made and the work was under way, driven along by hard work, enthusiasm, charm, persuasion and Ann's organising ability. It was to be a part-time post for many years – but it became apparent that Ann was not part time in her involvement and service; she always went the second mile.

Ann soon made contact with social workers and other professionals, many of whom she had already met through fostering and adoption. At the same time she began to amass an army of volunteers. She was supported and encouraged by the church at Poplars and by input from a total of eight churches in the town. This was seen as a demonstration of church unity – working together at practical levels of service; outstanding even in Christian circles. Volunteers offered their time whether they had church affiliations or not. Soon the number of volunteers topped one hundred and fifty and it wasn't long before the members (or users of the service) totalled two hundred. Such was Ann's persuasive power that two local independent schools, Worksop College and Welbeck, were actively involved, sending students as part of their social education sessions. It was not unusual to see these sons and daughters from "top-drawer" families, pushing wheelchairs, shopping or gardening, or just befriending a number of the elderly in Worksop. Ann sought to suitably match volunteer and user and made regular visits to establish a relationship, especially with new referrals. Where possible, she would encourage the active elderly to become befrienders and volunteers themselves, rather than mere recipients of a service.

It was not long before the scheme extended to provide a coffee morning and, later, a luncheon club that then became a day centre drop-in. Outings were planned, taking a leisurely cruise up the River Trent or visiting Castle Howard. Alternatively, holidays were arranged: to Great Yarmouth, Bournemouth, and Llandudno, for example. Nor was it

Ann's vision to keep to Worksop; she soon extended the work to encompass others in the Worksop Methodist Circuit, which included parts of South Yorkshire and North Derbyshire as well – the area within a ten-mile radius. Soon the numbers increased, such that the scheme that started with only local church backing soon became the flagship of the Live at Home movement. It became so popular and had so much impetus that very soon it drew the attention of headquarters, who restricted its further growth. This was also a time when the charity's bureaucracy started to intervene and remodel management structures several times, becoming PC in its appointments and, sadly, less effective locally.

Before all this evolved, however, Ann was able to introduce the Signpost Initiative in Carlton-in-Lindrick, offering a social meeting place, information on benefits and a contact point for the elderly, in liaison with the Parish Council and the Coal Board Rural Regeneration Project. At the same time she also saw another need and on each Friday introduced a group for those in the early stages of dementia. Ann appreciated the initial stages in this group, which always began and ended in prayer and a time of devotion. She enjoyed serving those who, through their age and condition, could no longer get regularly to worship. All this took five years under Ann's leadership; soon Vanessa Sumpton became her second-in-command and Sandra Whiteman her typist.

Tuesdays were busy days and meant an early start, for it was the drop-in day. Here Ann's powers of persuasion were most obvious. An army of volunteer drivers would transport the members to the base, whilst a myriad of others would commence preparation of the meals. So convincing was Ann that it was not unknown on asking someone what they were doing and why, to receive the response, "Ann asked me to!" One school governor, a retired lecturer from the local college, came for one hour each Tuesday morning solely to peel potatoes, whilst others came after lunch to wash up the pots and pans! Everyone loved her, especially the members. She was a "people's person", made everyone feel special and knew their needs and the needs of their family.

Annual General Meetings in any organisation are not the most inspiring occasions and are often sparsely attended. To overcome this, Ann made a feature of the meetings, arranging them on Tuesdays after the drop-in, with visiting speakers or singers and with tea, coffee and cakes to follow. Each year anything between one or two hundred were always in attendance.

As well as persuading volunteers to do almost anything, she was equally convincing with the members. One typical example of this was when she suggested that a gliding session be arranged. Several members and volunteers were interested and the local gliding club at Gamston near Retford hosted a group on a beautiful sunny Friday afternoon. By turns about a dozen of them were whisked up into the air in a two-seater glider, turning and weaving for a five-minute flight over the A1 and adjacent fields and runways. I declined the second invitation for a flight but member Frank Marsh, aged eighty-three at the time, volunteered for yet another go! The very thought of octogenarians taking to gliding was a scoop and the next session was filmed by Central TV as "now for something entirely different"! Ann did not, however, volunteer for the gliding sessions – I must admit it was the only way-out scheme I ever knew her forego!

There was one occasion, however, when she could not refuse. It was a normal Tuesday drop-in day and access was restricted because of a funeral service in the adjacent church building. The morning was as busy as ever and everyone was doing their work as normal, when Geoff Dougill, the minister, came into the office. It was five minutes before the funeral service was due to start and the regular organist had not turned up. "Can anyone here play the organ?" he asked; no one could so he looked even more worried. "Can anyone play the piano?" "I can tinkle a little," said Ann. She was quite able to play hymns but had actually not played for years. "Will you come and play for the funeral now?" he asked. Somewhat unconfidently she followed him, played music at all the right times and got Geoff off the hook. At the end all were relieved, but Ann's relief turned to utter amazement when she was given an envelope with twenty pounds in it! Her fee for playing! The regular organist turned up an hour later – he had written down the wrong time. Geoff Dougill said of Ann:

> She was a slight person with a big heart, a lovely smile and boundless energy. During those five years I tried to support and to keep pace with her. To have come to know Ann has been a great joy. As to so many people, she has been to me an inspiration. She translated for us all her faith into action.

CHAPTER TWENTY TWO

CRIME AND PUNISHMENT

The summer of 1995 saw our first visit to Newfoundland, Canada. Margaret, my sister, and her husband John had emigrated in 1973 to Lewisporte, situated on Notre Dame Bay on the north of the island. From time to time they had returned to the UK with their children Paul, Nicki and Chrissy to see my parents or for family weddings. The children were now growing and Paul's marriage to Judy was planned in August – it was our time to visit. Supply and demand always meant that it was expensive to visit Newfoundland but we knew we should be there – that meant we had to come up with the fare. Martin, Jenny and family, however, were not able to join us, but my parents were. This visit was one of several they had managed to make over the years since retirement.

The three-week break proved a wonderful holiday – we hired a car and visited as much of the island as we could. Not surprisingly Ann was able to make friends of many in Lewisporte and these generous people treated us like long-lost family. We were able to visit the tablelands of Gross

Morne National Park, and the Northern Peninsula to see the World Heritage site at L'Anse Aux-Meadows (the place of the first Viking and, therefore, European, landing on North American soil some hundreds of years before that of Columbus). We went whale watching and moose tracking and enjoyed the rugged scenery and the freedom of the Rock – as it is colloquially called.

Out of the blue in October 1997 we received an invitation to exhibit our work at the East West Christian Studies Conference held at Wheaton College, Chicago, along with other Christian organisations. It was recognised that we were making a practical contribution to the rebuilding of the former Eastern bloc. Our fees for flights and hotels were graciously donated. Again, Ann was very conscious of the need for her to be around for Peter and so she declined the invitation but suggested that Duncan accompany me. Duncan was thrilled at the idea and we flew from Manchester to the "Windy City".

We had been given instructions on how to make contact and quickly found our transit vehicle, which already had another conference delegate on board. The trip to Wheaton was both an eye-opener and a wonderful time of fellowship with our new found friend.

The conference was informative on what was happening, especially in other parts of Romania, and we felt a great encouragement from other delegates for the work we too were doing. One of the most personally endearing memories of the visit was the opportunity to visit the Billy Graham Museum adjacent to the conference hall. I went through the exhibits, longing in my heart for Ann to be with me for I knew she would appreciate its contents. Details of the Wembley Stadium event of 1954 were there, and I also found a photograph of associate evangelist Joe Blinco, the man who preached the day I too years later committed my life to Jesus.

One of the delegates, a former air pilot, graciously took us about in our spare time and I was able to visit the home of Frank Lloyd Wright, the world famous modernist architect. The following day we were driven to Willow Creek, a church on the outskirts of the city. Its emphasis was on user-friendly activities and services and some five thousand were present. The ministry was from Proverbs and those with marriages of ten, twenty and thirty years' length were invited to stand in thankfulness. I thanked God for such a lovely marriage and a tremendous wife. All too soon our visit was over and we set off once again to O'Hare Airport and our journey home. The visit had given me a determination to continue to serve the people of Romania and a determination somehow to bring Ann back to Chicago.

The mid-nineties also saw activity we could not have expected. Although Paul and Steve had left us some years before, we had not forgotten them. Occasionally we would bump into them in town or come across their names in the local press – not, I might add, for their services to the community; more along the lines of them doing community service.

It was in September 1994 that Steve was in court at Worksop charged with stealing vehicles, and driving without insurance. Steve pleaded guilty – apparently he had now become the local specialist in breaking into cars for others. He also became adept at taunting the police while driving the vehicles he had misappropriated. We did not condone any of this activity but we realised that for Steve this was more bravado than malice and when he broke into vehicles for others it was as a result of his having been intimidated by them, rather than for gain. However, the law is not soft in these areas and at first he was given a hundred hours' community service; later it was to be a custodial sentence at Glen Parva in Leicester.

It was quite interesting in court listening to his solicitor expounding his background and the extenuating circumstances that had led to his emergence into a life of crime. What was said was a mixture of truth and spin – but no reference whatsoever was made to the nine years he had lived with us. I wanted to shout out (but didn't), so I later said to the solicitor that I hardly recognised the person he was talking about. He smiled and admitted the omission but knew it would not help his client. Sadly, neither did his spin! A ten-week custodial sentence meant we made regular visits to Glen Parva, once again putting stability into the life of one of our charges. We were, as expected, the only visitors apart from his girl friend. After his release Steve moved from Worksop and, although this meant leaving two of his children, he did get employment and has continued to work. Some breakthroughs take much longer.

Paul on the other hand had particular problems with drugs and from time to time he would be arrested for shoplifting to pay for the habit. Forsaken by his family and again rejected by his girl friend, Paul became very depressed. He continued to be in and out of prison, with little stability in his life. For him too we remained available and he knew always to call in an emergency; something which he did and continues to do to this day. I recall people saying, "I could never foster, it's letting them go that's difficult." Somehow you never stop letting them go; commitment seems to continue.

Peter's presence at Bethany School had its ups and downs too. Not that the school was guilty in this respect – it was Peter who was beginning the teenage syndrome of knowing best. This was first evident in his last-minute rising in a morning. Since school started at 8.30, it was essential to be on the road by 7.30 so as to miss the traffic entering Sheffield – a few minutes either way led to disproportionate delays. Peter never saw it as his responsibility to ease the stresses of driving him there by being ready on time. Later, as he grew, we experimented with the train from Worksop – but, again, this ran to a timetable and entailed his co-operation. The train also meant a temptation not to take the bus to school from outside the station, but to go elsewhere. Driving to Sheffield, however lengthy, did mean that he arrived, and collecting him meant that he arrived at home!

Because of the excellent teaching from considerate and caring staff, Peter managed to obtain several GCSEs – a fact that others did not believe when his behaviour took an even more bizarre and downward turn. At school it was not unknown for items to go missing, minor damage to be done, absences to occur, all with genuine or plausible excuses. Lying and stealing could not go unconfronted, however, and for a number of years our family became prisoners in their own home. By this I mean we had to lock all bedrooms or private areas, otherwise, like a magpie, he would purloin anything of value. Since home should be a place to relax, the stresses that this regime imposed were tremendous for all of us. Without the Lord and without our understanding family and friends, I don't know how we would have survived.

As Peter reached the age of sixteen he was of the opinion that he had the right to rediscover his parents, whilst at the same time his mother had had a letter written to social services enquiring about her son. Somehow, legal adoption had never been fully understood by her. In a strange way, Peter also wanted to meet his dad. He too somehow was blind to the fact that we were mum and dad.

The situation at home again became tense and it transpired that Peter was, without our knowledge, investigating his past, initially by use of his life-story book and later by footslogging. In his last year at Bethany, in an experiment to allow him more freedom and reduce academic stress, Peter was allowed to take a day a week doing practical work. This he did with a former TA soldier, Andy, doing landscaping and other similar work. We thought this could not only assist in the short term, but might also offer employment after school, but again Peter became inappropriate in his actions and conversations. Sadly, it became an embarrassment to Andy to keep him employed and Peter had to leave.

For months Ann had been saying how large our home seemed to be and that she could no longer manage the housework on top of her job and her other responsibilities. The obvious solution was to sell – but Ann wanted the home to be sold within the church so that its facilities could continue to be used. On looking around the locality we saw many properties but none at which we felt comfortable. We discussed our feelings with Pete and Ruth and it was suggested that we did a house swap. This would mean us moving from a six-bedroom property with a half-acre garden to a smaller four-bedroom house with a pocket-handkerchief plot. We prayed about it and it somehow seemed right. At the end of March 1998 we moved a mile up the road – our second home swapped with friends rather than advertised. The difference in values gave us an equity that enabled us to make a number of alterations, which, with the help of John, Ann's brother, and Simon, a friend, we were able to complete in the next few months, even allowing for periods of rest between the various projects. One essential for me was at least to make the garden appear larger and when all the construction work was completed this was easily done.

The move to Carlton solved many of our problems. It did not, however, seem to solve Peter's. Unfortunately, he made a new friend from the estate, a lad of a good family, but at the time a bit of a tearaway. Secretly, these two were responsible for a number of petty crimes and our move into a new neighbourhood was christened by regular visits from police officers. The police were, at first, hostile, dubbing us as uncaring parents, until we explained Peter's needs and background. We then became a team working together for his rehabilitation. This friendship helped neither of these two boys and eventually led to our car being stolen and crashed by the pair. It proved to be a write-off. We learned that Peter had stolen the keys – his friend had driven the car. This was the start of Peter's record of crime, that ultimately led to him committing GBH whilst he was drunk, and several other more despicable cases of abuse.

All this was compounded by Peter's search for his family and his identity. Unknown to us he had discovered a half-sister nearby and on one occasion we lost him for a number of days only to find him again living in perhaps the worst house in the street. This initial contact with his family was soon to cease, but he then found other distant relatives and friends of his parents in Worksop. At the same time he also formed more undesirable friendships until he had no settled place of abode since, one by one, he had caused each location trouble. His mother visited from Kent and he went to her home too – but his relationship with her new spouse proved difficult. Within weeks he realised that his hopes concerning his mother were based on fantasy. Similarly, his father appeared for a number of weeks – only to leave when the court cases started. It was another hard lesson; the father who had been jailed for ABH because of his violence against Peter as a child was incapable of giving him the love and support he was searching for.

The local newspaper made a sensational reporting of these items and Peter went from court to court. Finally, he was given a sentence of twenty-one months, which would have been fourteen years had he been older. He was at the time a minor, an important fact which enabled the grace of God, rather than the justice of the courts, to be meted out. It was not an easy time for us as parents, nor for the family. Peter served ten and a half months at a number of youth detention centres, until he was ultimately discharged from Rugby. During this period we learned what it was like to be a family enduring the traumas of a relative in custody.

In a funny way his sentence relieved us of much pressure as a family, but it did mean that at regular intervals we were up and down the motorway visiting him. This experience taught us that families too are victims of the crimes of their relatives and that this kind of commitment involved suffering embarrassment at some institutions, which is hard to bear. With the help of our friends and family and the support of the church we were able to come through this whole experience blessed and joyful, a miracle in itself. These experiences were difficult for all of us but we were encouraged by a word from Isaiah 61:7: "Instead of your shame you will have a double portion, and instead of humiliation they will shout for joy over their portion.

Therefore, they will possess a double portion in their land. Everlasting joy will be theirs" (NASB).

Peter's detention meant that he was not available for our next trip to Canada for the wedding of our niece, Nicki, to Enoch, a young doctor with the surname Daniel – which meant that the majority of guests had almost identical names. This wedding was held in March 1999 and again proved a memorable experience. Duncan was asked to be MC at the reception, a position that he fulfilled admirably. It was an ideal time to reacquaint ourselves with John and Margaret's friends from Lewisporte. After the wedding the young people were able to get in some skiing at Newfoundland's Marble Mountain Resort. It was the week after the All Canada Games – the runs were ideal, the visitors minimal, the queues negligible and they had such a good time. We returned home via Toronto and made sure we called in at the Airport Christian Fellowship, to get a flavour first hand of what was happening in this expanding church.

Our journey home was remarkable in that on the TV it had been forecast that the weather was closing in and snowstorms were brewing. Organising the whole family to respond positively to such reports was not an easy matter. Margaret and John, from their experience of the North American weather patterns, suggested we pack and leave immediately. This we attempted to do and with hasty farewells set off on the journey to St John's for an overnight stay and an early morning flight departure. Along the Trans-Canada Highway we drove before the storm until the halfway stop at Clarendon. There the snow had already fallen and we arrived before the snow ploughs. After refreshments and toilets on we sped out of the snow belt, heading south-east to St John's.

Slowly the snow changed to heavy rain – fortunately we had missed the worst of the storm – but the deluge continued until the rain fell like stair rods in the capital. This was our opportunity to call on Chrissy and her fiancé Deon. Before we left, rivers of water flowed unceasingly down the hills of the city. Eventually, we reached the hotel and were off to bed ready for an early start to the airport. We had run before the storm and managed to miss most of it. The weather reports that morning showed the extent of what we had managed to avoid. Little did we realise then that in another sense we were running before a storm, the like of which we had never previously experienced

CHAPTER TWENTY THREE

INTO REVERSE

For several years Ann and I had taken advantage of her brother John's touring caravan, which he and June regularly parked on a farm close to St Mawes in Cornwall. Near to the sea, with only a few other caravans, it was an ideal spot from which to explore the Cornish countryside. Each year we visited we made a point of setting out to walk the coastal footpath, mainly to the south of the county, but also to the north if the weather was less adverse on that side. We managed to squeeze in a break in the July of 1999. The weather was good and we mapped the outstanding areas of the coastal path around Fowey and St Austell, which we had yet to complete. Areas of the footpath were more rugged than normal and Ann had difficulty in climbing up the hills. Although she never gave in she was struggling. We decided that on our return she would visit our GP to have a check up.

Our return coincided with the school holiday period and although an appointment with the doctor was no problem, the referral to a consultant was much more hit and miss. Ann had noticed too that some of her glands were prominent and deduced that it was obviously some sort of infection. Our GP decided she should go to Doncaster Royal Infirmary for a biopsy.

I dropped her off at the day ward early in the morning and was told to collect her later at lunch time. When I returned to the makeshift ward (the proper day ward was undergoing alterations at the time), Ann was still asleep. She was obviously taking longer than expected to come round from the anaesthetic. I went for a coffee to make myself scarce and came back half an hour later, by which time the staff had given her something to wake her up. Slowly she explained what had happened. One of the glands underneath her arm had been removed – what we had thought to be a minor problem was proving bigger than we had expected. I remember saying, "Wow! Do they think you have leukaemia?" By 29 July she had also had a bone marrow test. We were to wait a few weeks before the results were made known.

It seemed that everything was as normal as possible, except for waiting for the test results, and we both threw ourselves into work and home and church. I made final preparations for my imminent visit to Romania. We decided I should proceed to Romania and Ann would keep me informed of the results. She had her appointment at the hospital on the following Thursday and what we expected to be a normal consultation turned out to be quite the reverse.

It was some time later on the evening of 13 August that Ann telephoned me at the church's base at Sanpetru – fifteen hundred miles away. I had been there only a few days. We had discussed whether I should in fact make the pre-planned visit and we decided naïvely that, since it appeared to us both that all was well, my support at home was unnecessary. In a matter-of-fact rather than an emotional way – typical of Ann (nurse training coming out) – she recounted the details of her hospital visit to me, by now much more aware of the implications of the diagnosis. The situation was much bigger than I had expected and immediately I said that I would return home. Since Romanian time was two hours in advance of British Summer Time I could do very little there and then. It was well past office hours so we prayed together over the telephone. I reassured Ann of my love and my intent to be on the next possible aeroplane home. We would not know when that would be for a further ten hours or so but we would keep in close telephone contact.

I replaced the receiver and returned to the group of dedicated volunteers relaxing after the demands of another day's placement in the orphanages and hospitals of Braşov. In a lull in the conversation I shared the details of the telephone call. It came as a bombshell to them all, even though several were experienced professionals, since each of them knew Ann, having met her at one of the charity's induction days. Silence descended as shock set in. What do you say at a time like this? I made it clear that first thing in the morning I would attempt to book a seat and return home as soon as possible.

Meanwhile Ann was dealing with her own emotions and shared with the children the outcome of the visit, not in a sense of panic, but with calm assurance that this new phase of life would be like those before, one of trusting Father God who we knew was working all things together for good.

My attempts to obtain a return flight were, however, not without problems because this was the week of the total eclipse in Europe, with Romania being the prime viewing spot. Newspaper reports in Britain, even before the trip, pointed out that flights were busy and expensive both to and from Romania (one carrier increasing prices by three times, solely for eclipse-watchers around 11 August). Information like this tends not to aid faith, but to increase anxiety. I resisted the temptation to be anxious and next morning picked up the telephone to enquire on the availability of seats. The KLM offices were closed until 9.00 am so I tried the office of Romanian Airlines (TAROM) – three spare seats were available on the evening flight to Heathrow. Encouraged, I decided to reserve one of these and pay at the airport on arrival at Bucharest.

The weather that morning, uncharacteristically for the time of year, was heavy rain. The thought entered my head, "What about floods or landslides? You might have problems getting home!" Speculation, however realistic, can be yet another stumbling block to faith so I dismissed this notion. At this short notice our normal driver was not available for the transfer journey to Bucharest so another friend, Apolo, living at the base and already busy in one of the villages, was volunteered (and later informed by his wife, by mobile telephone, of my need). He was not planning to be back until about 11.00 am and with true Romanian timing he arrived just before 1.00 pm. Cutting it fine, but still possible!

Farewells can be interminably long and, eventually, I managed to get another volunteer (who was already booked on the same flight home), along with Viorica, our friend and cleaner at Sanpetru, into Apolo's car, and off we went with oodles of waves, tears and well-wishing.

Viorica enthusiastically shared the disturbing news of radio reports on landslides affecting the train network, which were making delays of up to four hours! Yet another opportunity to worry, but again I resisted it! Apolo drove his automatic VW Golf extremely carefully through town; we dropped Viorica off near her home, and left Brașov. Time was ticking away quicker than I wanted and the rain was still falling.

As we were travelling south, we had to negotiate the beautiful Carpathian Mountains, there being no reasonable or quicker way round. Very soon we were overtaking and being overtaken by vehicles on the hairpin bends (nothing new, this was par for the course). We were making good time; that is, until the whole line of traffic came to a halt still only halfway through the mountain section. The rain was pouring and the roadside gutters were full. Stationary, we were going nowhere so the engine was switched off. What could the problem be? – in those damp conditions people were not getting out of their cars to find out. A number of frustrated drivers eventually began turning their vehicles around and retracing their journeys. Time was continuing to race! It was 4.30 pm and we had done less than a quarter of the journey; the flight was due to leave Bucharest Otopeni Airport at 6.50 pm and we ought to be there by 5.00 pm or thereabouts, but we had at least another two more hours to drive! It's at times like this that your mind starts to tell you it's impossible and that you can also expect to pay for the ticket for the plane you won't now catch and the same again for the plane tomorrow you will need to catch. All of course paid for by money you don't have and worst of all you will have to telephone Ann in disappointment – it was a good try but . . .

It may be one thing being strong and full of faith at Sanpetru, but now what? Apolo placed a cassette tape in the radio system and the music of the song based on Psalm

36:5–7 filled the car. The singers sang, "Your love, O Lord, it reaches to the heavens, Your faithfulness, it reaches to the skies; Your righteousness is like the mighty mountains . . . how priceless is Your faithful love." My spirit soared . . . thank you Lord, You can do it, You're great; and I worshipped Him and praised Him for His great love, even to the skies. I remember saying, "I've waited so many times for TAROM flights in the past, now can they wait for me?" This was the turning point; I must trust.

Outside it continued raining; and then the spiritual breakthrough was followed by the material one. I do believe in angels, those biblical messengers from God, and in this instance they appeared in the form of four police cars with blue flashing lights! From nowhere, it seemed, driving in a convoy the vehicles came past us down the centre of the road, speeding in our direction. As quickly as possible Apolo tucked in behind them and off we sped, past miles of other stationary traffic, slowing only to get round vehicles sticking proud of the main traffic flow. Lines of vehicles were solid in both directions and we travelled down the centre of the road, apparently under escort!

We came into the mountain town of Busteni, and were waved along by other traffic police through a fast flowing torrent crossing the road. Earth-moving equipment had already been brought in to remove trees and boulders to clear the way for all the other vehicles. We had been escorted through!

The police vehicles pulled over, but we carried on. Leaving Busteni and the mountains behind, we descended first to the foothills and then to the plains where it started to rain even harder. These conditions didn't stop Apolo who was able to drive along what was by then a wider road and we went for miles, hardly being able to see through the windscreen. Time was pressing too, and we still had many miles to go. Unbelievably another police car with flashing lights passed. Again Apolo tucked in its wake, clinging as close as possible through several towns at a good speed, even passing stationary police cars positioned on the road to prevent speeding! Eventually, just short of Bucharest, the rain stopped and we raced on to the airport, arriving at 6.30 pm, twenty minutes before scheduled take-off.

Passing quickly on to get our seats and to register, things seemed less stressful; then on through customs and down to the departure lounge. The flight had been delayed and actually left an hour after our arrival! Praise the Lord for answered prayer. I had expected a two-hour wait for a coach home from Heathrow; so waiting at Otopeni or Heathrow was six and two threes.

The flight seemed long but was uneventful, whilst at London the plane had to circle to find a landing slot because of its delayed arrival. All went well and, eventually, I made my way through the labyrinth of corridors, through immigration and off to collect my case. Fortunately it was the first case out, so I hurried on, making good time and heading for customs through the "nothing to declare" section. The ordeal, however, was not yet over – it was my turn to be stopped by customs officials, just doing their job! I was questioned, had my passport and charity papers taken, was questioned more, my case emptied and was given the full works. Why are you here? What were you doing in Romania? How often do you visit? Anything to declare? What is this? A barrage of questions, each asked at least twice. Psychological pressure, a lovely time-waster that found nothing! I kept thinking of the last coach of the

day to Sheffield that I intended to get at 10.20 pm – it was
now 10.10 pm and I still didn't have a ticket or seat and here
I was stuck in customs like a criminal. Eventually – and it
seemed ages – my things were all put back into the case and
was told I was free to go. I then had to ask for my passport,
which had to be fetched from the supervisor's office elsewhere in the building! "Thank you sir, just doing our job,"
said the officer, and the passport came back into my pos-
session.

Out of customs as fast as I could – was anyone waiting for
me? No, couldn't see anyone so off I ran to the central bus
station – finally making it just before 10.20 pm to find the
coach had also been delayed. Thanks, Lord! I rooted through
my pockets and managed to find one ten pence coin and
quickly telephoned Ann, who by this time was anticipating
that I had missed the connections. The coach arrived as I
replaced the handset.

Four hours later I reached Sheffield to be greeted by our
son Martin, arriving home half an hour later to hugs and
kisses – home to a lovely wife and the promise of a celebration for my birthday (the following day) with my family.
Home at last, tired from the physical, emotional and spiritual demands of one adventure . . . home to the physical,
emotional and spiritual demands of another which was to
last much longer. Another adventure in the long list of
those we had come through since our meeting at the age of
fourteen.

Although the journey had started as a personal one it was
not a private one. In view of my departure from Sanpetru
and our involvement in so many lives, we were to receive
letters, cards and telephone calls of encouragement from
many sources. One such was from one of our senior volun-

teers, Thelma Wilford, who wrote, "I wanted you to know that my prayers are with you at this time and to send you the words of a Graham Kendrick song that have meant so much to me over the years."

For the joys and for the sorrows,
The best and worst of times,
For this moment and tomorrow,
For all that lies behind,
For this I have Jesus.

Fears that crowd around me,
For the failure of my plans,
For the dreams of all I hope to be,
The truth of what I am,
For this I have Jesus.

For the tears that flow in secret,
In the broken times,
For the moment of elation,
Or the troubled mind,
For this I have Jesus.

For the weakness of my body,
The burdens of each day,
For the nights of doubt and worry,
When sleep has fled away,
For this I have Jesus.

Needing reassurance,
And the will to start again,
The steely-eyed endurance,
The strength to fight and win,
For this I have Jesus.

Graham Kendrick
Copyright © 1994 Make Way Music

In spite of Ann's professional knowledge, she was not up to date with cancer diagnosis and its clinical care. Her diagnosis was unclear, so too was the prognosis and in a naïve but determined way we set out on this journey of discovery that was to touch our whole being – physical, spiritual, emotional and psychological. The storm was already brewing; we were now going before it.

CHAPTER TWENTY FOUR

DESTINATION AND DESTINY

By early September Ann had commenced her regular visits to the consultant haematologist. Our joint ignorance of the illness meant we would investigate as much as we could. I decided to take my filofax with me to all consultations, which were usually held every three to four weeks. This was obviously not the normal procedure for as I wrote down the essence of his observations and our conversations the consultant queried what I was doing. I duly put him at ease, for I found this method essential, even though I spelled things phonetically rather than correctly. My experience in visiting doctors, and that was not very often, was that I usually forgot what was said as I was overawed by the consultation. Since this was a matter of life and death and neither of us knew much about the technical areas, these notes would help us negotiate the possibilities and problems. Gradually we were all at ease and we built up a credible patient/doctor relationship with both him and the many housemen who assisted him through the periods of our visit.

Early September was also the time at which we commenced a bulletin kept at the office, so that those who were praying, or those who were interested, could be kept up to date with Ann's progress. It also meant that we did not receive constant telephone calls.

Very quickly we were trained into the Bassetlaw Hospital procedure: register at reception; book in for a blood sample (having taken a numbered card and having waited further until the number was called out); give the sample (immediately dispatch to the laboratories); then relax, have a drink and return in forty minutes or so and then wait. This waiting could go on for another hour; somehow appointment times were rarely adhered to. During this time Ann was weighed and her weight recorded at each visit. We met the same patients, all going through similar personal agonies; we struck up conversations with fellow sufferers.

The hospital visits were every three or four weeks – except for leave and bank holiday periods. Initially, the consultant compared current haematology readings with previous ones, explaining their significance. He did this by means of a computer – and at each visit I would record the salient facts for later perusal and enquiry. Very early he asked if we had any holidays planned; if so, we should go ahead and take them.

Irrespective of all we were going through emotionally we still had duties to perform, work to do, a life to live and, with a mixture of naïvety and trust, we went about our "normal" lives. The hint about holidays should have been a clue. On one occasion the consultant confidently shared a statistic on recovery from cancer, namely that fifty per cent of patients survive eight years after diagnosis, but each patient is unique and predictions are difficult. I was quick to realise that fifty per cent did not! Ann in her exuberance had initially made the statement "People ask me, can I live with cancer? I reply, can cancer live with me?" Much later she felt this was an arrogant, brash comment. I personally felt, however, that it was typical of her life. Problems would not faze her; she would trust God for the outcome. We were entering uncharted waters as far as we were concerned, a journey over which we had little control. It inevitably drew us nearer to God; desperate people do pray more! Such was the enormity of the situation that "nothing is impossible to God" took on deeper meaning.

At the diagnosis of the disease I asked Ann to keep a journal of her journey through the illness – a journey of how she personally dealt with the ups and downs of treatment. One of her entries read, "Can't look after mum, what a blow! She has to stay at John's. Somehow I must tell her but how, Lord, can I explain? She is so confused, have I let her down?" During this period and with some reluctance from Ann, I managed periodically to take some photographs of her, for which I am very grateful. These later gave me a record of the ravages of the disease and Ann's resolve through it all. Ann was obviously conscious of her appearance being less than normal.

By the end of September it was confirmed that the disease was at stage four, not an early stage as previously thought. A recent chest X-ray indicated an enlarged lymph gland in her chest – which meant she was also to have a CT scan. On asking about the possibility of a bone marrow transplant we were advised that these had not proven successful; we were highly unlikely to get a match and in any case the treatment was not usually given to patients over forty years old. (Later Ann's brother John, averse to hospitals and things medical, even volunteered to give bone marrow – if he matched – but his age of sixty-one was against him.)

A further appointment was made for late October and in the meantime a Macmillan nurse would be contacted to discuss any queries. Ann found these discussions particularly helpful and learned facts that were not down in print. This next appointment, however, indicated that chemotherapy tablets were needed, for immediate use. Ann took these for the first time a week later.

With the encouragement of Ann and the support of the family I again visited Romania at the October half-term so that Peter Hardy and other teachers who would like to visit could be available. We had arranged the official opening of the renovations, especially of the two units of accommodation that we were going to use for residential respite care. Because so many of our staff – Ann, Anne Hemsall, Anne Backhouse and faithful volunteers Anne Lemm and Anne Walker – had similar names, I felt it right to honour them all by naming one chalet after them. Since Ann(e) was derived from a root meaning "grace" we named chalet two Har ("grace" in Romanian), whilst chalet one was named Bucurie ("joy", to mark Joy Winks' contribution over the years. We invited the Mayor of the village, doctors, nurses, teachers, families, users and all we knew. Pete sang yet another of his Romania-inspired songs and Rodica Costuic translated for us. Eventually, after a speech from both the Mayor and myself, we cut the ribbon (blue, yellow and red, the colours of the Romanian flag) and declared the premises open.

Inevitably this was a time of commemoration as well as one of celebrations. We thought of all those people who had made this day possible, our supporters in prayer and finance. We remembered the hundreds of volunteers who had given time, skill and energy to see a vision realised. We were grateful for the encouragement of the church and the welcome of the Romanian people. Together these made up a vast crowd of ordinary, unnamed individuals and organisations, but to us a host of people who were pleased to recognise our success. Naturally, we had a celebration afterwards, with organised tours and a book for comments from our visitors. Many of these were poignant and heartfelt, such as the one written by Catalin, one of our users with special needs, and his mother: "Good people, thank you for your big hearts. Thank you for thinking of us and creating a world in which we feel human too – a world in which we feel well." The local newspapers and TV had a field day too – plenty of copy, pictures and coverage. Our new facilities were described in their non-PC language as an "ultra-modern centre for handicapped children".

On completion of this emotional time, full of thankfulness for what God had achieved through us, rejoicing along with our Romanian friends, tearful that Ann was not there to enjoy the events, we prepared to return home eager to share the details of the opening, but more eager to be with Ann. She had missed this milestone – a realisation of a vision that she had initiated and worked for as unto the Lord.

Whilst I was away Ann took advantage of a weekend break and, along with our daughter and granddaughters Jessica and Rebekah, spent a "girly" weekend at Buxton in the luxury of a four-star hotel. They had a wonderful time, but not without Ann having problems with the effects of her tablets, but of course she hardly mentioned the discomfort.

Initially Ann had chemotherapy tablets to see if these had any effect and, gradually, doses were increased. As time passed she became more and more tired and prone to infection, until by the end of the year she was forced to take time off from work and stay at home. Her priority was her health, but all through the year from time to time she visited the office, though she preferred to respond to questions via the telephone. Her presence and drive were obviously missed and it was ultimately decided that she would work up to the end of 2000 and then the scheme would appoint a new co-ordinator.

In February we decided to visit Chicago for a few days and we actually were able to fit this in in April between hospital visits. It was a special time for us both, visiting Wheaton College, the bookshop and the Billy Graham Museum. Ann was thrilled to see the details of the Wembley Crusade plus all the other exhibits. We greatly enjoyed swimming in the hotel pool, which we did as often as possible and also fitted in a visit to Willow Creek Church. We walked as much as we could along the waterfront of the lakeside. The weather was kind to us and we enjoyed our freedom, which so soon was over, but not before we had seen the overhead railway and been to the top of the Sears Building and seen Chicago from above.

We had also promised ourselves to visit the Moody Memorial Church and the Moody Bible College situated also in Chicago, both established in the city as a direct result of the ministry of Dwight Lyman Moody, who along with Ira Sankey was famous for his gospel ministry in Victorian England as well as in the States. It was at the College Museum that Ann's eyes lit upon one of Moody's quotations:

Some day you will read in the papers that D. L. Moody of East Northfield is dead. Don't you believe a word of it. At that moment

I shall be more alive than I am now. I shall have gone up higher, that is all, out of this clay tenement into a house that is immortal, a body that death cannot touch, that sin cannot taint, a body fashioned like unto His glorious body. I was born of the flesh in 1837. I was born of the Spirit in 1856. That which is born of the flesh may die. That which is born of the Spirit will live for ever.

These were her sentiments too and I was to use this quotation on her behalf just a few months later. At last Ann was able to see the very things she had given up three years before when Duncan had taken her place.

In late April we were also able to take a three-day trip to Amsterdam by coach. It was dry and cool but we enjoyed it tremendously. Amsterdam is a small city, so we walked around the centre, seeing most places of interest: the flower market, museums, a ride on a boat through the canals and, of course, the Anne Frank home. What a marvellous time together on our own.

Easter time was marvellous for another reason. We took a family holiday together – all of us, something we had never really done before. Devon was the destination and although it was a little damp we enjoyed ourselves. We took three residential caravans adjacent to one another, which gave us room and space to be alone when needed. We had decided to take the break, conscious that we might not be able to do it again – and how right the decision proved to be. One of the outstanding memories was our visit to Woolacombe Beach, so near to Mortehoe, where we first became an item forty-one years before. Ann decided, along with the young children, to go swimming. Both the air and water temperatures were cold – but she did it and we all covered her up as she came out of the water, so she didn't die of hypothermia!

Another first experience for us was in May. Our niece Chrissy from Newfoundland visited us on her way to Aberdeen for a job placement with a petroleum firm as part of her university course. She came with three of the largest bags and suitcases you ever saw. They were also the heaviest. Her visit was soon over and it was our pleasure to take her to Doncaster station to catch the train to Aberdeen. After waiting some time it eventually arrived, but work on the tracks meant it was way up the platform and so, since Chrissy's reserved seat was in carriage one, we had quite a hike with her massive baggage. Eventually we managed it, put Chrissy and her bags on to the train and succeeded in finding luggage space. To our shock, with us still on board, the train doors closed and without my spectacles I couldn't read how to open the door. Miming to the porters, we were told to stay on board until the train reached York. Well, we were laughing at being caught this way and so too were the other passengers. Twenty minutes later we alighted at York station, waving goodbye to Chrissy. Since the train to Doncaster was due in thirty minutes we had a coffee and as I sat drinking I saw a notice on the platform, which read "Don't get taken for a ride". We did get a train back and the ticket inspector was sympathetic – apparently it happens frequently, but for us it was a first!

We enquired about the disease from friends and via the local Lymphoma Society in Sheffield, which we visited, but treatment cycles and Ann's health meant very few further visits resulted. As time progressed Ann's condition also became more obvious. The effect of the lymphoma was visible enlargement of her glands and for Ann this involved those in her neck especially. From time to time, following treatment, they would reduce, but always seemed to return enlarged. It was obvious that the small doses and oral treatment were not proving effective.

Ann's intravenous chemotherapy treatment first commenced in August at Doncaster, about a year after her first visit. It was the summer holiday season so again no designated consultant was available. Ann was also given stronger painkillers plus permission to visit the hospital when necessary, which was just as well since the pain level increased owing to a chest infection. We had to make another emergency journey to the hospital over the bank holiday, when Ann was kept in and treated intravenously with antibiotics and a saline drip. On being discharged she was directed to go to Bassetlaw Hospital on 4 September prior to intravenous chemotherapy the day after.

This visit revealed what was to be a regular report and the blood results indicated that her neutrophils and platelet levels were inadequate and so she was given additional injections. The following day she was also given blood and her chemotherapy was delayed for a further week. After that she was told that general human contact was possible for seven days but was then to be limited for the following two weeks. Then the cycle commenced again.

The next major change was the insertion of a Hickman line so as to enable several injections to be made at the same time straight into the bloodstream. The insertion was to be done by an anaesthetist who explained the procedure. A small tube was to be placed straight into the heart! With the aid of a monitor he made the first attempt without success and then, not having read her notes, asked whether she had lymphoma! He tried again and Ann was able to work the monitor and see what was happening. She said that she never prayed so hard for success, and successful it was. The operation, however, was painful, Ann said later. She never usually revealed such normal reactions; therefore, we concluded, it really must have been painful.

It took about three weeks for the insertion site to heal – but the device was a great help medically. It did, however, always come between us from then on, for the last thing we wanted was to make it come out. Bathing was quite comical since we had to secure it in a plastic bag to prevent water entering; we were pleased that neither of us was squeamish.

From time to time the drugs were changed, but the swellings remained. Platinum chemotherapy (the most powerful) was now under consideration and was actually given a week or so later at Doncaster. Alongside this, Ann received further blood to boost her haemoglobin count. Her blood group was B-positive. We always laughed at this since it was so appropriate, whereas mine was O-negative – again said to be appropriate by some!

Ann suffered little nausea but slight hair loss had commenced. Eventually she decided to have her hair shaved off and to wear a wig. She had been advised that it would eventually grow stronger that way. Her platelet readings registered nine, whereas they should have been about fifty and it was decided that she should have steroids for a week. The consultant said to Ann, "We need a miracle – and that's your department." Her glands enlarged again and started pressing on her veins, and hospital was the place to be in case of bleeding.

In the midst of all this to-ing and fro-ing we had a small respite – 1 November was Peter's birthday and he had now come out of prison and settled in Mansfield, away from his Worksop contacts. We decided we would visit him and his girl friend Claire and take them out for a meal. Before that we decided to travel into Derbyshire and we visited Lady Bower reservoir. It was a lovely afternoon, just the two of us. Though we didn't realise its, it was to be our last trip, but we took it all in and enjoyed every minute. From there we went to Mansfield and celebrated Peter's birthday.

That same weekend was the Poplars Ladies' Day at Carlton. In view of her illness Ann had cancelled all her speaking engagements, except this one, which she knew she would be able to do. So Saturday morning she spoke for over an hour (most remarkable in view of her condition) and it proved to be her swan song, a review of the goodness of God and an encouragement for those present to press on. Her theme was "The Treasures of Darkness", taken from Isaiah 45:3a.

The fifth of November was our daughter Liz's birthday and we went out for a meal together. The following day Ann went into hospital for a further course of platinum chemotherapy. Again, her platelet, haemoglobin and neutrophil counts were low and alongside this her temperature was high and there was a risk of pneumonia. Barrier nursing was recommended, but fortunately she had a private room. After treatment the situation seemed to improve, but then crisis days arose, with a rapid heartbeat creating the possibility of clots on her lungs, plus water retention. Through it all she showed continuous medical interest.

Ann's illness gave her time that she had never previously enjoyed and apart from reading and praying – obviously only possible when treatment allowed – she took the opportunity to write to those who were on her mind. She also took the opportunity to share her experiences and faith, especially with the staff with whom she had by now developed a good relationship. She sought to put other patients at ease, including many who were fearful of both the treatment and the future. However, when isolation and barrier nursing became necessary Ann could no longer attend day care clinics and the number of visitors she could receive, apart from the family, was restricted. Those who dared to brave the embargo merely put their heads round the door, smiled and expressed their love before departing.

By the morning of Friday 10 November the chemotherapy was completed and since there were no apparent problems Ann was discharged from hospital that afternoon. In spite of her being physically exhausted, coming home was a tonic, providing a familiar and comforting environment bigger and more personal than the private hospital room. Again, for immunity reasons, general access was restricted but inevitably the church expressed the warmth of their love and concern by telephone calls, prayers and cards.

After a five-day respite it was time to return to the hospital for further platelets. X-rays, however, showed patches on Ann's lungs, which necessitated antibiotics and careful medical attention. Within a further ten days Ann started to feel better, though she had to be given oxygen through a mask, and could begin to read and write once again. She now seemed to be permanently connected to saline, anti-biotic and blood drips.

On one of our previous visits, about a year earlier, to the church that Jo and Russ attended in Leeds, Bobby Ball had given his testimony. Not only was this amusing (a gross understatement), it was so real and communicated the love of God to everyone. Ann's immediate desire was to invite Bobby to Worksop. This she did after the meeting; again, in no way fazed by his popularity. She asked whether he would be happy to share in one of our local working men's clubs.

Bobby graciously agreed and after months of preparation the event took place on Saturday 25 November at the Whitwell Middle Club. Although Ann could not be there in person it was uppermost in her thoughts and prayers – yet another one of her inspirational initiatives.

Locals were a little apprehensive of attending the event, thinking that we were to field a look-alike – why on earth would star Bobby Ball come to obscure Whitwell? They did, however, with persuasion, fill the music room to capacity. Bobby was surprisingly nervous – admitting that this was his first return to a working men's club for nearly twenty years. He had learned his craft in such establishments prior to his conversion to Jesus years before. Within seconds of hitting the stage he had everyone eating out of his hand. Needless to say several individuals responded to his prayers at the end of the meeting. Ann was obviously thrilled to hear of the outcome.

Basing our observations on previous experiences, although it was obvious that Ann was weaker in her body, we expected that she would soon emerge from the ominous decline in her blood constituents. But the signs were not good and she was not appearing to overcome the effects of the chemotherapy. In fact she seemed to be slipping into a permanent sleeping state. The medical staff assured me that it was a matter of getting the correct balance of painkillers – a process they were constantly monitoring. By Wednesday 29 November I had asked if anything could be done since all I seemed to be doing on my visits was to watch her sleep. Since the consultant's round was scheduled for the following day I was invited to attend and ask my questions.

It was, therefore, an unexpected and pleasant surprise to enter Ann's room on the Thursday to see her sitting up in bed, fully alert and radiant. All questions somehow evaporated and the consultant's visit was "normal". What a thrill to talk and hold hands, to communicate and share one another.

Unbeknown to us, this was the high point, for little by little (since she was still under the delicate balancing of medication) Ann's vitality began to decrease, but not before I managed to have a private chat with the consultant. A lovely, gentle professional, she explained the gravity of the situation, but was unable to say with certainty whether Ann's demise would be in weeks or months – who was to know? I thanked her for her understanding help and asked whether I should notify the family, especially Kate and Duncan in Canada, bearing in mind the difficulty of obtaining plane tickets in the approach to the Christmas season. How long is a piece of string? She could not be any more precise.

It was good to be together, attempt a crossword and listen to extracts from books and all the personal trivia of family and home. Ann had particularly made a point of writing to those who she knew needed encouragement – it was my job to add stamps and post the mail.

On Tuesday 5 December we spent what was to be our last evening together and, as I left about 8.30 pm, in walked our son Martin who, on his return, informed me that the staff had agreed further steroid treatment. I was thrilled at this since, during the last course of platinum treatment, it was the introduction of steroids that had raised Ann's blood levels and resulted in her recovery. It all sounded hopeful. However, I was told later that they had done further tests for the laboratory – but the consultant's own rule-of-thumb analysis showed that the red blood cells were few and far between – it seemed that her very life blood was ebbing away.

The following morning Ann woke at 8.00 am for breakfast, laughing and joking as normal with the staff. However, she soon declined and by 10.30 I had the call to go quickly to the hospital. Aware of its tone and implication I managed to telephone the family and made contact with Liz, Martin and Jenny, and Jo and Russ in Leeds – a miracle in itself. The day before, John and Margaret had arrived at our home from Canada. They did not respond to my telephone call. I could not contact Kate, Duncan or Peter.

I left the office and made the hospital by 11.15; within minutes Liz arrived and then the rest of the family, including John and Margaret. Already Ann had been given morphine and was semi-conscious. We held hands and I spoke to her. There was a little response but gradually the drug took over. We excused ourselves when the consultant came and we chatted, and raised again the question of whether we should have notified Kate earlier. We were called back into the room, at which point Ann passed into eternity and a trickle of blood emerged from her mouth. None of us had been in denial that this would happen – we just did not expect it. I suppose God was insulating us from contemplating it.

I had several times been present when friends had died; it was, however, the first time we all had been present at the death of a family member – the first in our family for thirty years. And this was no distant family member – this was Ann. What do you do in circumstances like this? We did what we knew – turned to Father. We celebrated a life, the like of which none of us had ever known; we thanked Him, each one of us, for what she was to us and we rejoiced that pain no more had control and that her hope of glory had now been realised. We stood, watched and thought and tears trickled down our faces. We didn't know why this had happened; we didn't know why she hadn't been healed in this life, but we knew we could trust the One who does all things well.

We retired into the almost adjacent family room for a time of quiet and were waited on by a nurse with a cuppa, but not before I had telephoned the church office on my mobile telephone to ask Derek to let the church know. It was 1.40 pm, Wednesday 6 December 2000. By the time we returned home the news had been shared with as many as possible.

The news itself and the suddenness of the events of the day were a shock to everyone, especially to those who were recipients of Ann's letters of the previous few days. It now became my duty to inform our parents and relatives, Ann's family, our friends and, of course, Peter, Kate and Duncan.

We chatted together and decided to arrange the funeral for 13 December to allow Kate and Duncan to at least try for plane tickets. In spite of the seasonal demands they were able to do this and we sensed God's presence even in the details.

So too in the arrangements for the funeral. Ann's favourite hymns came to mind and I asked Pete to sing Jim Cowan's song, as sung by Robin Mark on the *Revival in Belfast* album, "When all is said and done". Ann had listened to the tape whilst in hospital and suggested that Pete should sing it (not specifically for her funeral, but I wondered later whether that was what she meant). Peter Fenwick rang me on another matter and was more than happy to give the address. I wrote a thumbnail sketch of Ann's life for the funeral order of service, and this inevitably included D. L. Moody's words concerning his own demise.

As the funeral service came together so did my own feelings about the question of burial or cremation. I was aware that Scripture speaks only of burial, but Ann had always asked for cremation whenever the topic occurred. I prayed about my personal dilemma and God granted me the revelation that gave me peace. I felt that God said it was the resurrection of the body that constituted the miracle, not the elements of which it was composed. I was at ease to proceed. I wanted to make the funeral a time of thanksgiving and celebration for Ann's life, to involve everyone and be as practical as possible, especially for those who had travelled some distance. I discussed with the family my desire to avoid any of the theatrical touches that I had seen at so many funeral services. They all agreed to my wishes.

We met at the service and took our places. During the singing of the first hymn the coffin was brought in. Some four hundred people were present, a fantastic turnout for a working day, with seven church leaders from every denomination in the congregation; there was standing room only as all around the building people crowded in. After that, Derek and Pete led the service, with Martin and Duncan praying, Pete singing and Peter Fenwick speaking. As we stood and listened to the recording of "Holy, holy, holy" played by trumpeter Phil Driscoll, the coffin was taken out to cremation at Mansfield, whilst we as a family spent time with our guests and had refreshments to follow. The family had a private committal service at the church yard in Carlton-in-Lindrick the following day, led by Derek; Pete was involved in school activities, but he just happened to be at a carol service practice at the church building as we finished.

The next few days we talked and talked as a family and had a precious time together until Kate and Duncan returned to their new home (which they had only occupied in September) and their girls, to explain about Granny. Tributes flooded in from around the country as well as from abroad and £2,500 was collected for the Poplars work in Romania and the Worksop Live at Home Scheme. The local newspaper had already adopted the Live at Home Scheme as its charity for 2001 and subsequently Ann's name and achievements were trumpeted in the press.

Christmas and the New Year were precious family times, but it was different, as was the whole new experience. We coped magnificently, even joyfully, but the fun generator was no longer with us. I felt I was beginning to know how the disciples of Jesus felt between Calvary and Pentecost. Somehow, as the days passed into weeks and months, I began to appreciate more than ever the meaning of the words "intimacy" and "presence" . . . God was showing me in the reality of my life what these things meant. I'm still learning, but what an excellent teacher! On the matter of Ann's early death and the question, "Why this waste?" I recall Jesus' response to the same question at his anointing at Bethany (Mark 14:3–9, NASB). Verses 6–9 are especially meaningful: "She has done a good deed to Me . . . She has done what she could . . . that also which this woman has done shall be spoken of in memory of her." Ann was able to break the treasured perfume of her life for her Lord. No longer do I feel it's important to know why – I sense that when I see Him I'll be taken up in His glory too much to want to have my current questions answered.

EPILOGUE

For Ann the journey is over, the achievements of the past are behind; so too the tears and the pain, the mourning and death. The words of *Pilgrim's Progress* come to mind – the testimony of all fellow pilgrims:

I see myself now at the end of my journey, my toilsome days are ended. I am going now to see that head that was crowned with thorns, and that face that was spit upon for me.

I have formerly lived by hearsay and faith but now I go where I shall live by sight, and shall be with him in whose company I delight myself.

I have loved to hear my Lord spoken of; and wherever I have seen the print of his shoe in the earth, there I have coveted to set my foot to.

His name to me has been as a civet-box; yea, sweeter than all perfumes. His voice to me has been most sweet; and his countenance I have more desired than they that have most desired the light of the sun. His word I did use to gather for my food and for antidotes against my faintings. He has held me, and hath kept me from mine iniquities; yea, my steps hath he strengthened in his way.

It took some time for the church to come to terms with Ann's death and their individual loss and grief. I believe we're mostly through it now, although grief emerges, from time to time, when we're not expecting it. There have been many situations since her death in which we would have loved to have had Ann's vision, spirituality, professional expertise and wisdom – but this has thrown us all on God – sufficient to say that new ministries are emerging. Not surprisingly, they are being seen in the lives of individuals into whom she poured her life – mentoring in reality – the kind of legacy she sought.

Ann's death too has opened up many opportunities for me to minister; when I take meetings or funerals I no longer do so in a merely professional capacity, but am able to come alongside others who grieve too. I have been able to share my experiences, empathise and assist as a fellow traveller along the journey of life, which not only includes pain and grief, but also love, joy and peace. This was not a ministry I chose, but one given to me . . . I feel I can now say, "I know something of how you feel, how can I help?" It's the comfort that Paul speaks of in 2 Corinthians 1:3–4: "Blessed be the God and Father of our Lord Jesus Christ, the Father of mercies and God of all comfort, who comforts us in all our affliction so that we may be able to comfort those who are in any affliction with the comfort with which we ourselves are comforted by God" (NASB).

In another way, oddly, nothing has changed. Yes, I miss Ann tremendously, my soul-mate and friend for most of my life, but God does not change and that commitment I made so many years ago to my Saviour in response to His love for me still holds good. I am very blessed in every way and par-ticularly blessed to have shared my life with one whose sole ambition was to live for God and seek first His kingdom. I suppose it's all summarised in the three words I placed on her memorial, "ALL FOR JESUS". I wonder, is that your ambition too? It can be – indeed, I would love you to be able to say "yes".

DO YOU WANT TO KNOW MORE?

If you are wondering how you can know the heart-warming experience of Jesus sharing your journey through life, please contact Poplars Church at 46, Watson Road, Worksop, Nottinghamshire S80 2BQ England; on e-mail at admin@ poplarschurch.co.uk; or telephone 01909 530171.

Our trained personnel will be happy to assist you in your search for truth.

ANN'S JOURNAL EXTRACTS

20 September '99

A great time at Rhodesia on Faith . . . I felt a real freedom to speak and how it did my soul good . . . Faith comes by hearing and hearing from the word of God. How true this is. I am so blessed by reading Smith Wigglesworth's book *Ever Increasing Faith*. Lord, I want to see the glory of God come down. I am going to plead and keep knocking until I see it – how I am getting hungry and thirsty to see it. Lord, keep the appetite going.

21 September '99

I have felt a spirit of death on my life. Feelings during the summer that this would be my last with Norman – lying awake fighting off gloomy thoughts of death despite my spirit being full of faith . . . Derek, Pete, Norman, Kenny, Bob and Jude [all Poplars Trust Committee members] prayed for me.

24 September '99

Consultant again ... not good. All my tiredness and symptoms of "flu" due to the body fighting the disease. Suspect treatment sooner than later. Widespread disease, stage four – the advanced stage ... good gracious, time is precious.

How I love my Norman, he took it all so bravely yet I know and see the pain. I have no fear to die and recognise that my life is hidden with Him. I cannot die until I see the glory of God here – Lord please give me this desire. I want to see the kingdom of God.

My family is so precious.

25 September '99

Saw Peter today ... he looked much cleaner and very chatty – a little worried that he will be out on 24 December – he needs the right accommodation, Lord – give us direction. I remember Psalm 30:5 – weeping may last for the night but a shout of joy comes in the morning.

Lord, I am waiting for the morning to come when Peter is completely delivered and set free from himself, his past and he decides to give his life over to You.

26 September '99

Tearful in the night – dwelling too much on this body of mine – the swelling of the glands is painful. I am holding onto You, Lord, and know You are with me. Norman is a tower of strength but I know the news on Friday has knocked him.

27 September '99

The weekend has been particularly difficult – having to take captive thoughts, fears and apprehensions. Obviously concerned for Norman; we are so close – how will he be without me? Trust God, Ann. But a good week and back on track.

4 October '99

All should read *Ever Increasing Faith* by Smith Wigglesworth. I am so hungry for a new sphere of service on a new dimension of power and an outpouring of the Holy Spirit into my life. I want to repent of all the wasted time and years – I know they have been years of service, caring for others, taking on responsibilities for others and fulfilling the command of true religion in looking after the orphans and widows, but the time now is at hand to go on and seek for a greater measure of the Holy Spirit. Am I hungry? – Lord I repent – I want to be filled and I will seek You until I am and then I want to preach, both with Norman and on my own. You know, Lord, what I mean, I tarry Lord . . . I am expectant.

Nearly forgot abdominal ultrasound at Bassetlaw Hospital.

5 October '99

Spoke to Macmillan nurse and then contacted Weston Park Hospital (Sheffield), speaking to the clinical nurse responsible for lymphoma – very helpful and therefore went to support group CAMEO at night. Met Bill and Ann Peel – Ann has the same but stage two.

6 October '99

At Leeds, quiet day with Live at Home led by Father Simson
. . . Anxiety is imagining a place where Jesus isn't. Be like a
child, leave the tangled skein of worry in Father's lap.
Terribly tired at night.

8 October '99

Very tired – somehow feel poisoned.

9 October '99

A little better.

10 October '99

My body seems to become more and more exhausted.
Symptoms – extreme tiredness and a creeping poisoning effect. Wedding at Hemel (Ruth's and Robert's
son, David) and then saw Peter at Young Offenders'
Institute, plus Peter and Sandy Seeley at Lincoln. A
lovely weekend but have desperately battled against the
body. Considering going to Heart Cry conference at
Swanwick at the end of November . . . I want to go but my
body is weak.

12 October '99

Met at Derek's for dinner – shared about the cancer possibly
being a demon – take up the full armour (Eph 6:10–14).
Woke up early (4.45 am) due to tickly cough.

13 October '99

Heard today Norman and I have a free weekend offered for the Swanwick conference – praise God, we know it's right to go. A busy day but I feel on top of my body. Maggie Mirfin shared 2 Corinthians 1:8–11 and Ann Jackson, Mark 9:24–29.

Went to bed weary but very well in spirit.

22 October '99

Hospital appointment again. Consultant very rushed . . . saw his second-in-command – must pray for him. Ultrasound showed raised glands around the aorta plus enlarged spleen. Oral chemotherapy will start on Norman's return from Romania and delay it one week. Feel very well after taking mum away for a few days to Lincoln.

Very rested and actually felt normal since all the prayer.

23 October '99

Norman off to Romania – felt bloated and sick most of the day.

Faith for Dark Days by R. W. Emerson (given by Eddie and Janet Roper)

> When dark days come – and they come to us all –
> We feel so helpless and lost and small.
> We cannot fathom the reason why,
> And it is futile for us to try
> To find the answer, the reason or cause,

For the master plan is without any flaws,
And when the darkness shuts out the light,
We must lean on faith to restore our sight,
For there is nothing we need to know
If we have faith that wherever we go
God will be there to help us bear
Our disappointments, pain, and care,
For He is our Shepherd, our Father, our Guide,
And you're never alone with the Lord at your side.

Quote (R. W. Emerson): "All that I have seen teaches me to trust the Creator for all that I have not seen."

24 October '99

Woke up with enlarged glands in the back of the head – unwell. Made a decision to take the chemotherapy tablets in faith. Away to Buxton – felt sick and vomited only once – had a good rest and no real problems. Sleeplessness but otherwise well – praise God.

31 October – 3 November '99

Very tired, went to work but asleep in the evening; otherwise the lumps appear to be going down. I continue to believe God.

7 November '99

Visit to Northern Ireland for Uncle Ron's birthday with Norman and his Mum and Dad – a very good time, feeling much better and getting stronger and less tired.

19 November '99

Glands gone right down – this past ten days, I have felt really well and normal. Back to the hospital and expecting to be left until next year. However I have another two courses of chemotherapy – return in two weeks (whoops!). Blood levels dropped but platelets too low for the drugs to be given yet . . . X-rays of sinus mean I may need a post-nasal drip! To see ENT specialist and trust you Lord.

I feel really well.

27 November '99

Conference at Swanwick with Heart Cry. Beginning to feel the tenderness again – trusting and feeling at peace. Very concerned for Peter – we need the right abode for him. I am trusting, Lord, and feel worried but must hold on and have faith.

6 December '99

Derek, Pete and Norman – prayer about the anxiety re Peter . . . Every enquiry had brought a dead end. No safe house for him. I felt there was no hope. I had to will myself to know the word – my hope is in God. The burden was there fourteen days until tonight when the men spoke with authority and then I really knew God was in control of this.

10 December '99

Surprised that I needed another course of chemotherapy but the consultant was insistent – can have up to six sessions but it becomes more toxic – hopefully will get away with three. Very nauseated.

13 December '99

No news from probation . . . long way to go but we visited Peter at Rugby.

20 December '99

Sheila Soar informed Norman that prayers had been answered – Somerset had refused Peter but Bradford had accepted him. The treasure of hope has shone through at such a dark time. He was released on 24 December, brought up by Duncan and Norman and bedded in by Norman and myself. Very emotional time but praise God.

Father, I give You thanks, my health feels a hundred per cent.

31 December '99

Christmastime was a joy – meeting together and being together, Kate and Duncan here. Praise God, a real blessing. Liz with her servant heart.

1 January 2000

Writing in bed . . . chest infection . . . everything on hold, waited on by my hubby – Liz popping in and out, I have slept and slept.

As I dwell on the New Year and the century ahead my spirit has been fed by Ezekiel 37 – how exciting to discover that on the command of the Lord Ezekiel obeyed and prophesied and the bodies came together in the valley. He was told to try again to prophesy the breath into the bodies so that it came from the four winds.

It reminded me of Pete's prophecy from Song of Solomon chapter 4 verse 16: "Awake O north wind, blow south wind." The cold wind needs to be around to keep any premature buds from opening – how this can be painful. The south winds opens up the buds at the right time.

Perhaps we have had the north wind but not the south; perhaps we are here to speak to the four winds for the breath to come, the Holy Spirit, as we look to the risen Christ. I want to listen and know the time when He tells us, His people, to prophesy breath – the bodies are coming together but more is needed, Lord, in this next century.

Perhaps I could pray this for our leaders. O Lord, may a mighty wind embrace them all four! Let me quote from the diary of Lilly Trotter: " 'Awake O North Wind' has been the word in my heart these days – the North wind put back the buds that are wearing out prematurely – they are getting ready by the repression for a stronger life when the south wind blows."

Isn't that something!

5 January 2000

Back to GP, two weeks' note off work – what a surprise, I think I now have to submit and allow God to do His work of healing and restoring – at peace. Feeling very tired and got bronchitis so no wonder!

7 January 2000

Visit to consultant – blood levels really low, no more chemo until six months plus, but I'm susceptible to infection at the moment. Immunity low. Chest X-ray in two weeks if necessary.

12 January 2000

To see GP today. Norman and Pete yesterday prayed for the blood to be over our lintels, that the Angel of Death will pass by . . .

13 January 2000

GP very concerned about my health but eager to tell me that the cancer was under control. Two weeks' sick note – to get built up!! Very absolutely exhausted on my return, very, very tired but resolved – no contact with anyone with infection, to be very careful.

I think back to when children have left our home and the pain has been indescribable. The loss causing a void which I could never express. But the joy in knowing that it is given to God – He only knows and He takes the loss and compensates by filling the void with the joy of knowing that you have been part of the will of God – for however short or long in that child's life. No person or situation can take the wealth of the experience away – perhaps again it is like treasures in darkness (Isaiah 45:3); that is, a gem finely carved through cost, sacrifice and love. Father, bless all those children that I have had the privilege of mothering and bring them from the kingdom of darkness into life. Norman too has been so faithful in being a dad – a man who walks with God. Genesis 5:21 – then Enoch walked with God: he was also the father of Methuselah – other sons and daughters – praise God.

21 January 2000

Back to the hospital, weight up, 1lb gain. WBC and HB up, not normal but nearly there. Injection was to be given to boost the immune system but not needed, praise God. Still not mixing but at peace.

22 January 2000

Hebrews 12:6 – the Bible talks about chastening (AV) or disciplining – the word comes from a Greek word that means "enforced hearing". God has a way of teaching us lessons.

26 January 2000

See GP – another two weeks off! Realistically he feels that fifteen hours a week is enough, not thirty. He says that my body will always be fighting the infection. It will get tired – then I need to rest. Decisions – praying and waiting on God. Reading *The Anointing* by R. T. Kendall.

1 February 2000

Rang my line manager at Derby – and shared about the GP's remarks and the future. He was most caring and will talk to personnel to discuss options . . .

Also spoke to Jane, lymphoma cancer research nurse. G-CSF are subcutaneous injections, they are naturally occurring growth hormones and given daily for a week to raise the blood levels before chemo is given again. She also said fatigue is normal after chemo.

1 Don't expect to return to normal
2 Majority never get back to what they were
3 Don't expect too much of yourself
4 Protect yourself
5 Rethink about the future
6 Put yourself first

Fatigue will always be a problem, energy one day and completely tired the next! I am listening, Lord – will obey – adapt accordingly. Help me to know what is the best for the future. Thanks.

7 February 2000

A lovely birthday last Friday – Jo and Russ stayed – blessed with such a wonderful family and also friends galore. Saw Peter on Saturday, very positive time. Praying for the future – my energies – support for Norman. I'm still not mixing, will wait now until blood test – patience!

18 February 2000

Been to Kate's Wed-Sat – lovely, lovely time. Saw GP – I'm off for one month.

Last night wept and let myself (and Norman) down, Bill and Pat's engagement and I was not able to go. Missed it terribly – I try not to make Norman feel guilty but missed him and wanted to be there with him. Today is

Sunday, a new day and hopefully I will be back to church next week.

Hospital appointment. Blood levels still below normal – a little up. Hb very good. Wt down. Nose bleeds. Dizziness. Feel positive and recognise limitation. Goal: to find the book I wrote, get together past diaries, consider GN Broadcasting and *People's Friend* – articles – learn to type, continue with quilts. Thank you Lord.

No news from Trevor.

23 February 2000

Very concerned about Peter – supposed to be returning to Worksop to get a flat. Very little communication. In debt due to not paying his board money at Bradford, we only knew through ringing his key worker. Tried to help sort this out but he is determined not to. In court ten days ago; he was then unsupervised, seemingly, in a home with children. However, first night here yesterday – shared a flat with others for one night. Under-age, who knows! Verse that has stuck out to me this morning, 1 Samuel 16:1 – "Now the Lord said to Samuel, How long will you grieve over Saul?".

I just know that at the moment Peter will do what he wants to do and not listen to the risks to himself or to others. Lord, I know I cannot care or keep as I would want to at this time. I must release.

Pat and Cliff from Elkesley have been helpful but realise Peter's attitude is poor and he has a will to do only what he wants. Lord, please give us wisdom so that we know how to act, how to protect Peter and others from him but also to release him.

3 March 2000

Peter has moved to Worksop and he went to Cliff and Pat's for the day. Birth father seeing him regularly.

7 March 2000

Peter quiet over the weekend – no contact. Peter's birth mother rang Norman at the office. Spoke to Peter who said his birth father went with him to court that day. Spoke to Peter's birth mother on the phone and Peter there with her – we were unaware of it. No court appearance (must have lied) – already at Kent – sent back by social services.

8 March 2000

Jude verse 24: "Now to Him who is able to keep you from stumbling . . . AND TO MAKE YOU STAND IN THE PRESENCE OF HIS GLORY BLAMELESS WITH GREAT JOY."

Seeing GP today, still no news from M.H. Feeling very tired at times but more energy in between – no dizzy spells for two weeks.

Peter this past two weeks caused a lot of concern because birth father and mother now in the picture – contact and with it deceit. Probation officer says he is lying through his teeth. His exploits have caused front-page news in the *Worksop Guardian*. My dilemma is always: Does he go this way because he is not here at home? OR would he have gone anyway (like before) because of the restriction here? He owes money and when he has it drinks it away.

LORD have mercy, where we have not been able to take him further may You do the rest and may he be convicted by Your Holy Spirit so that he seeks You. Peter phoned on his way back from Kent – social services sent him back.

PRAY FOR LAURA.

10 March 2000

Peter and birth mother in Worksop court.

11 March 2000

Deferred to 10 April; in the paper again. Peter seeing his birth mother on that day. Peter very confused.

17 March 2000

Story in *Worksop Guardian* again.

17–19 March Amsterdam Weekend

Wonderful time – feel well – no problems seeking the future – how to release, proceed forward – help us to know, Lord.

Peter once more in the *Worksop Guardian* this week. Have written to his solicitors and probation asking for letter to be sent to his address.

26 March 2000

We feel settled here on Windsor Road. Mum moved to James Hince Court on 7 March and settled very well. Try and see her and, now I am driving, take her out for a while.

God is good.

27 March 2000

Three days of feeling really tired.

Good news on Friday 24 March at the clinic: WBC up to 4.4 now, just normal. Glands still enlarged – more or less told not to worry.

Went to the wedding of Richard and Diane.

Went to the meeting at Carlton-in-Lindrick.

Parents' Sunday – children overnight Saturday.

30 March 2000

Norman has booked for Chicago! – praise God. Peter's mum and the girls staying in Worksop, very little contact now.

Keep remembering the verse "How long will you grieve over Saul" (1 Sam 16:1); was I being prepared? [see 23.2.00]

7–13 April 2000 Chicago

A tremendous spiritual experience, a holiday and a rest. A gift of £300 encouraged us to go and also a need to go before my insurance expired.

Billy Graham museum – at Wheaton College; 1954 video shown of my conversion in London – praise God.

Also visited Willow Creek Church and Moody Bible Institute . . . wonderful time.

April 21–1 May 2000 Easter in Devon

A family holiday – the first but hopefully not the last. For me it was just so good to be together – hopefully everyone else felt the same. It went smoothly – it was encouraging to have the children around, what a delight they are. I was conscious that due to the diagnosis of having cancer this could be used as a manipulative tool for family to "go along with me" – but Norman and I felt it was an investment particularly for the grandchildren.

Healthwise I felt well – not under any pressure and rested when necessary. Everyone was helpful and did their share of cooking etc. What a blessing they all are. Liz, Jo and Russ sharing the work in the caravans and what a delight to be with. Will it happen again? – hope so.

30 April 2000

Noel and Lesley came to stay at Kate and Duncan's caravan. He gave me Psalm 103:1–5.

7 May 2000

Staying at Kate and Duncan's whilst they are at Toronto. The girls are wonderful, such a blessing. Praying for Kate and Duncan's future – Chrissy also here from Newfoundland and going off to Aberdeen for her scholarship.

19 May 2000

Consultant – seen today. WBC lymphomas again on the increase. Swollen glands, plus in the abdomen? Treatment next time.

High Leigh conference with Maureen Gray. Generations – three generations walking together.

25 May 2000

Prayed for at the ladies' conference, that Satan would get his hands off me – a real manifestation in my stomach – cramping pains – believing for a miracle. All praying for salvation for Peter.

26 May 2000

Holiday with Pete and Ruth in Northern Ireland – excellent.

4 June 2000

Very enlarged neck glands – sub-cranial. Swelling left side and abdomen becoming more and more uncomfortable and swelling getting larger there.

5 June 2000

Prayed for tonight, Monday, by evangelist Chowdri – no evidence, but what a joy that Peter went. Thank you Jesus. Prayed for yesterday – bottle of oil over me – what joy to be loved of the Father and the church.

6 June 2000

Psalm 118:17: "I shall not die but LIVE."

John 6:27: "Do not work for the food which perishes, but for the food which endures to eternal life, which the Son of Man shall give to you, for on Him the Father, even God, has set His seal."

Prayed for again by the evangelist. Asked for forgiveness for the generation line that despised the Jews. Read this morning Psalm 120:6 – "Pray for the peace of Jerusalem." This was mentioned last night.

Praying for a church for Peter.

12 June 2000

Glands very enlarged – uncomfortable. Maureen Gray – healthlessness in the body – pray against it.

Deuteronomy 29:29: "The secret things belong to the Lord our God but the things revealed belong to us and to our sons forever." Isaiah 59:21: "Covenant for me and the following generations."

27 June 2000 (Tuesday)

Hospital last Friday, WBC up, chest infection. Antibiotics and chemo given. Despite feeling lumpy and uncomfortable I am OK and very blessed. Read today Psalm 144:4 – "Man is like a mere breath, his days like a passing shadow." Time is endless – eternal.

Peter – crisis at weekend. B & B for two nights. Norman has been wonderful. Bed-sit obtained. Gone to church!

Psalm 144:12: "Let our sons in their youth be as grown-up plants" – promise today.

28 June 2000

Couldn't sleep – last day of chemotherapy tablets. Glands very uncomfortable, still enlarged, wondering how long this will go on for? Will the glands subside? Is the treatment really effective? Shed some tears (poor old me's) – got up in the end and felt more comfortable.

6 July 2000

A few days in the Lake District, a wonderful peaceful time, plus couple of days with Jo and Russ, very relaxing and so good to chat and share. They are gems and have their feet on the ground. Sickness now gone but just very tired. Swellings improved but glands are still enlarged. I have many questions and I must trust God.

Went to Retford Baptist to hear Brother Perez from USA; word of knowledge for a bad neck, so I was prayed for. Lots of laughter. He spoke on the wine and water at the wedding. It can happen at anytime. Look and feel no different BUT trust God.

13 July 2000

Norman away in Romania, appears to be having a positive time – so pleased. Liz in Cornwall. I am coping but have to keep my eyes on Jesus, He is my support, not Norman. Thank you Lord – my abdomen is so uncomfortable, causing backache and sickness. I trust you, Lord.

28 July 2000

Scan of abdomen and pelvic region. Saw GP (new lady) yesterday – due to back pain, pressure on the ureter. Spoke to consultant Friday, more chemo 4 August – tablets, but if it fails to bring glands down, different method needed. All week glands getting very large, felt so tired and the girls and boys visited – lovely to be distracted from one's illness.

6 August 2000

Exodus 23:25: "And I will remove sickness from your midst"; v 26: "I will fulfil the number of your days." Thank you, Lord.

8 August 2000

Heard from the hospital re results of the scan; to see Dr B at Doncaster next Wednesday, 9 August. Feel this is in God's purpose. No chemo tabs this weekend, praise His name – so we'll see what's in store to get these lumps down!

Filled in disability allowance forms. Whoops, what a come down!

9 August 2000

Attended Doncaster Hospital to see Dr B, she was very understanding and compassionate. My abdomen hard and distended – all glands enlarged. She was very concerned – query high grade lymphoma? To start drugs, 30mg daily, and anti-gout tablets to stop the build-up of lactic acid. Felt reassured to go in on Monday for three days as outpatient or to stay to give chemo injections. I know God is in control and accept this.

10 August 2000

Janet Smith rang, amongst many others – Zephaniah 3:17: "The Lord your God is in the midst, a victorious warrior. He will watch over you with joy, He will quiet you in his love, He will rejoice over you with shouts of joy."

Vomited seven or eight times all day. Anti-emetic given by GP; will space tablets out tomorrow. Thank you Lord.

12 August 2000

Finished reading *Amy Carmichael* by Sam Wellmen. The old Reverend Mr Webb-Peple had won Amy's heart when he spoke of the joy of the Holy Spirit. "Joy is not gush," he said emphatically. "Joy is not jolliness. Joy is perfect acquiescence in God's will."

Amy Carmichael about prayer, pages 178–79:

1 We don't need to explain to our Father things that are known to him.
2 We don't need to press Him as if we had to deal with an unwilling God.
3 We don't need to suggest to Him what to do, for He Himself knows what to do.

14 August 2000

Celebrated Mum D's birthday yesterday with a family tea – Chrissy here from Aberdeen, so she saw the family. Looked at *My Combat with Cancer* by Peter Crawan who is the brother of Pat Thomas and had lung cancer. Diet important – plenty to drink, radishes, garlic, red wine, pips of grapes, broccoli, brussels sprouts, spinach, kale, tomatoes, carrots, dried apricots, pulses, tea, dark chocolate, selenium vitamin (brazil nuts).

He did not badger God for his healing but knew he had to seek God first and then all will be added. Keep focused on Him and refuse to be anxious. Refuse to let the affected part of the body (disease) touch the spirit.

Went to the hospital, saw Dr B and again had bloods done. Hb from 9 to 11, platelets up; very pleased with me. Two more days on cortisone. Start Wed five-day course of steroids. Injection.

16 August 2000

IV treatment at Doncaster Hospital; stayed in overnight – sailed through it. Praise God. Feel fine but very tired. Gill Colton popped in to say we are having a prayer chain for me. Ruth and Pete – Psalm 41:1–3.

18 August 2000

Home – read this morning about how low grade lymphoma, if transformation occurs, is dangerous and prognosis poor – not disheartened.

20 August 2000

Home and feeling so well, yesterday spoke to Jessica on the phone and felt very emotional – first lot of tears for a long time. Reunion and farewell service at Maltby Methodist. My heart went out to the ex-youth club members – please make it possible, Lord, for a reunion where we can testify! Hope so. Lumps going down by the minute.

21 August 2000

Still on steroids, feeling well – Duncan, Kate and the girls arrived safely. Jessica inspected me closely to see if my hair was still on. She confided on her own that she knew I had cancer but not the others . . . She asked me lots of questions: 1) Grandad sleeps with you – won't he catch it? 2) Will I need a wig? 3) Will my lumps go? Kate said they were playing families one day and one of them said, "You be Granny and have pretend lumps." They are wonderful.

22 August 2000 (Tuesday am)

Abdominal pain starting but steroids decreased now, nearly finished them. Felt very uncomfortable and abdomen enlarged, hard and painful.

25 August 2000

Saw consultant today. Neutrophils low, only 0.3%; should be between 2.5–9.0. Given pain killers – lachilose? – and anti-sickness drugs. Felt ill, pain, coping at home – just. Violently sick at night – all up but felt better then. To return if no better on Tuesday for five daily injections, GCSF.

26 August 2000

Pain still there and realise I was unable to eat properly; there didn't seem to be any room in my stomach. Beginning to realise I was constipated. Kate and Duncan at Grapevine.

27 August 2000

Woke with wheeze – slight cough. Kate and Duncan's family farewell at the Smiths. Norman preaching at the URC Rotherham. By lunch time I was hot.

Admitted later to Bassetlaw Hospital as a precaution with impacted bowel and swollen stomach. IV saline and IV antibiotics. Put in isolation room. Very much relieved and at peace. Enema given at 11pm. Temp remained spiked all week. First few days just slept. Said goodbye to Kate and Duncan and the girls, I cried for Kate rather than me – but all was well and I know they felt better that I was being looked after.

Felt overwhelmed with God's love – my own en-suite was a haven! All week I heard praise music in there, angels were singing and I thought at first it was the Christian music coming from the room attached, where the Christian gypsy was quite ill; but no – that was country and western music. Discharged Friday, but very weak.

Grapevine weekend; a bath towel brought home with my ID name and prayed over by everyone and wept over too by John Brewster and Simon Matthews. I really appreciate the love of the church.

4 September 2000

Returned to Bassetlaw – bloods down, platelets down. Treatment too risky. Very pale and the consultant said a blood transfusion would be given tomorrow.

The words God gave me in hospital which at first I was too ill to read: Matthew 5, The Beatitudes, from the Message version of the Bible which starts, "You're blessed when you're at the end of your rope. With less of you there is more of God and His rule."

5 September 2000

Returned to hospital in the morning when three units of blood given – home at 6pm. No problems; this will make me feel better.

6 September 2000

Couldn't sleep after waking up in a hot sweat; hair falling out everywhere and abdominal discomfort. Read Deuteronomy 25:25–26: "I will remove sickness from your midst. There shall be no one miscarrying or barren in your land."

11 September 2000

Blood test results up; chemo tomorrow.

12 September 2000

Consultant concerned about my "swellings". Ankles now swollen, armpits very painful. He is to consult with Dr B re swellings. Hickman line in as my veins are thrombosed. Not sleeping well – very painful but I AM BLESSED. Kate Bristow and Maureen stayed at the weekend.

14 September 2000

Feeling much better this morning – no pain and not so tired – wonderful. Slept since chemo!

Deuteronomy 31:14: "Then the Lord said to Moses 'Behold the time for you to die is near . . .' " This has not been said to me yet! Broke bread with Derek last night, feel a need now to do this regularly.

22 September 2000

Doncaster Hospital – Hickman line put in. Quite a performance – enter near the shoulder under the clavicle and then into the right atrium of the heart. Two openings with stitches. Difficult to do due to the enlarged lymphoma near the blood vessels; it had pushed the vein out of position. Medical photographs to be done. Platinum IV chemo given five days during admission – to start 3 October.

23 September 2000

Very painful but coping – surprised at the loss of mobility. Temp up slightly, raised over weekend, nothing much.

26 September 2000

Bassetlaw – bloods reasonable – dressings and flushed out – everything OK. I know I might have to have the toxic regime and will again trust God.

29 September 2000

Stitches removed – fine. Photographs done. No problems, bloods reasonable. To come in on the Monday.

30 September 2000

High temp but soon went down.

1 October 2000

Didn't go to the induction day yesterday or to the celebration today but feel OK – my time will come.

2 October 2000

A runny nose – blood results low but consultant eager to start. A print-out given of all the drugs – started at 9.30am. Everybody wonderful. Emma here while Thursday and it's been good to chat to her. June has seen my SN, very competent. A little side-room given, quiet and well stocked! Read and prayed – watched TV and had Norman here, wonderful.

4 October 2000

Woke up early but slept well. Busy morning, a different treatment – Dr says home Monday but I am peaceful. God is good and no sickness yet – but starting to blow up.

6 October 2000

All the treatment off now – no leads!! Chest X-ray and a slight cough. Very bloated with fluids but feel fine – still awhile. Today read about Deborah in Judges (4:14) – Arise – the time to attack – she gave the command to Barak, she saw that God was ready and in front.

9 October 2000

Monday morning – all being well, discharged today. The weekend went very quick – slept a lot but feel well today.

10 October 2000

Home!! Colin and Derek popped in to pray – significant, I feel.

"God is too kind to do anything cruel, too wise to make a mistake, too deep to explain Himself. I'd rather go to heaven sick then go to hell well" (testimony of David George of Houston, Texas).

24 October 2000

I have been in Worksop Hospital for a week now, and feel well enough today to write something down. My temperature has been high and is still spiking. I have been given replacements of blood, magnesium etc, trying to get the immunity up. Physically things are not good. Consultant had a good chat yesterday and said the disease was beating us and if something was not soon found it could be a grim future, a matter of months. Blood stem transplant was an option so John came in this morning to give a sample of blood. It will take a week to see if there is a good match (a one in four chance). Tomorrow, consultant will discuss with Doncaster team the way forward – will let me know the outcome. His parting comment was, "What we need, Ann, is a small miracle" – but that was my department!

Praise God, I trust, remain at peace and know He is in the driving seat.

26 October 2000

Praise God, first night with no temperature and does it make you feel better? The temperature helped me to sleep which gives my body the rest it needs but I've just not been fit for visitors. Yesterday they took me off IV antibiotics and changed it to steroids. Repair for the blood clots in my arms and today will let me home for the afternoon. God is good, particularly meaning that my time with Norman will be quality time today. Thank you Lord.

27 October 2000

Home again – praise God. Temperature down

28 October 2000

Jo and Russ came, so good to share. Feeling stronger, attended meeting Sunday morning.

29 October 2000

Monday – Christmas shopping.

30 October 2000

Bassetlaw Hospital visit – counts up, platelets = 36, amazing! Church praying for this – praise God. Received letter from Joy re youth. Very encouraging. O Lord, how I want this illness to only glorify you.

Determined to speak at the ladies' day next Saturday – got the word! Need the strength, trusting God. Weekend spoke to Kate and Duncan; prayed for by John Arnott and his wife. Monday able to contact their daughter at Birmingham – ministry set up for two weeks time after the treatment – praise God.

1 November 2000

Maureen Gray rang up and read out Psalm 91.

Out to Derbyshire today with Norman – praise God for sunshine after so much rain. Picnic by Lady Bower reservoir. Showed Norman the hotel at Buxton we girls had stayed at and then went on to see Peter – took him and Claire out for a meal. A wonderful day.

2 November 2000

Norman and Liz took me shopping – most of the Christmas shopping now done!

3 November 2000

Back to Doncaster Hospital for blood counts – everything up – testified how the church had been praying – start chemo on Monday. Such small miracles this week – renewed strength every day – platelets up, temp remains down, feel so much stronger. God is good. Out for lunch with Liz for her birthday – a good time.

6 November 2000

Start of chemo – here early, got going quick! Chatted and sat next to Glenys (with myeloma) who recently had a similar infection to me in hospital. I shared about my prognosis and experience in hospital and told her about the small miracle. She then shared about her experience when ill in hospital. A man came into the room several times and said he was a protector and guide. This frightened her at first but he gave her specific instructions to get her temperature down and said he would watch over her. Meanwhile her auntie came to see her, who is a Christian, and she instantly sensed there was a presence of God. What an opening!

After that she had to go but another lady came and chatted – a carer, her husband has leukaemia. Again, quite naturally, I shared about my stay in Bassetlaw and the small miracle needed. She opened up straight away about her need for spiritual things – obviously a church goer – but again such a privilege to speak to her.

What a wonderful day – able to tell nursing staff that the church had prayed for blood counts and they were up again!

7 November 2000

Woke up early but after a deep sleep. I have spent some time writing to Maureen. She phoned Norman yesterday after a long chat with Vanessa at LAH. Vanessa had shared with her the talk I gave on Saturday at the ladies' day – she was challenged with her attitude towards caring for her mum with cancer.

I wrote The Beatitudes down for her from The Message. I still get great reassurance from this and praise God for the ripples of last Saturday. Vanessa came, which was a blessing, and brought Christine P. I was absolutely thrilled.

8 November 2000

9.45pm – going to the phone and called by a young woman in a four-bedded ward. Younger than me but quite distressed. She had seen me walking up and down, had seen that I was quite cheery but also bald! – so knew I was on chemotherapy. She needed someone to talk to; that day she had been told that she had cancer of the oesophagus. She was very upset, nervous and was told she needed radio-therapy and perhaps chemo. I sat for a long time with her and comforted her as much as I could – trying to reassure her. She was greatly encouraged that I had no side effects and that her growth seemed isolated. I told her about my faith and how the Lord was seeing me through. She con-fessed too of believing, as she was a Jehovah Witness!! Anyway, again I just felt privileged to be used. She was with other elderly ladies who couldn't be of any help to her. God is good and I will keep contact.

9 November 2000

Saw Joan S. previous night from St John's Church. Walked past our house. I asked how she was, to which she said she was very much like me, putting on a brave face! Consultant came to visit and chatted! He is becoming more and more human – Holy Spirit, touch him. I know he thinks I will be in the box soon!

I am continuing to seek God for a real visitation of Jesus and am believing for the miracle of healing. It is becoming more of a reality – home tomorrow, praise God!

10 November 2000

Last day of treatment, everything went well, no problems. Discharged late afternoon but very tired and exhausted; so good to be home – returned Monday. Still weak and very tired – fell asleep, checked TPR but fine.

14 November 2000

No hospital visit; instead met Lori Lawlon, the daughter of John Arnott, and Chris Ginn. They came from Birmingham, very friendly sociable couple, chatted a little. We had lunch with Norman – in the afternoon they wanted me to release all anxiety and just to soak in God's love – tapes were put on and I lay by the settee, relaxed and fell asleep! It was a good time and they felt I was perfectly at peace.

15 November 2000

Visit back to the hospital for more platelets and again injections for platinum were started. TPR up, arrangements for admission; only symptoms were pain at night when I breathed in! Chest X-ray done – white patch on each side of the lung – double pneumonia. TPR remained up; but did go down after the weekend. Mobile X-ray called for ECG – concern about raised high blood pressure and pulse. X-ray showed the left side clearing up but the right side was full of infection, possibly on top of a blood clot. No treatment to worry about, so sit tight and will try new antibiotics to hit the right side.

25 November 2000

Temperature went down, making me feel much better. Up until now I have not been able to read or concentrate but I am waking up now! I am on continuous oxygen which has helped my breathing and three times a day have a saline nebuliser – it's all easing my chest, making me feel better. I am praying for Bobby Ball's visit to Whitwell tonight – O Lord, that men and women will be saved!

This was Ann's last entry into her journal.

"WHEN IT'S ALL BEEN SAID AND DONE"
by James A. Cowan

Chorus:
When it's all been said and done
There is just one thing that matters
Did I do my best to live for truth?
Did I live my life for you?
When it's all been said and done
All my treasures will mean nothing
Only what I've done for love's reward,
Will stand the test of time.

Lord your mercy is so great
That you look beyond our weakness
And find purest gold in miry clay
Making sinners into saints

I will always sing your praise,
Here on earth and ever after
For you've showed me Heaven's my true home

When it's all been said and done,
You're my life when life is gone.

When it's all been said and done
There is just one thing that matters
Did I do my best to live for truth?
Did I live my life for you?
When it's all been said and done
All my treasures will mean nothing
Only what I've done for love's reward,
Will stand the test of time.

Lord I'll live my life for You.